Red Car Long Legs

Jennylynd James

Copyright © 2015 Jennylynd James Enterprises

All rights reserved.

ISBN-10: 150589316X
ISBN-13: 978-1505893168   www.JennylyndJames.com

DEDICATION

This book is dedicated to my parents Gloria and Kenneth James for paving my path to success through education, patience and constant guidance.

Jennylynd James

PREFACE

When my postdoctoral research fellowship at a University in Tallahassee, Florida had run out, I managed to get a managerial position at a fresh produce company based in Oxnard, California. I was recently divorced with a toddler, and determined to start a successful industry career. Moving to California provided unique challenges such as first time home ownership and learning Spanish to communicate with staff. My responsibilities took me to Mexico and throughout the United States participating in industry conferences and auditing growers. This exciting career was punctuated by the search to find love, with many episodes of dating. Romance in California, however, proved as fleeting as the population that ebbed and flowed. Joining an organization for single parents helped me to find new friends and people with whom to socialize. It was a materialistic society with many hoping to become famous in Hollywood. A person's worth was evaluated by his zip code and the type of car he drove. I bought into the hype and moved to Westlake Village, California.

As my skills increased I moved on to a more senior role at a multinational company. I enjoyed the corporate company culture of private aircraft travel to remote locations in Central and South America and I ate my way around Latin America experimenting with exotic dishes. Eventually disenchantment with the system and the money-orientated society set in. I became restless with the inability to find a suitable life partner. It made me question whether the grass was greener in another land. I decided to look for work experience in Europe with the hope of finding a solid culture, with real people. This quest set the stage for a new life's adventure.

Many thanks to my daughter, Tiffany Lukawski for helping me recall some of our adventures in California, and her patience during the journey of writing and editing this memoir. I owe a huge debt of gratitude to Daniel Parkinson, my chief editor for the long hours spent reviewing details of the manuscript. Your experience, wisdom, and insight in editing were greatly appreciated. Sincere thanks also to

Linda Vachon and Monica Crane for their dedication and countless hours spent editing and providing support during the development of this work. Thanks also to Felice Gorica and Aurélie Taufflieb for your support in developing summaries for the cover and preface. Your ideas were greatly appreciated.

CONTENTS

	Preface	v
1	Juevos Rancheros - Introduction to California	1
2	The American Dream and Money Pancho	28
3	Pollo Con Mole	63
4	The Rules of Life	96
5	Singing through the Millennium	138
6	Planning a Move	161
7	Changing Houses, Changing Jobs	190
8	Gallo pinto and the Costa Rican Adventure	237
9	A Mom's Life	253
10	You May Kiss the Bride	266
11	Higher Ground in the Industry	322
12	Chicken Gudgeons	375
13	Escape to Eire	408
	About the Author	433

1

JUEVOS RANCHEROS – INTRODUCTION TO CALIFORNIA

The Motel

I ran swiftly into my room, locked the door, and then fastened the latch. Out of breath, I peeped through the key hole to see two robust men with big muscles and long beards. They passed in the corridor shouting at each other. Their expletives frightened me. They joked and laughed about going into town for food and to look for chicks. Turning with a sigh of relief behind the safety of the locked door, I scoped out my little room.

It was January 1999 and I had recently started a job in Oxnard, California. Reflecting on my situation, all the memories came back. A few months before, my plane had touched down at the Los Angeles airport at 10:30 pm. It was my first time travelling to LA and I was fortunate to get an interview with a company based in Oxnard, California. All I had to do was rent a car and find my way to the motel located close to the main office. I planned to wake early and arrive at 9:00 am for my interview.

I looked around the Terminal to find the airport rental car service. Even though it was late at night, thousands of people filled the terminal. LAX had more terminals than any other US airport I visited in the past. I could not figure out which direction to turn. Eventually I saw someone in uniform and asked for directions to Dollar Car Rental. He pointed at the sign that said "Car rental shuttles this way" and ran off. Rushing to the centre island, I watched as one company van after the next arrived and left. As soon as one crowd gathered and boarded the vans, more people arrived. A group of five men with multiple tattoos and piercing gathered at the curb, cursing and swearing as they waited for their van. They reeked of stale beer and their eyes looked blood shot. As the Dollar Car Rental van pulled up, to my disgust, they also boarded with me. I cracked the window slightly to get relief from the smell of alcohol and tried hard not to make eye contact because I felt afraid and a little unsure of myself. The rental car offices were in fact located outside the massive airport and were not in walking distance. When we alighted from the van, the check-out line was very long, with all manner of tourist and traveller.

After 11:00 pm I finally got the keys to my car and asked for a map of Southern California. The attendant showed me the best way to get onto Highway 101. It was the highway that would take me to Oxnard. When I jumped into my car, the rowdy group of men shouted across the yard, asking if I needed company. I stepped on the gas pedal and rushed out as swiftly as I could. I did not want them to follow me in their big cruiser, and hoped they were going in a different direction. Being a bit paranoid, I checked my rear view mirror repeatedly. North on Sepulveda Boulevard and onto Highway 405; this Highway was supposed to meet the 101. I turned on the light and looked at my map to be sure I was heading in the right direction. Mounting the ramp onto 405, it was evident nobody would give me a chance to enter. This highway was said to host at least 400,000 vehicles a day as did Highway 101. The drivers were fast and furious. I sped up and still could not enter. Wondering if I would drive into the side wall, a split second of clearing finally came and I joined the speeding masses at 120 km/h freeway.

There were no roadside lights and bright lights from oncoming traffic was blinding. I had to stay alert, ignoring all thoughts of sleep and pushing my body into high gear. A cold sweat from nervousness broke out and I cracked the window to let in some cool fresh air. In fifteen minutes I saw a sign indicating an exit to the right for Highway 101. Again, it was a challenge to get to the right. Mad drivers were overtaking on the right side too. They left no space for folks like me to enter. As a car passed me, I dashed into the lane behind him, barely missing him by a hair. This caused distress for the car following him in hot pursuit. The driver behind me blew his horn long and hard. He was upset by my sudden move, and let me know it. He then proceeded to drive as close as possible to my bumper. Tailgating at 120 km per hour on an unfamiliar highway made my heart race. I wondered how and when I would be able to shake him off. At the junction to Highway 101 he went east as I drove off in the direction of 101 North.

I breathed a sigh of relief for this momentary reprieve only to find the stunt would have to be repeated to get into a lane on Highway 101. It was the biggest freeway I had ever seen; seven lanes and counting. An extra lane was added and removed at exit ramps. Getting into the first overtaking lane I could not keep up the pace. I tried desperately to move to the second-to-last slow lane. This was safe for me. Changing each lane was a yoyo of emotions from tension to relief. Finally I reached a lane where it did not matter if I drove at the speed limit. Nobody would be too upset.

It was then I realized I had not planned carefully how to find the Rose Avenue exit in Oxnard. I could have kicked myself for not memorizing this information. Passing through the San Fernando Valley, then Conejo Valley I tried looking at my map while driving, but this was a challenge. I was afraid to stop since it was close to midnight. If I came off the highway, there was no guarantee I would be able to find my way back on. Not all of the exits had entrances to the highway. I scanned the map while driving and saw that Oxnard was the town after Camarillo. Flying past Newbury Park the traffic descended a steep hill leading to the Oxnard plains. The car sped up so quickly I almost veered into a car in the lane to my left. *Focus and hold the wheel.* This was my mantra.

Flying at top speed, I eventually saw signs for Ventura, and then signs for Carpentaria. The freeway had become a two lane highway. Something was wrong. I tried to look at my map but it was too dark. My heart skipped a beat when I realized I'd passed Oxnard completely and had to turn back. I pulled off the highway at the first exit and ended up at a beach. There was no way back onto Highway 101.

My God, I thought, how was I going to find my way back to the highway going south? I did a U turn on the small beach road and started heading in a southerly direction. The road was dark with no nearby buildings. Just then, I noticed a rusty old pickup truck with one head light was following close behind me. It was after midnight. I questioned what this person was doing on a small beach road in a rusty pickup late at night. Trying to stay calm and take deep breaths was not easy. I passed a side road down to the beach. Still no highway entry was in sight. I became more anxious and continued to watch in my rear view mirror as the one-eyed truck followed closely. I sped up thinking he would not follow so closely. However, he sped up too. My heart raced. Was this some sort of game? Just then I saw a sign that said, "Highway 101 South". I rushed onto the ramp and built up speed quickly to 100 km per hour. I knew the old truck could not go as fast as me. Racing to safety in the overtaking lane, I headed back in the direction of Oxnard, looking closely at the signs for the Rose Avenue exit.

First Ventura, then four Oxnard exits, I finally found Rose Avenue. My roadside motel was situated on the service road near the highway. It was unbelievable how excited I was to see the Holiday Inn Express. It was not the grandest choice in accommodation, but it was close to the company's office. With the motel in sight on the North side, I made a quick detour South to be sure I could find the company's office next morning. There was nothing worse than showing up late for an interview. Using the excuse of not being able to find the place was not an option. I had received directions from the HR department, so I drove a short distance on the dark quiet roads and circled around on some side streets until I spotted the office. The town was dead quiet and the area around the company was filled with warehouses.

Re-tracing my drive, I got back to the slip road with the Motel and entered the yard. One truck after the next could be seen parked in a row. This motel was probably a welcome rest-stop for long-haul truck drivers. Several other vehicles entered the yard after me. I tried to find parking near the main office to check in. As I parked and came out, two truck drivers looked me over and whistled. I looked away, kept my head down and swiftly removed my bag from the trunk. It was important to appear brave and bold in this situation even though I was falling apart inside. I locked the vehicle and bolted to the office to check in. Unfortunately, the office door was locked. It was 12:30 am. 'Hello? Hello? Is anyone here?' I called out anxiously.

I heard whistles in the background and saw two big truck drivers jump down from their rigs. After ringing the doorbell a few times, a sleepy looking man emerged from the back office to open the door. I rushed in quickly telling him about my one-night reservation. He searched the list but could not find my name. 'Come on. Come on,' I wanted to say, but had to calm down. 'Can you please check again? This reservation was made since last week.' He looked again at the list. By that time, some people had also entered the office and waited to get keys to their rooms. I heard someone whispering behind me about "this fine looking woman". Not wanting to turn around, I kept my composure and asked the attendant to check again. Eventually he found the booking and gave me the key to room 10 located upstairs. I wished he had not yelled out my room number to everyone in the lobby. After all, I did not want anyone following me upstairs. I grabbed my key and headed for the door. 'Oh this one's serious,' said one in the group as I whisked past. 'Hello darlin',' he said, but I didn't answer him.

Mounting the staircase, I was not sure which direction to turn: left or right. A lucky turn left brought me to room 10 down the open corridor. I tried the key and it would not go in. My hands were shaking and sweaty. I tried again and finally got the key in the lock. I heard footsteps as some loud people advanced up the staircase. The key had to be jiggled in the lock before the door finally opened. I ran swiftly into the room, locked the door, fastened the latch and set my alarm clock for 7:30 am before hastening to bed.

I heard banging on the door. It got louder and louder. They were laughing at me. I was so afraid. I dialled zero on the little telephone near my bed to call the front desk, but there was no answer. What was I going to do? I started screaming and screaming!

Then suddenly as I screamed, I opened my eyes. It was just a bad dream.

I was still in the little motel room and the sun was rising. There was a queen-sized bed, a small television, a tiny kitchen counter with a sink, and two overhead cupboards. A microwave, kettle, and a small refrigerator under the counter completed the kitchenette. I rushed to my job interview and managed to perform well. A few weeks later, I was offered the position and given a contract for the role of Director of Food Safety at a large fresh produce company in Oxnard, California.

Leaving Tallahassee

After working as a postdoctoral research fellow for two and a half years at Florida A&M University in Tallahassee, I had the task of packing our belongings to leave. Tallahassee did not hold fond memories for me. It was where my marriage fell apart and I was anxious to get away. Just before Christmas, a moving company was hired to load everything, including my red Mitsubishi Eclipse with the sun roof onto a 40 foot container bound for California. The car and auto loan were part of the divorce agreement. All my furniture was disassembled and loaded onto the 40 foot container. My friends who worked at the university all came to say farewell. I was going to miss them since I did not know anyone in Oxnard, California. As we drove out of town in a rental car heading to Miami, to catch a flight, I told my toddler, Tiffany, 'Don't look back. We're going to have a new life!'

Of course, she did not understand what this meant. As long as she was with her mommy, she was fine. In fact we were heading to Trinidad for Christmas holidays. I would leave Tiffany in my mother's capable hands for at least six months so I could get settled in California. I felt sad to leave my child behind, but it was customary in our culture for grandparents to take care of grandchildren while their parents prepared a way for them in foreign lands. I had to work fast to find a home, school, childcare, and activities, in a strange town.

Introduction to Oxnard

My job took me to visit farms throughout the Oxnard plains, Salinas Valley, Baja California and Yuma, Arizona. As an avid traveller, exploring the California coastline and enjoying the long drives up Highway 101 beckoned. I had six months to find a home and find childcare before my mother brought Tiffany to me. With limited resources, my only option was to stay at the motel close to the company. I made a reservation at the Holiday Inn Express. It was next to a Harley Davidson store, the landmark proudly given to me when I called to make a booking. This was to be my temporary home for a few weeks. In January 1999, the land looked bare. But, it was always bare in this dry, Mediterranean climate. I planned to buy a home and climb onto the property ladder, part of the "American Dream".

The company was gracious enough to store my belongings in the container on their grounds. They had dozens of containers onsite. One more did not seem to make a difference. It was one benefit of working for a family owned business. They offloaded my red Mitsubishi Eclipse from the container right away, and I had my own car to drive.

My neighbours at the motel were rowdy truck drivers, bikers, and other travellers from Highway 101. Small trucks, medium sized trucks, and large trailers; it was distressing to think too much about it. I planned to spend as little time on site as possible. The motel would just be a place to rest my head at night. The company's moving allowance had stretched far enough to pay the moving company. Now I just had to pay for my first two weeks' accommodation from savings until I actually earned a salary. My budget was tight in those early days.

Oxnard had a mild temperature in the winter and very cool summers. Onshore breezes kept the coastal communities cooler than inland. The average minimum temperature reported for the region was 52 °F (11 °C) and the average maximum temperature was 69 °F (21 °C). This meant there would always be a chill in the air and a great deal of sunshine; it seldom rained. The sun was very bright and daily weather reports included the ultra violet index or UV index, a standard measurement of the strength of UV radiation from the sun at a particular place and time.

The Oxnard Plains were reported as one of the most fertile in the world, with large areas dedicated to agriculture. The area was also famous for its strawberries. Oxnard was said to produce one-third of California's strawberry volume.

From the end of September through the end of October, strawberries were planted. This was followed by harvesting from mid-December through mid-July. Row after row of plastic covered soil was observed with small strawberry plants emerging from the plastic. The plastic was called mulch and it controlled the growth of weeds. I was there in time to see hundreds of workers hunched over rows of strawberries in the fields. As they picked the ripe fruit, it was placed immediately into clear plastic containers.

In the Plains, one could also see rows of neatly planted vegetables: lettuce, carrots, tomatoes, peppers, cabbage. Every imaginable vegetable was planted there. My first free day in town was a Saturday spent driving through the fields aimlessly staring at the expanse of agriculture. Then using my simple regional map I found my way to Main Street, the centre of town. The town of Oxnard was a mixture of British settler homes and Little Mexico. I came upon Heritage Square, a historic part of Oxnard where 15 restored Victorian mansions were nestled in a landscaped garden. The buildings gave a hint of the history of pioneer families who moved to the area.

Downtown Oxnard, most of the people were of Mexican descent. In passing town squares, old Mexican men with sombreros were observed sitting on benches socializing. I imagined myself being taken back to a pueblo somewhere in Mexico. It was hard to believe this was actually in the United States. Many Mexican restaurants and shops graced the major streets of Oxnard. From Third Street to Fifth Street, the fashions in the shop windows appeared to date back to the 1970's in a rural desert town.

In addition, just south of downtown was home to hundreds of Filipinos and African Americans who worked at the Army base at Port Hueneme (pronounced Y-nee-mee) or had family working there. I drove down Ventura Boulevard past the base and looked with curiosity at the fenced area wondering what mysteries lay behind. Coming back North and turning left onto Channel Islands Boulevard, I came across a corner spot with wooden shops and restaurants. It looked quaint and I decided to stop for lunch. Fast food restaurants advertised fresh seafood and this was tempting.

The staff handled raw fish and cooked food at the same time. It was a food safety nightmare. Ordering fried seafood at one fish monger's hut, I hoped the boiling oil would kill the germs. I had a side of fries and coleslaw. As soon as I returned to the motel, I made a mad dash to the toilet with a bout of diarrhoea. It may have been the salad ... Eating that meal was not a good idea with so few hygiene controls in place. I should have known better as food safety director for a big company. I remembered seeing a server happily licking his fingers as he tasted fried fish, and then continued to work.

On Sunday, I continued exploring the area. Heading back to Fisherman's Wharf then over a small bridge I saw houses interspersed with canals. Home owners had small boats and a mooring in front of their homes. What was impressive was that houses were also accessed by small roads that came off another large road. This was a beautiful part of Oxnard. It reminded me of a wealthy European housing area with the canals. It was a small Venice, with water taxis taking people around to Fisherman's wharf and other neighbourhoods.

On the other side of the bridge, the left side in the fork of the road led to more shops and restaurants for the beach and boating community. This area was called Channel Islands Harbour. Many sail boats and power boats could be seen in the water. Since winter was mild, people could use their boats in the winter, unlike some other parts of the country. Oxnard was notable for a coastal area of 20 miles (32 km) of scenic, relatively un-crowded coastline. The beaches were said to be big with soft, brown sand and massive sand dunes. These dunes had been featured in movies over the decades. I had a rough map of the area and managed to find my way to the coast road.

The beach community was like the typical US beach communities we saw in Florida. Large and stylish wooden homes rubbed shoulders with ram-shackled, but overpriced wooden houses. The buildings did not match. They all looked like master plans of random artists. The faces of the beach population were mostly of European descent, different to the Mexican population in downtown Oxnard. I parked on the roadside between two houses and hoped nobody would mind a stranger in the neighbourhood. I could not find another way to get to the beach. Walking across the sandy clearing, the expansive beach came into view. It was majestic with sand butting onto the Pacific Ocean. It went on for miles and miles in front of the long row of beach houses. It was a beautiful sight. Who would have thought Oxnard had such a beautiful neighbourhood? From the highway, there was no clue of the beaches and coastline. In addition, the Oxnard Beach was never advertised like other parts of California. The beach would certainly provide for many hours of exploration and walks to escape from reality. I walked to the water's edge and put my toe in the water. It felt like ice water and I shrieked. Driving around would have to suffice until summer.

Following the coast road in the direction of Ventura, I happened upon an area called Ventura Harbour with its quaint restaurants, shops and fishing boats. Further up the coast near the town of Ventura, surfers swam happily in the frigid water. I had heard some people surfed religiously every day. The surf pilgrimage started early in the morning before getting ready for work. It was supposed to be the ideal preparation for a day at the office. This ritual continued in the winter when wet suits were worn.

As I turned east along West Gonzales Road, I discovered the Oxnard Golf course community, with houses built around and through a large golf course. These houses were larger and more expensive than those in the downtown area. I drove around briefly, got lost, then found my way back out. I needed to make a decision about where to live. There was no chance of getting too comfortable at the motel. On Ventura Boulevard, a large Ralph's supermarket beckoned and I went in to buy a stack of microwaveable dinners, juices, fruit and bread. My budget was too tight to eat out every day. For someone who usually cooked her own breakfast, lunch, and dinner, eating packaged food was not my cup of tea. However, it was temporary and I consoled myself in knowing my own home would come in a few weeks.

Company Introductions

Monday morning finally came and the excitement mounted as I approached my first day on the job. I questioned whether I knew enough about the fresh fruit and vegetable industry to be giving advice. My last job in Florida involved working with fresh grapes. It was going be a steep learning curve to transition to vegetables. Management put faith in me, supporting my move all the way from Florida to California. However, the challenge facing me was overwhelming.

Director of Food Safety meant being responsible for developing and implementing food safety programs. I had to ensure the company's vegetables were grown, harvested, packed and shipped under sanitary conditions. The development of Good Agricultural Practices (GAPs) was a new and burgeoning industry in California back in 1999. Many companies were developing auditing schemes for GAPs. And supermarkets and large restaurant chains joined the band wagon by demanding third party audits as a requirement of doing business. The company's operations had to be readied for a slew of audits and I was the "fall guy/woman".

My first day at the company was a whirlwind of activity. Dressed in my finest interviewing suit I arrived early. The receptionist, Daisy was the first person I met on entering the office. She was a pleasant, skinny Filipina girl with large teeth, glamorous make up, and long brown hair with highlights. Her telephone greeting to customers was like a strange song. Over and over she would say the company's name and then sing, 'Hold a minute please'. Calls came in fast and furiously, and she knew exactly where to transfer them. I hoped people were easy-going and I would make some new friends. I did not know what to expect. 'Please have a seat and I'll call Manuel in HR,' Daisy chimed.

He came promptly from another location nearby. Manuel was a sharply dressed Mexican man with a crisp shirt, neatly pressed denim jeans and cowboy boots. He wore a cowboy hat to complete the ensemble. He was slim built with a moustache and talked non-stop. It was like being at a rodeo. In fact being at the company's premises and seeing all the outfits reminded me of the set in an old Western movie. I was waiting at any moment for someone to say, 'Lights, Camera, Action!'

Manuel took me to the HR trailer to sign some paperwork and get introductions out of the way. Excessive chatter was good in public relations. He spoke about the company, the staff, the owners, the crops, the workers and other details worth knowing. He blurted out, 'You don't need to know much. You just have to be able to talk!' I responded, 'Point well taken Manuel.' I then wondered if this type of bragging was typical of the California man.

Maria, his assistant was also of Mexican heritage. She had an interesting and beautiful long nose. Her slanted eyes showed mixed heritage, probably Aztec and Spanish. Her long hair had been swept into a tidy bun. She conversed effortlessly in Spanish and English on the telephone as calls came in from clients, employees, and others. The HR department was in a trailer away from the main office which housed the sales and marketing group. The offices were small and modest despite the apparent large size of the company. From my research, the company was one of the largest vegetable growers and shippers in California.

What a unique adventure. Learning to converse in Spanish would be a benefit since everywhere I turned, the staff spoke

Spanish. I loved languages and was ready for the challenge. Manuel took me to meet Mabel who was leaving the job. We crossed the busy yard dodging forklifts carrying pallets of vegetables from the packhouses to massive coolers. Trucks entered the yard from different directions carrying freshly harvested produce to be washed, packed, and sold to wholesalers for supermarkets and other large operations. The fresh vegetables were shipped nationwide. The large scale of the operation taking place before me was impressive and scary at the same time. Mexican men of all sizes passed on forklifts greeted Manuel and kept an inquisitive eye on me.

Their eyes seemed to ask 'Who was the new girl?' They smiled and drove past. Most workers looked contented. Packhouses were made of galvanized iron walls painted grey. We approached a warehouse with several rows of washing equipment. It was full of vegetables awaiting washing and those being removed from the water flumes. Never had I seen so many fresh vegetables. The noise of the splashing water and equipment drowned out our conversation.

We entered through a man-door and then walked up a narrow, wooden staircase leading to offices. When we got to the landing, we entered a small hallway. On one side there was a small kitchen with basics for storing and re-heating meals. Manuel said I could sit in there and heat up food if I brought lunch. In the middle of the hallway was receptionist's desk and central point for the department. 'That'll be your office,' said Manuel, pointing to a narrow office crammed in between a washroom and a larger office to the right. Another large office was situated in the left-hand corner of the area. My name plate had already been installed on the door of the narrow office. It felt great to be assigned my own office. The space looked like it was slipped in as an after-thought when the new position was created for my predecessor. However, I didn't mind. It was the first in my life I had my own office, and it felt really special.

I was then handed over to Mabel, the departing Director of Food Safety who graciously stayed to help with my orientation. She sat amidst mountains of files and papers ready to go through everything with me. After two days, she would be on her way to a new job. Mabel was a short, young woman with stout legs. She wore brown shoulder length hair. Her round face was punctuated with a tiny mouth with thin lips. A small, slightly hooked nose emerged from her face. She wore a simple business blouse with a scarf around her neck and a straight skirt. Flat sensible shoes were ideal for walking around the large facility. She greeted me with a big smile. I owed Mabel everything for helping to create this job opportunity when every other company had turned me away. She recognized my potential and I was determined to work extra hard to prove myself. 'Hiya. Haw wuz yer flayt?' she sang in the strongest, Southern drawl.

I was tempted to answer back in a Southern drawl too, since I was good at imitating the Southern accent, having lived in Tallahassee, Florida for almost three years. 'Oh it was fine. Just trying to get settled,' I responded in a neutral accent. 'Good to see you again.' Mabel was a friendly, well educated food scientist from Georgia. Her accent, I was to discover had been the subject of many an office joke behind her back. She suggested we walk around to meet the bosses and other key people in the company before reviewing the documents.

We turned the corner into a big room full of books and papers, with desert paraphernalia decorating the walls. I saw two old leather tires suspended from a branch, an old saddle, and some horse shoes. Why would anyone save these?

'This is Bob,' said Mabel. Bob was the Operations Manager who was going to be my boss. Bob was a kind-hearted Californian with possible roots in Oklahoma. I had visions of his predecessors arriving as prospectors during the gold rush when the area became part of the USA. Of course I could have been wrong. He had large blue eyes and a mop of medium length brown hair. He looked extra tall and strong. He sported a neatly ironed, striped, long sleeved shirt, and denim trousers. Bob wore work boots and a hard hat. I later learned Bob wore a toupée! He may have been a cowboy, but not without vanity. Bob walked about with many rolls of building and construction plans in his hands. He said with a smile, 'I don't quite know what you are supposed to do. Just do it well!' With that he laughed and went on to his next project. Yikes! With Mabel gone, would anyone know what I was supposed to be doing?

As we left Bob's office, we met with the receptionist, Alma who had just arrived. She was as cute as a button. This pint sized secretary/receptionist was a curiosity. She was a pale skinned Mexican with green eyes, stylishly coiffed light brown hair and a stocky build. She had a round face, thin lips, dimples on both cheeks, and neat thin lines for eyebrows. As Mabel introduced us, Alma said 'Hola. Hello. Welcome to the company. Have to fix my makeup. Can't let anyone see me like this'. She then rushed off to the wash room and shut the door.

Later in the morning, she took calls with her face fully made up. Alma slipped happily from the typical Californian accent, to fluid Spanish, depending on who was on the line. She was born in an area in Mexico where French had settled centuries before. That may have explained her pale skin colour compared to other Mexicans I had met. She spent some of her childhood in Mexico and told me her old aunts taught her poise and elocution. She wondered why that was necessary at the time. She then moved to Camarillo, California where many Mexicans lived in basic middle class housing. They lived in their own world with restaurants, clubs, radio stations, and television stations, barely needing to cross over into the English-speaking world. Alma wore fashionable street clothes with platform sandals. She was ready for a fabulous party, except this was a small office in a warehouse. She had the happiest smile and I imagined could make a nice friend.

Alma reported to Mel, or the 'little red rat', as she referred to him behind his back. Mel was responsible for purchasing. He was a short, loudmouth from New York. It was believed he could get the best deal for everything. He would cut the price from under any supplier and he was a force to be reckoned with. Mel had a mop of red curls with a hint of a bald patch that was developing with time and he had a red moustache. His New York City accent was strong. When Mel screamed at a supplier, the whole office knew. Mel moved from New York with his wife and son a few years before. It seemed many people moved from all over the United States to California in search of fame and fortune. It was the golden state of opportunity. Mel had a spacious office next to mine. As I was introduced he took a short break from screaming at a supplier to say hello. He let down his noisy front, chatted for two minutes, and then continued with business as usual.

We then met with Glenn who was responsible for maintenance at the facility. He was skinny, casually dressed, and wore spectacles. He was possibly of British descent. Introductions continued as we went across the yard to the main office. I had too many names to remember and just said hello politely. Another day I would have to walk around again on my own time and speak with everyone. I wished my office was in the main building and not in the warehouse. The girls in the office were pretty and well-dressed and I had to be stuck with the factory folks.

I met my other boss, Tom, the President and CEO of the company. He was over six feet tall, good looking, and with a thick head of black hair. His green eyes and chiselled jaw reminded me of another character on a movie set. He wore a shirt and trousers, not too dressy, but not too casual. I could imagine how the ladies of California would faint before this man. He had good looks and he was the President of his own company.

Tom was third generation Eastern European. His grandfather had emigrated at the turn of the century and started a fresh produce company. This company had grown significantly over the years and many family members had key roles in the business. On his desk, Tom had a photo of his beautiful wife and several teenage children. He held out his hand out for a firm handshake.

'Welcome to the company Jennylynd. Ask Mabel as many questions as you can. When she's gone, she's gone. Gotta learn everything now,' he said.

Getting Directions

Later that day, Mabel took me to visit the vegetable processing plant on Camino Del Sol, only a few miles from the main facility. Remembering directions after she left was going to be a challenge too. We were moving swiftly. This plant was recently purchased from two brothers, Ken and Edmund. Management decided to leave them in charge of running things while bringing in additional sales staff. It was an interesting concept, but at least the guys took ownership to make sure the business ran smoothly. Ken was the plant manager and took care of day to day operations. He had a mean streak and was strong-headed. Edmund took care of maintenance and worked on the evening shift.

The facility was a large grey, concrete building with glass windows at the front. On entering, we were hit with a smell similar to rotting vegetables. Mabel told me to get used to the smell. It was the pervading smell throughout the plant even though no vegetables were rotting anywhere. The smell of cut vegetables persisted in the air and would cling to your skin, bags, documents, clothes, hair etc. I was cautioned not to wear fancy clothes when spending long periods of time at the plant. Everything would smell like old vegetables.

The building looked only a few years old and the polished concrete floors gleamed. At the front near the street were offices, a quality assurance lab, and the lunch room with tables, chairs and refrigerators, and a large maintenance room with tools. Then, a wall enclosed the refrigerated interior from the rest of the building. It was a building within a building. All processing was done in the refrigerated space. We walked around meeting and greeting the staff.

The factory workers were predominantly from Guatemala with a few Mexicans thrown in for good measure. Everyone looked related. Two brothers, Paco and Ramon ran the production floor. Various spouses and cousins also worked in the plant. Everyone had to follow Paco without question. I was advised to make friends with him in order to implement new programs. If he did not agree with what I said, nothing new would be implemented. I had my work cut out for me. Sylvia managed quality assurance (QA) and also took orders, going through volumes of paper work. She was a good natured blonde from Ventura. She tried to keep track of what was going on outside the production floor. I had to get to know the staff and see where improvements could be made. Everyone stared at me as Mabel mentioned I would be taking over. She told Paco, 'You have to listen to Jennylynd!'

Paco watched and nodded. In his eyes I could see him saying, 'Who is she? What does she know? She can't tell me what to do. I'm the jefe.' Paco looked mischievous and not easy to work with. We put on white lab coats to walk around the processing floor. It was cold and damp. In the future I was going to have to wear a sweater, when returning to this facility. I also knew I would have to brush up on my Spanish language skills for effective communication, because a fact lost in translation was not an excuse.

After watching the process from raw material to chopping and washing and then the automated bagging of product in plastic film bags, we proceeded to the farming office. This was located in the nearby town of Camarillo. I drew small maps of the main roads in my notebook to help me plot my way around, so I could find the sites in the future. The ranch, as the farm office was called, was large facility with office buildings, a few old houses and sheds, and larger buildings for storing farm equipment and chemicals. A landscaped area at the front of the building had lawns shaded by large trees and park benches for picnics. The area was available for company picnics and other events.

As we entered the main gate, we saw field after field of vegetables. Dirt roads separated plots with different types of crops. In fact, many of the fields we passed along the way belonged to the company. Each was in a different stage of preparation: tilling, sowing, weeding, irrigation, and some harvesting. I was eager to meet the farm managers. The overall boss or jefe of the operation, Frank, was part owner and cousin to the president. He was tall and lanky and told many jokes. 'Well they could put me on a slow boat to China …' I heard him saying on his telephone as we approached.

'Hi there. Welcome to the company.' He gave me a warm handshake and had to leave. 'Dave'll tell yah whatever yah need to know.' Dave was responsible for pesticide application in the fields. As we were introduced, I noted how easygoing this man of such wealth and stature acted. He was less arrogant than many people I'd met in the past who had little money or power. He was tanned from many years in the sun and of course he wore his work boots and a cowboy hat. This was fitting for a day at "the ranch". It was another Hollywood western movie set, but this time we had the dust from the dirt road to add special effects. As Frank drove off in his big pickup truck he motioned to a few other gentlemen out in the yard to come for introductions.

I was then introduced to Dave and Hugo. Dave was a tall red head with a beard, moustache, and spectacles. He had a slight paunch and carried many papers and maps. He plotted where pesticides were applied and sent reports to the California Department of Agriculture. He looked a bit worried with so much work to do. Hugo took care of all planting and harvesting activities. He was a round Mexican man with years of experience in agriculture. He was so heavy that he seemed to have difficulty breathing as he stepped from his tall pickup truck and up the short staircase to the farm office.

'Hola. Que tal Mabel? Quien es?' he asked. Mabel reminded him she was leaving the next day and introduced me as the new "boss" for food safety. I sheepishly shook his hand and pondered my fate again as the "boss". These gentlemen had key roles in running farm operations and would be instrumental in teaching me what I needed to know. The experience was going to be thrilling.

The following day, I met with Mabel early to review food safety documents. We examined one pile after the next. She then signed me up for workshops in Plant Sanitation and a Train the Trainer course. She advised me to go to all the fresh produce conferences and serve on committees to learn about the industry and interact with industry people. It was sound and valuable advice. I was to see her again at many industry events in the future. She told me stories and many observations about the people, the area, and the staff. And then she was gone.

I felt a strange emptiness in my stomach when she said farewell. We had only spent two days reviewing my duties. It was good to have had a fellow scientist to hold my hand and guide me. When she said farewell, I was on my own and had to make all the decisions. This was in addition to finding a home. It was a strange overwhelming feeling of too much to accomplish and not enough time. I tried to maintain composure and push myself into action.

Don't Use My Internet

In 1999, most people did not have cell phones. The company gave me a beeper and I was asked to check it regularly and find the nearest landline or pay phone if I were to be beeped. That included when I was out in the field or driving four hours to Salinas Valley. I thought nothing of this because that was the way things were at the time. Internet in small companies was brought in using dial up modems. Mabel had insisted on having internet access in her tiny office and I happily inherited this privilege. Email messages were still relatively simple using the DOS language. And conference calls could be conducted only by telephones with no internet conferencing.

Internet technology was so new that sometimes employees would come into Mabel's office to send an email or check something online. I listened as Mel recounted a funny story about Mabel. 'Who's bin using mah indernayt!' She screamed so loudly one day that the whole warehouse heard the noise. Mel, Alma, Manuel, Bob and everyone came to see what had happened. It was a tense and serious situation in her mind. They laughed quietly at her accent and wondered how to keep a straight face and appear concerned. Bob said she was to lock her office door when leaving and he would be sure to speak to all the engineers and staff supervisors about her privacy.

Mel laughed hysterically as he told me the joke and repeated. 'Who's bin using mah indernayt!' It was one of the standard company jokes. Looking around the office I studied my new environment. Mel was screaming at more suppliers, 'Get awda here!' Alma was plucking her eyebrows and re-applying her make-up and lip gloss. Bob was pouring over building plans and a cup of coffee. And I cowered in my narrow office, trying to determine my strategy for reviewing mountains of files Mabel left behind.

Miguel worked with me as a lab assistant. He looked Aztec with his long nose, pony tail, dark slanted eyes, and dark sunglasses. Why did we need dark sunglasses in this tiny loft of an office? 'How are you today Miguel,' I asked cheerfully later that day. He shrugged and swaggered off to "his" lab; the little den downstairs. I followed closely to get an idea about the capabilities of our lab equipment and supplies. The lab was well equipped and Mabel had done a great job in teaching Miguel how to perform microbial analyses on product samples, swabs, water tests and a host of other tests. I tried to be friendly with him by making small talk, but this was not easy. He obviously missed his last boss and resented the fact that I had taken her place. This was going to be tough, I thought.

'What Mexican dish would you recommend I have for breakfast Miguel?' I asked, making light conversation. 'Juevos rancheros,' was his short answer. The next morning I went to a small restaurant off the highway in Camarillo and ordered juevos rancheros. It was a dish made of fried eggs smothered in spicy tomato salsa. This dish became one of my favourites while living in Southern California.

2

THE AMERICAN DREAM AND MONEY PANCHO

First Time Home Buyer

Driving back and forth from the motel to the office every day, I had one thing in mind: get out and get my own home. Oxnard was home to a wide variety of restaurants. Of course, there were many were Mexican restaurants: fast food, casual, and fancy dining. The few times I ate at traditional American style diners and restaurant chains, I became ill within a few hours. It may have been the water or the unsanitary conditions in the kitchens, but my stomach did not adjust easily. Or it may have been a case of nervousness while trying to cope with living alone in a strange place.

I wanted to experience the "American Dream" which was home ownership. From a distance my immediate family told me not to buy anything. According to them, renting was the best option while scoping out the new environment. Being strong willed I forged ahead with my plan. A few signs from real estate companies were displayed in front of various properties in Oxnard and people in the office gave conflicting advice on where to find a good place to live. The town was dotted with several pretty housing developments. However my knowledge of to get a mortgage loan was nil.

During my first week in town, I decided to call a real estate agent whose mature face smiled back from a sign in front of a house. Sam was a tall, middle aged, well groomed gentleman with salt and pepper hair. During my lunch break the following day, we met to view a two bedroom house in

Oxnard. I told him about my recent move from Florida, about wanting to buy a house right away, and the fact that I was living in a motel. This first time buyer was in need of advice. The kindly gentleman took me under his wing and became an amazing resource for the weeks ahead. He may have felt sorry for me and became my substitute father. Sam set up an appointment to visit his friend Mike who worked for a mortgage brokerage and escrow company.

'What's an Escrow Company?' I asked. He knew I was totally green and had to become knowledgeable on home buying in a hurry. Mike's office was a one-stop shop for all home buyers' needs. He asked me to return with a job letter showing proof of salary. The next day I was in Mike's office completing a host of application forms. 'You can't buy a home until you are pre-approved for a loan,' he explained. 'We need to know how much you qualify for, before you can go shopping.' Mike completed the application for the mortgage loan and in filling the profile he put "White, Male, US citizen". 'Mike, that's not correct' I said cheerfully. 'Don't worry about it. I know what I'm doing. Just sign here. Your salary is high enough, so I know you can pay'.

It was a rude awakening for me about how the profiling of people for mortgage loans worked. I was on a work permit and a black woman. I would probably never have qualified for a mortgage loan at the time. My Guardian Angel was at work helping out. That week a photo and write up about my joining the company had been published in several local newspapers and produce industry newsletters. This was a public relations program run by my company. Mike had seen the local news article. He knew my position was secure because it said so in the newspapers.

With pre-qualification in hand, I had to sign up for mandatory mortgage insurance, as well as lessons on money management and mortgages. This was a small price to pay for a hasty loan and little credit history. I completed the classes and went on home viewing expeditions with Sam almost every lunch hour during my second week. 'This area is great. Don't even bother with living over there. This one may have a good resale value,' Sam counselled as we looked at various properties.

Oxnard as a whole did not have a good reputation with neighbouring towns; however, some parts of Oxnard were considered good and others were not. Sam was a valuable resource. The property market had hit rock bottom in January 1999, so this was to my advantage. Home owners were willing to agree on an offer, even if one came in at a few thousand dollars lower. There was no big rush for home purchases at the time. I heard people tended to look for homes in the summer months, so a seller who had to leave in a hurry would be happy to negotiate.

Eventually we saw an advertisement for a beautiful two bedroom townhouse on Moby Dick Lane in a gated community called California Lighthouse, Oxnard. 'You and your daughter would be safe here. Not everyone can enter. You must have a code to get in,' Sam advised. We met outside the walls of the fortress on a cool mid-winter's day. It was quite impressive. California Lighthouse had Mediterranean style, peach-coloured townhouses with red tiled roofs. There were townhouses of various sizes, from two bedrooms to four bedrooms. The homes all had a living room with a vaulted cathedral ceiling, white inner walls and beige coloured carpets. We looked at two units and immediately I fell in love with a two bedroom home on Moby Dick Lane.

The property was advertised as 1222 square feet in area with 2.5 bathrooms. 'What's a half bathroom?' I asked Sam. 'This is really a powder room on the ground floor with a sink and toilet,' he said. 'Each bedroom upstairs would have a full bathroom with a bathtub.' I had never seen so many bathrooms squeezed into a tiny house, so it was something worth looking at.

At the entryway to the property was an archway with jasmine vines. There was a small concrete patio and a flower bed with some dead flowers. I had visions of bringing that flower bed back to life. The front door opened into a smart, neat living area with beige carpets and white walls. This colour scheme was popular in California. 'Always keep it neutral for re-sale,' everyone would say. My beige sofa and love seat would fit well to the right. And my dining table with four chairs and matching dark wood china cabinet would fit expertly on the left. The place was completely empty, so we would not have to wait for the occupants to move.

The property market had recently crashed so I arrived at the ideal time to California with my small budget. A neat kitchen with a gas range and beautiful, wooden, built in cupboards, an ample fridge and burgundy ceramic tiles graced the kitchen. All I had to do was wipe away the dust and move in. No repairs were needed. As one walked down the small corridor next to the kitchen, to the left, neatly hidden behind a folding wooden partition were a washer and dryer. The owner had included the appliances in the sale. That was brilliant for me. Being new in California, I had no idea where to go to buy appliances. To the right of this was the cutest powder room with a pedestal sink and tiny toilet. Over the sink was a beautiful oval mirror. I was sold on the townhouse immediately.

As we walked up the carpeted staircase, we came to a large landing. In my mind, it would serve as a cozy TV loft. The loft overlooked the living room and dining area and was ideal to house my large dark wooden wall unit. All the dark wood furniture purchased in Florida was dismantled and stored in the forty foot container. Continuing upstairs we found two bathrooms, each equipped with a bathtub and shower. Tiffany would have a kiddie bathroom decorated to her liking, and I would have a girly bathroom. Tiffany's room was quite small, but it had potential. I planned to create a ballerina themed room. We would be starting from scratch in decorating the bedrooms since only beds were brought from Florida. The garage had an automatic roll up door which was exciting for me. I pressed the button and watched the door roll up with delight and pressed again to watch it roll back down. This was a new toy. Mental plans were already being made for the extra space in that enclosed two-car garage.

I told Sam how perfect the place looked. The community seemed lovely too. There were two heated swimming pools with hot tubs. Californians loved their swimming pools. This was a must in many townhouse complexes. The grounds were neatly manicured and each home had its own small garden and patio which home owners could develop to their unique tastes. The home owners' association charged a monthly fee for maintenance of the pool and grounds. Little did I know this home owners' fee usually went up each year and not down. It was to pay for maintenance of the complex and new problems that could developed every year. The fee was large for someone on a limited budget. I would also have to pay the mortgage and mortgage insurance. However, the pretty peach colours on Moby Dick Lane and the swimming pools blinded me. I envisioned entertaining family and friends at my home.

I drove back to the neighbourhood during the night one time just to check out the residents who would not have been there during the daytime. The complex seemed relatively quiet. It was going to make a good home.

Asking Sam to make an offer for me an offer on my behalf, I witnessed for the first time the lengthy 'song and dance' of offer and counter offer; sign this document, sign that document. I wondered if I was signing my life away. Half of the time I was not quite sure what I was signing. Naïve but sure of my agent's need to sell and my need to buy a new home, the offer was accepted.

When it was time to get the mortgage loan, Mike asked what sort of down payment I had to offer. 'Yikes. You mean I have to pay down some money?' I asked with the stupor of someone green to home buying. 'Yes of course. What are your assets and collateral?' I had reached an impasse and didn't know what to do. I could show some remnants of mutual funds I still held after the divorce, but that was it. I started earning a wage at my new job, but nothing was saved for a down payment.

I went back to Sam with my story and he appeared baffled

by my lack of knowledge. All I knew was that I wanted to buy a house. Realistically no research was done on the details. I was learning everything like a young child at preschool and hoped everything would fall into place by magic. The good man decided he would lend me $5000 which was the minimum one could put as a down payment for the loan. 'Don't worry about it. I know where you live,' he said jokingly.

Good natured Sam gave me a loan for the deposit and I promised to pay it back swiftly. I did so in two months never quite liking to owe anyone a cent. Getting the keys to my house on Moby Dick Lane was a happy occasion. I arranged to have all belongings delivered in a van from storage and started the slow process of unpacking. Hopping and skipping, I left the old motel. My real estate agent gave me a list of 'Things to Do' as soon as I moved in. The first thing was to change the lock to the front door since many people: the last owner and numerous real estate agents would have used the property's key during showing. I looked in the yellow pages and immediately found a locksmith. He gave one price to change the lock and another to re-key the lock.

What did "Re-key" mean? I had never heard such a term in my life. Extra clarification was needed since re-keying was certainly cheaper than having a whole lock installed. It turned out to be the changing of some parts of the lock without changing all the hardware. Was it secure? Of course it was. That was the answer the service man on the other end of the telephone line gave for my simplistic question.

The main lock was to be re-keyed after work that first day. I had jitters about someone entering the place with a copy of the old keys. I didn't think there anything worth stealing. We didn't own many assets at that time, but everything had a history and sentimental value. The locksmith arrived just after 6:00 pm as instructed. He was a young Mexican man who sized up the lock and proceeded to take it apart as soon as he arrived. He made one adjustment after the next and then put it back together.

After he was done, he looked around and asked, 'Where is your husband?' I was shocked at being asked such a silly question. It was only then I realised where I lived. Oxnard was as much a Mexican stronghold as any other town in Mexico. In a typical macho environment, a woman seldom owned her own house, far less ordered repairs for the house. I decided to give him the answer he needed to calm him down. 'He hasn't come home from work yet. So have you finished?' There was no need to give this man the impression that I was living alone. No need having unwanted alerts going out to bandits about my circumstances. 'Thanks a lot,' I said. 'Take care. Bye, bye.' I paid and ushered him out swiftly.

When everything was unpacked and decorated, I invited everyone from the office for lunch: my boss, the secretary, sales people, anyone who could take an hour off. I prepared a simple meal and salad and set up everything before leaving for work that morning. It was going to be a case of re-heating when we got there. Trudy, the sales coordinator asked, 'Why are you doing this? Nobody invites people over.' Well, I said, 'You are my new family since I have no family in California.' She was shocked. What better way to celebrate a house warming? The office staff pooled funds and bought me a gorgeous hamper in a large stainless steel colander. They also gave me fancy candles on tall stands and I kept these gifts for many years.

Everyone was impressed with my beige leather sofas and wooden furniture, the high cathedral ceilings, and the pretty powder room. I learned later that people seldom invited others to their homes. It was an unspoken rule; plenty chatter in the office and goodbye at the end of the day.

The Oxnard Auction

Getting used to the many bills that came with home ownership was difficult. In addition to the mortgage, I had to pay the mortgage insurance for not putting down a 20 per cent deposit. Since I lived in a gated community$300 went into home owners' association dues paid monthly. The gardens and pools were certainly beautifully maintained daily by a crew of Mexican gardeners. They watered, and pruned, and trimmed, and cut grass, and cleaned and did all that needed to be done to make California Lighthouse look beautiful.

I also had to pay separately for electricity, water, garbage collection, the telephone, car note, and car insurance. I did not dare add any more bills to the list and decided to live without home insurance and cable television. In addition, cell phones were a new phenomenon and I was not going to add yet another monthly expense to my list. At the end of the month I had to write many checks and mail out the envelopes with a stamp so they would arrive before the due date. Such were the joys of home ownership in the 1990's. Cheque books were always used and re-ordered frequently.

My esteemed friend and real estate agent told me I would be

able to get paintings, antiques and unique decorations to furnish my whole house by going to a Friday evening auction that took place at a warehouse in North Oxnard. I had always assumed auctions were snobbish affairs for the wealthy. But this one was different. It was a casual event run by Kathy and "Mom". Previewing took place from 5:00 pm – 7:00 pm on Thursday evenings. This was the time when potential buyers could rummage through miscellaneous boxes; review the furniture, size up the items on offer, and plan ahead for a night of bidding fun.

The warehouse was dingy with rows of old tables onto which objects where placed with brief descriptions. The Auctioneers would empty estate homes and be responsible for selling the contents. They took 10% on top of the sales price. This was something to remember when bidding furiously. It was an auction for ordinary people and nobody wanted to pay too much for anything. I needed table lamps for all the rooms. In newly constructed condominiums and townhouses, ceiling lights were not provided in bedrooms. That was a revelation. With so many beautiful walls, paintings were needed for decoration. Why settle for prints when oil or acrylic paintings were cheap and available. I had to furnish Tiffany's new room and decorate it too. All I had for her room was a twin size mattress and box base. In my room, there was a queen size bed on a metal frame; no furniture.

The auction game had begun and I went every Thursday for the preview to find treasures for the home. Items changed every week depending on the house or estate that was being auctioned. Sometimes the goods were beautiful and sometimes they were not. One had to return every week to find new options.

My first Thursday, I approached the warehouse nervously. It was on Wagon Wheel Road, a quiet slip road in North Oxnard, just off Highway 101. The old Wagon Wheel Motel: a bunch of ramshackle wooden buildings dating back to the 1950's and a few other buildings were situated along the roadway. The motel had a giant neon sign that included an animated stagecoach driver and galloping horses. It was near the Esplanade Shopping Center, a number of industrial buildings, a trailer park and an ice skating rink. This road also hosted an old roller skating rink and a bowling alley from the 1950's. I wondered if it was safe but many others came for the preview. Many tables stored bric-a-brac. Some objects were lit by small lamps. I smiled nervously at the folks who seemed to know what they were doing. They were the regulars. A few items had a price on them and were marked "reserve". 'What does reserve mean?' I asked one passer-by. She knew I was a novice and helped me along with more information. 'Reserve is the minimum price an item could sell for. The seller would not accept a bid any lower than this,' she said.

I spotted three solid wooden chests of drawers that would be ideal for a little girl's bedroom. If they could be painted white, I would create a ballerina-themed room for my little ballerina, Tiffany. The plan had begun to take shape in my head when I spotted a framed print of ballet shoes. I walked around the warehouse looking at paintings and old books. There was even an old pop up doll's house and story book. So many treasures, so little time. I made notes of the interesting items and looked forward to my first auction that Friday night.

Proceedings started at 6:30 pm but when I got there at 6:00

pm, spaces were already filling up. A large area had been cleared for the audience to sit. Everyone needed to see the items and the auctioneer. I sat quietly near the back to take in the scene. People sat on plastic lawn chairs, wooden chairs, and all manner of chairs. The crowd was dressed casually for the most part and looked like John Public. Some wore shabby clothes. Others portrayed the illusion of wealth in vintage jackets and other clothing that may have been purchased at this auction. We paid $10 for a bidding card and the price would count towards any item purchased.

Kathy, the auctioneer, was assisted by her mother, "Mom". Kathy had short dark hair, wore a T-shirt and track pants and spoke faster than I could understand. 'This is a beautiful set of crystal glasses. It's Waterford Crystal folks. Come on, do I hear $10? Opening bid. Beautiful for entertaining. Do I hear fifteen? I see a hand up in the back. Do I hear $20?'

People raised their cards when they placed a bid, and everyone had a number. I was too shy to raise my bidding card and wanted to see what other people would do. After observing a few winners, I decided to risk a bid on a box of books and miscellaneous items. I had not rummaged through the boxes, but since the bidding was low for this item, there was no harm in taking a chance. I raised my number 26 card when the bidding started at $5.00. Kathy then proposed $10. No card went up. She challenged the crowd to bid on the interesting box and nobody bothered. 'Yes, sold to number 26!' Yippee. I had won a box of Lord knows what. It was exhilarating to be a winner. Kathy and Mom provided a great deal of entertainment during the night too.

Mom would sometimes hold up the items we were bidding on. The room had at least 100 clients, maybe more. Mom walked with a stick, had grey hair and glasses, and looked quite ill, despite her role of displaying items. If she forgot to show a new item, Kathy would yell, 'Hello. Are you NEW? Where is the item?' Vendors situated in a tent outside sold hotdogs and soft drinks. If you are out for an entertaining Friday evening, there was nothing better than a greasy hotdog and soda pop to pass the time. Another character who displayed items was nicknamed "Doc". He ambled around with the assistance of a walker. He obviously enjoyed his important role at the auction. He was fat and weathered, wore glasses and sported greasy shoulder length hair. He wore track pants and an old leather jacket. Kathy would ask, 'Doc, what're we bidding on?' He would respond 'Forty Ah'. This meant forty "a" in Doc's language.

People would bid frenetically on the item if it was worth anything. Then he would shuffle over to the next item. The auction characters were just as interesting for me to watch as the whole auctioning exercise. Some folks did not even bid. They bought hot dogs and pop and looked around. What an odd bunch they were. Watching people gamble on items was a thrill in itself.

And so began my addiction to the auction. I would go every Thursday night after work to preview items and then to the auction on Friday night to bid and buy. Eventually, I became better at the bidding game. My mission was to get anything I needed to furnish my new townhouse. It had to be a gem and not cost much. Even though I was on a shoe string budget and starting out in unknown territory with no support network, I felt surprisingly comfortable.

Neighbourly Love

I had moved into my peach coloured townhouse on Moby Dick Lane and was settling and decorating. However, I did not have any friends and wondered what I should do to make new friends. On a few occasions as I sized up my patio flower bed, I spied my neighbour on the right looking out and longing for conversation. I waved and went inside. He was tall, possibly over six feet. He wore small glasses over his beady eyes and seemed to be in his early thirties. He was reasonably good looking. His dark brown hair was neatly cut and combed into place. He had a long nose and thin lips with a small mouth. He was slim and looked fit with some muscle tone. He was obviously bored and nosey all at the same time. To work, then back home, to work, then back home; did this man not have a hobby?

One day, I decided I would actually speak with the neighbour over the wall. Sure enough it was a half an hour conversation about this and that - the neighbourhood, his rose garden, the other neighbours, our jobs, and other topics. He asked so many questions. They were obviously well thought out after staring at me curiously for a week. The neighbour, George was an engineering technician. I looked up his designation and in my snobbish mind he was not actually an engineer. He was at the half way point with a Diploma and not a full degree. However, since I did not know anyone and he did have a good job, I decided he could be a potential friend. George worked at a multinational firm based in Oxnard. It is amazing how judgemental I had become after emerging from seven years in academia into the real working world.

George said the people on the other side of me did not speak much and were not friendly. They could barely even muster up a hello. George had been living on Moby Dick Lane for almost one year. He got his townhouse for a favourable price and had started to slowly furnish the place but did not yet have much. He had started cultivating roses in his front garden. George had started and put in several rose plants with layers of black plastic mulch ground-cover to retard weeds. His garden was flawless and he was obviously obsessed with neatness.

One day, the doorbell rang. I wondered who could possibly be ringing my doorbell. I did not know anyone. I was a bit afraid to open the door. I walked quietly to the front so as not to make a sound and peeped through the key hole. It was George. First I saw his spectacles, and then I saw him. He had a neat smile across his thin lips. What did he want?

I opened the door and smiled with delight. George had brought me one of the first roses from his garden in a little glass of water. It was a beautiful orange coloured rose with red tips. He beamed with pride as he presented his offering. Was this George making a pass at me? Was this his first attempt or had he tried and I had not noticed? What were the implications of accepting the rose? Should I invite him into my home or let him stand at the door for conversation? A million questions went through my head as I tried to plan my next move. 'Hi George. What a lovely rose. Thanks so much.'

Would you like to come in for a cup of tea? The man did not have to be encouraged twice. He barged right in and took a good look around. 'Your place is the same size as mine. I like your furniture. I don't have a large sofa and love seat yet. My living room is bare. Where did you buy that?' I told George I had moved from Florida with my furniture and would probably have to get bedroom furniture. I was contemplating why I had let him in as he continued to examine everything and ask more questions, forever comparing my place to his. He was competitive. 'Oh, a dark wood china cabinet. Wow that's so pretty. You need more crystal to fill it up. You have a matching dark wood table and chairs. Nice. Did you get them in Florida too?'

Oh the nerve of him, I thought. I would have to limit the tour to the living room and dining room to avoid further scrutiny. After one cup of tea, I decided to find a way to send 'Mr. Questions' home gently. I stretched and looked at my watch. 'Oh, look at the time. Well, it's going to be an early start for me tomorrow. Must get to bed!' It was only 8:00 pm, but I did not want to prolong the interrogation. 'Nice of you to come over George. And thanks for the lovely rose'. I had put the rose in a small vase and gave him back his glass, to avoid his having to make an extra trip to collect it.

The last owners had done nothing with the old flower bed and the bushes had to be cleared away. I hated gardening unlike some neighbours and thought of what I could plant so that it required no care at all. The arch over the gateway had a jasmine vine which required little care. George informed me that in the summer I would be happy to have lovely jasmine flowers and they smelled great. In fact, I enjoyed the smell of the cedar trees that seemed to grow wild in the pathway in front of my home and also along the sides of the highway. One day I brought in a bag full of cedar bark and leaves cleared away from the patio and left them in the garage for the next day's garbage removal. As I drove into the garage after work, I was greeted by the most delicious aroma of cedar.

I bought a few bulbs of miscellaneous flowers. The bulbs should last for a long time I thought. George peered over the wall as I planted the bulbs. 'You should really put in some plastic ground cover to keep out the weeds,' he said. I was hoping he would mind his own business. I could fix my own flower bed, thank you very much. And in fact his garden looked too neat, and too sterile. I wanted something wild to match my character. George informed me he was handy and could do a little bit of plumbing, a little bit of carpentry, and could even lay tiles. In fact he was fitting his own bathroom and toilet. If I were to ever have anything go wrong at home, I was to call him first to see if he could repair it. That was good news of sorts. My place looked almost new but I was happy to know I could count on George for emergencies.

Well in fact it so happened I noticed a leak behind the washing machine one day. I opened the utility closet and water was slowly leaking out during the wash cycle. I did not want to have to go through the expense and inconvenience of finding a plumber. Later that day, I mustered up the courage to invite George over to fix this for me. He ran over with wrench in hand. 'I'll take a look. It's probably something simple.'

I hoped it was simple. I knew absolutely nothing about home repairs. I would usually walk around the house in a tank top and short shorts. As George knelt down to fix the hose, he looked up at my short shorts and most certainly got ideas about fixing me too. Yikes, I should have worn a long dress with long sleeves before asking him over. What was I thinking? 'I have to change the washer', he said with great excitement. 'I just might have one in my tool box!' He hurried home by jumping over the wall and quickly sprang back over the wall with washer in hand. 'That was easy. I told you I could fix anything!' he said after ten minutes of repairs. 'Thanks a million George. That's great.'

Then he stood staring, trying to muster up the courage to ask a question. 'Ah Lindy, if you're not busy tomorrow, can I take you out to dinner?' I pretended to have to check my calendar, knowing full well I had nothing to do and no place to go. 'Let me get back to you a little later'. 'I'll call you,' I said, as he lingered a few seconds. 'Bye bye'. I sat and thought for a few seconds. The following day would be Saturday. I had planned to buy groceries, fix the garden and explore a few shops, literally driving around Oxnard, Port Hueneme, and Point Mugu to see what I could see. I supposed I could go out with him. He looked ok. He was tall so I could wear high heeled shoes, and he was an engineering technician. 'Hi George', I said when I called back later. I'm free tomorrow night. Where would you like to go?' And so our neighbourly love started. George was fast with everything. And so was I.

Perhaps it was out of loneliness. Perhaps I was bored. I didn't think too long and hard about anything. We went out a couple times. We went to see a movie, and then we went to walk around the mall. George showed me Santa Barbara and a beautiful rose garden near the Old Spanish Mission. Then we went out on the Pier for ice-cream. I learned a great deal about the area from touring with George: Ventura,

Camarillo, and Santa Barbara, and every place in between. One evening he asked to see how I had decorated the bedrooms. I showed him that I had started a ballerina theme for my daughter's room before her arrival. I showed him my dismally empty bedroom which was still in need of furniture. George cornered me in a passionate kiss and we hopped into bed to test the mattress. It was comfortable by all counts.

George was an expert at DIY. After looking at my beautiful powder room on the ground floor, George decided he would redo his own dismal toilet. He bought tiles, a new bowl, faucet and sink, and even a tile cutter. Brrrrrrrrrrrrrrrrrrrrrr … was the loud noise I heard from the vicinity of George's kitchen and garage many an evening. He was working fast and furious. His goal was to have the bathroom ready for a summer barbecue planned at his home. Brrrrrrrrrrrrrrrrrrrrrrrrrr … would he ever finish in time?! 'I took a class at the Home Depot store,' he chimed as I asked one day what the racket was all about. 'My lovely bathroom will be ready soon. It might be nicer than yours!'

I had no intention of competing with this man, but he had the conviction of a small child trying to win at marbles. My neighbourly lover came over many evenings for a visit. We spent weekends exploring the California coastline and also gardening. California was certainly more fun with another person to drive around enjoying the sites. We cooked at my house, and then we cooked at his house.

The time was approaching when Tiffany would be coming to live with me. How would I explain this unknown person to her? He was eager to meet her and do family outings.

George was moving at the speed of light with everything and I barely knew him.

Planning for Tiffany

I had to find the best child care in Oxnard and had no clue where to look. A few people at work gave me ideas, but most were negative. 'Don't put your child in the Oxnard public school system', they said. 'The schools are no good. You'll regret it!'

Florida had been little better and I had already made up my mind to find a good private school, had I stayed there. I combed the yellow pages for ideas and came across several private schools in Camarillo and in Oxnard. I made appointments and went during my lunch break to visit and ask questions. I had many questions to ask at these private schools. Most of all I wanted a school with flexible times that worked with my office hours of 9:00 am to 5:00 pm. If the pre-school dismissed students at 2:00 pm, then I would have to find after school care. Everywhere I went, the story was the same. One could drop off the child after 8:00 am, but they had to be collect 1:30 – 2:00 pm. The system was not built with working people in mind. I was told the school day could not be too long for pre-schoolers. They needed their rest. The dilemma of the working parent was huge.

I met Dana while 'shopping around' for a childcare facility for Tiffany in Camarillo. I had made an appointment to visit a pre-school in Camarillo during my lunch hour that day. The person in charge said I could come after 12:30 pm. This was when the children would be settling down for an after lunch nap. She came out to the gate when I buzzed the door bell and spoke to me at the gate. The building was an oversized house in Camarillo with a large front wall and gate. A flower garden decorated the front of the home. It seemed comfortable and I imagined Tiffany would settle well there. 'Hello, how are you?' she asked. Dana was a cheerful looking black woman with curly dark brown hair cut into a short bob. Her olive brown skin shone in the sun and she had a bright happy disposition. She had round piercing brown eyes and a small mouth with pouted lips. She was slim and pretty by Caribbean standards; average height and long limbs.

When did she move to California? Why was she working for a small child care facility in Camarillo? These were questions I had as we spoke about the daycare. 'Are you from the Caribbean?' she asked. I listened to her accent and tried to guess which Caribbean country she could be from. 'Yes I'm from Trinidad,' I responded. 'Fancy meeting someone from the Caribbean in Camarillo, California.' 'Yes, I'm from Barbados, but I've been living here for years.' I could hear the slight Bajan twang but it was diluted by a West Coast Californian accent.

We went inside and did a quick tour of the house. She explained the fees and their security processes. I was then given some paperwork to take away to read and sign. The papers would have to be submitted if I decided to take the vacant spot that was coming up. Dana suggested I look at a place called Mary Law Private School in Oxnard since I lived in that town. She wrote the name for me and said it would be more convenient than trying to drive out to Camarillo everyday. This certainly made sense. Dana and I exchanged telephone numbers and promised to keep in touch. I made an appointment at Mary Law Private School which offered a pre-school and elementary school in the south of Oxnard. The Private school was situated on Albany Drive off East Channels Islands Boulevard. It was a 15 minute drive south of my house with all the traffic lights. If we left home early we could possibly get there before rush hour traffic. The buildings looked like refurbished 1980's structures. I saw several brick buildings, as well as temporary, pre-fabricated trailers. There was an ample wall and secure gates. It was important to prevent intruders from entering the school. One had to go directly to the office on entering the school. All the students wore uniforms. Girls wore a navy blue skirt and white blouses. This was a welcome respite for me since I did not want to have to think how to dress the child every morning. We would have several uniforms and that was it!

The owner and school principal was a short, East Indian man called Mr. Da Silva. One had to get past the short bleached blonde, middle aged secretary, to speak to him. It was the same at all schools. The secretary was 'God'. As she scheduled an appointment for me, I was told I was lucky because a vacancy was coming up soon. Usually I would have to get on her waiting list. I just wanted to meet with the principal and find out what kind of school I would be waiting for. Da Silva had a mop of salt and pepper grey hair, wild eyes and a big smile. One of his eyes winked now and then. It was a nervous twitch. I secretly nicknamed the fellow 'Wink Eye Da Silva'. I had nicknames for everyone I encountered.

He described how his school was "Da best". They had strict policies and discipline like 'back home'. Their curriculum was second to none. They offered music and French. One would never get this in the public school system. I wondered why they were teaching French when every second person in the neighbourhood spoke Spanish. However, the French language was supposedly the language of class and sophistication, so one had to know French. From a survey of the classrooms, it seemed some of the teachers were from the Philippines. In fact Oxnard was home to a large population of Filipino descent. The teachers seemed strict and responsible. My Tiffany would have to be enrolled there and I would find the money to pay for it. I would also have to pay for after school care. I spoke to one of the pre-school teachers, a robust black woman. She directed me to one of her church friends, Ms. Cheryl, who ran an after-school program at her home. She also gave me the number for a young substitute teacher, Carol, who lived nearby and was always looking for babysitting jobs to supplement her income.

Armed with a telephone number and address, I made an appointment to see Ms. Cheryl. She lived a few blocks from my home so this was going to be useful when I had to collect Tiffany after work. On entering Ms. Cheryl's home, I felt the warmth of a well run household. Ms. Cheryl was a middle aged black woman with two daughters in their late teens and a supportive husband. The family was religious by all accounts since there were framed religious passages around the house and black angels were also prominently placed in various stations. People came from all around Oxnard to pick up and drop off their children. Children were treated like part of the family. They were given snacks and activities like art and reading while waiting for parents to collect them. This was going to be Tiffany's home away from home.

Arrangements were beginning to fall into place. However I still had to make sure her room was beautiful and comfortable on a shoe string budget. I decided to go back to the auction to find some treasures with which to furnish the room. I returned to the Friday night auction collecting crystal glasses, oil paintings, lamps, books, and a series of ceramic plates with certificates. I could not understand why anyone would want a series of ceramic plates that came with certificates. I was not familiar with the concept but was told they were valuable because they were limited edition plates and the certificates said it all. These miscellaneous plates were used as wall hangings where a painting could not fit. They were images of flowers, cherub children, and landscapes.

I was on the lookout for wooden furniture suitable for a tiny bedroom. At last, one day I spotted a set of three chest of drawers; all solid wood with faded paint. They would be perfect. I had visions of sanding and painting them white so they would match. Two were to serve as side lockers next to the bed, and the other which was wider, with four drawers would be ideal for storing clothing. I was determined to outbid everyone for these wooden treasures. When they were brought before the crowd, the auctioneer split them into two bids. The larger chest of drawers went first. "Do I hear $20? Yes $20. Do I hear $30? This is a nice chest of drawers for a little girl's room."

That was precisely why I wanted it. I wished other people were not so intent on bidding for MY treasure. I wished they would focus on other more precious objects in the auction. But, however, there were two other families who wanted the damn chest of drawers. I set my upper limit to $60 and not a cent over. After all, I needed the pair of side lockers too. Eventually we reached $40 and one family dropped out. I put in a half a bid at $45. The other family bid another half at $50, then $55. I bid $60 and held my breath. 'Do I hear $65? Come on. This is a really nice, solid wood, chest of drawers.' Kathy the auctioneer teased. 'Does anyone want this treasure for $65?' She asked one more time and at last ... 'Sold to the lady in green; number 40!' This was my first big purchase and I was proud and excited.

When the pair of smaller lockers was put up for auction, the others seemed not to be too interested. I managed to get the pair for $40 without much of a fight. So I had my set of chest of drawers and another day I would look for a pretty matching head board for the little girl's twin size bed. They were always auctioning off head boards and bed frames so I knew one day I would get the ideal one.

This furniture was the most difficult to haul home. The chest of drawers had to be dismantled into pieces. I packed the drawers onto the front seat of my tiny red Mitsubishi Eclipse, flattened the back seat and left the top up so I could put in the frame of the large chest of drawers. I had to make two trips back and forth from the warehouse to my home to remove the items. On my second trip back to the warehouse, most of the other customers were long gone and the helpers were just packing up. 'Just in time they yelled,' as they loaded my car and closed the roll up door. I had a few bruises and aches from hauling the furniture but I was contented at not having to pay full price for pre-fabricated wood chip furniture. It was real wood, I consoled myself. The lot would stay in the garage awaiting repair and rejuvenation.

California Driver's License

Since I had moved to California from Florida in January, I was driving around with my Florida license plates on my red Mitsubishi Eclipse with the sun roof, as well as driving with a Florida driver's license. I tried to see how long I could get away with it while dodging police cars as they spied my red car. The thought of spending the extra cash on car registrations and other non-essentials had me hemming and hawing. I decided if the police stopped me, I could always pretend I did not know the law.

Unfortunately, red sporty cars always attracted unnecessary attention and one day I was stopped by a cruising police officer. 'Ma'am, you are driving with a Florida license plate. Do you live in town?' 'Yes I do. Just move here two weeks ago.' I winced as I tried to contrive a plausible story, feigning ignorance when he asked where I lived. I said I had recently moved to Oxnard from Florida. 'Ma'am you need to change your license plates as soon as possible and get a California driver's license.' 'Really? I wasn't sure I had to do this so soon,' I said. 'Yes,' he said, 'And if we see this Florida license plate again, you will get a fine.'

Those were the magic words: "Get a fine". It was better to swiftly get the plates changed than spend money paying fines. When I explained the situation to colleagues at work, they told me I needed to pass the fuel emissions test to get the California license plate. Pollution levels were a serious issue in the State and they had special rules. Not everyone could show up and get a license plate. One colleague recommended getting an oil change as soon as possible and having a pre-screening fuel emissions test done before I went to the Department of Motor Vehicles (DMV). I had one day to do everything and my brain was in a whirl. Fortunately, places remained open late in the area and I was able to get an oil change and spark plugs replaced at a garage in town. I had purchased my car brand new in Florida in 1997, so two years later I did not think there would be any problem with fuel emissions. That would surely only apply to old gas guzzlers.

I decided to take my chances and go directly to the DMV the following morning, taking time off from work. I tried to get there early before any rush, but still had to wait in line. Two applications were filled, one for a license plate and the other for the driver's license. I was able to get an appointment that morning to have my car tested. The vehicle proved sound in terms of the low level of emissions and I was told to return in a few days for my license plates. A letter of temporary approval was generated and I could produce this if stopped by the police.

The California driver's license required filling form DL 44, giving a thumb print and having my photo taken. I had to verify birth-date and proof of residence, which was my home purchase information. After paying the application fee, I had to pass a vision exam and set an appointment for the test on California traffic laws and signs. The test had 36 questions and one had three chances to pass. On passing the test, which was graded by computer on the spot, I would exchange my Florida license for the California license. There was no need to take a driving test on the road.

It seemed simple enough. I received a copy of the road signs and other rules for driving. Scanning the document briefly, I imagine everything looked familiar and booked an appointment during my lunch break the following day. When I returned next day, I settled down to take the test on the computer. As one question after another flew in front of me on the screen, I discovered that some of the multiple choice questions were tricky. In addition, I could not remember what I had seen in Florida and what was new in California. I was guessing one question after the other and the future looked bleak. 'Stand over there and wait for the results,' said the attendant when I had finished.

I looked around at the crowd with a smirk on my face. Hmmm lots of Mexicans, they probably did not even understand the questions the way I did. Look at that one. He just crossed the border; Ha! In ten minutes, attendant called us one by one. "Mr. Mexican" passed and went over to receive his temporary permit. The laminated version would be sent in the mail. 'Jenneee Leee James,' she mispronounced my name. Why did everyone have such difficulty saying my name? All they had to do was read the letters. As I came to the counter with confidence, she said, 'You did not pass! You can allow two weeks before booking an appointment for the re- test.' 'What? Is there some mistake? I... But I've... I've been driving at least 15 years!' I knew I had not studied, but this was so humiliating. Even "Mr. Mexican" passed the test. I hung my head in shame and said I would call to make an appointment. 'Next!'

I had to go home and study the traffic regulations and road signs for California. They were indeed different to Florida. In addition, the exam included many situations needing assessment and judgment to choose the best answers to tricky multiple choice questions. This was the first in many lessons in not taking anything for granted. After studying for a whole week, I returned to do the exam and passed on the second try.

The Church Choir

As I settled in my new home I longed for the opportunity to go out and socialize after work. Coming home to an empty house was not much fun and unpacking and fixing daily was wearing me thin. When in doubt, find a church choir. That had been my strategy to find friends and a community. Being alone in a strange place had been taking its toll and there was only so much the job could satisfy my attention. I needed to do more from an artistic standpoint. I was unsure which choir to join in this area. I didn`t know which one was good and which wasn't. In addition I had been an occasional Anglican Church-goer and needed some spiritual satisfaction and more contact with people other than the office crowd. I combed the newspapers to find a church and one with a decent choir. I spotted an advertisement for a call to worship by the Episcopalian or Anglican Church in Camarillo.

The town was just south of Oxnard on Highway 101. It was relatively close so I decided to go to church on the Sunday to spy on the choir. I called their office during the week for directions and a friendly lady gave me the details. 'Take highway 101 south and go past the Las Posas Road exit. Don't exit there.' I wondered why I should not exit on that street when the church address in the book said Las Posas Road. 'Exit at Carmen Drive and turn left. That will take you over the freeway. Then keep driving until you come to Las Posas Road,' she continued. 'When you get to the intersection turn left and we are a few yards down on the right.' Armed with this information, I knew exactly where I was going. I was determined to get to the service early.

I dressed in my Sunday best and left Oxnard for Camarillo, arriving twenty minutes before the start of mass. The directions were exact. I pulled into the driveway and took a good look at the surroundings. The modern church structure was made up of a main church building of brown bricks which stood at the back of the church parking lot. The mostly flat structure with a small metal sign on the brick wall was punctuated by a lily white bell tower on one side. Joined to the left side of the building was another brown brick building which I assumed was the parish hall. This too was bungalow style with the two buildings forming an 'L' shape. The end of the 'L' closest to the road had a dark cross engraved into the light concrete brick on that side. The car park was quite big and decorated with flower beds, shrubs, and rose-bushes in front of the church. Large evergreen trees partially hid the building from street view. I guessed they were expecting big crowds with such a sizeable car park.

On arriving early, I walked sheepishly to one of the pews at the back of the church and sat quietly at the end. The choir was just finishing a pre-service rehearsal and would have a short break before the mass began. They were a small group, about ten women and eight men. However, using microphones, at some key stations they were able to magnify the sound to fill the church. Many of the singers were elderly. This was typical of church choirs with volunteers. It wasn't easy to get young people to join.

A few minutes before the mass started, the church filled up

quickly with many families. Suddenly the organ was booming and the choir processed down the main aisle in full red and white gowns. The service was similar to the one I grew up with in Trinidad. Some of the wording and melodies of the Liturgy were different, but easy to follow nevertheless. I watched the organist as she made her way up to the organ and back to the front of the choir to conduct an unaccompanied piece. She then scrambled back to the organ. The little lady was a power house of energy. I wanted to get to know her.

During the announcements they mentioned that they were always looking for new singers. Anyone interested was to speak to Mary, the organist, after the service. Well, it was a sign from above. As an avid classical music singer, I was only too motivated to oblige. I had sung in choirs all my life: community choirs, school choirs, and university choirs. While living in Tallahassee, I sang with the large and reputable Tallahassee Community Chorus. They were a superb choir and I would have to seek out one of a similar calibre. The answer, however, lay in getting to know some other singers who could point me in the right direction of a big choir.

I followed the liturgy and sang out loud during the mass then watched the choir carefully as they recessed to the back of the church. After the service I walked toward the organist as she finished her last piece for the mass. 'Hello, my name is Jennylynd,' I said. The organist was a short plump lady with a short haircut, a round face and a tiny mouth. She was so short; she wore high heeled shoes to press the pedals of the organ which she played with great skill. She looked like a stocky, older version of Betty Boop and she even carried her namesake's bag with her belongings. 'Hello. How are you?' she said.

'I'm fine. I've just moved to California and would like to join the church choir,' I explained. 'That's great,' she said. 'We're always looking for new singers.' She was pleasant and positive. I had a good vibe right away. Mary asked me to sing some scales. She seemed pleased with my voice and range and told me about their Thursday evening rehearsals and early Sunday morning rehearsals. She asked if I was familiar with the Anglican Liturgy. Of course I was raised in the Anglican Church and went to an Anglican girls' high school. I knew it well. That was it. I was in the choir and eagerly looked forward to the Thursday night rehearsal.

Money Pancho

After organizing my choir membership, my achievement was rewarded with a tasty Mexican lunch at a restaurant called Money Pancho. Several people at work had mentioned the unique name of this restaurant when advising where to take visitors to the company. I wanted to try their food first hand so I could make the recommendation. Having lunch was like a visit to Mexico. The menu was baffling and my choices might as well have been done closing my eyes and pointing. I did not recognize the names of the dishes and certainly had never tasted them before. I ordered a tortilla soup (fresh chillies and other vegetables blended and served with onions, Pasilla chilies, cheese, sour cream, avocado and topped with tortilla strips), fish ceviche (fish served in a sauce of tomato, cilantro, onion, lemon juice), a taco salad with chicken (lightly toasted flour tortilla shell filled with homemade rice, refried beans and chicken), and carne asada (Steak Jalisco style grilled over an open fire the served with a beef enchilada).

The waitress opened her eyes and asked, 'Is that for you alone or are other people joining you?' 'No,' I said. 'It's just me. I'm really hungry.' She said, 'OK' with a smirk, and whisked away swiftly with my order. I understood afterwards why she looked surprise. It was way too much food. I had to ask for boxes to take home the leftovers. There was food for two lunches and two dinners the following days and I began to relish Mexican food.

In the Office

Alma at the office became the first person I observed intensely. This pint sized secretary and receptionist did what she wanted. She started teaching me Mexican slang while I practised my text book Spanish. Her hair always looked stylishly coiffed yet she would fuss as soon as she arrived. Her eyebrows were the neatest thin line I had seen on anyone, yet she would spend time plucking to re-enforce the thin line before applying makeup. If only she knew, I spent no more than 15 minutes getting ready after a shower. Putting out the outfits in advance made the process even shorter. No makeup, just some lipstick and wads of moisturising cream, and I was ready for work. The dry California air was notorious for depleting moisture from the skin. I had no intention of becoming a prune after a few years.

'Why do you spend so much time on your make-up'? I asked one day. 'Well, you never know which client would pass through the office'. One day, Alma was so distressed over her eyebrows, she disappeared for some hours. She later told me that she and her mother had gone into the city to have her eyebrows tattooed onto her face. Never again in life did she have to worry about the shape of her eyebrows. It was the first time in my life I had met anyone obsessed about the shape of eyebrows. I barely even noticed mine. The day after the tattoo job, Alma strutted with the confidence of an accomplished woman with a new lease on life. 'You need to get acrylic nails,' she told me. 'What?' I asked, surprised by the statement. 'Your hands look like a man's. You should really get your nails done.'

I noticed many American women had long acrylic nails permanently glued onto their own nails. Many people when using a computer keyboard would go "Click, click, click". I made it a point not to participate in the madness. In any case, I love to cook all my meals. How would that be possible if I had long nails? I had a small child. How could anyone take care of a child while wearing nails? 'No, I'm not doing it. I hate not being able to cook my meals and I don't like the feel of nails anyway.' 'But …' she interrupted me. I jumped in, 'Anyone who doesn't like me because my nails are short will have to deal with his own personal problems. I don't have a problem.' I shut her up right away and changed the subject.

Alma always got the tallest cup of coffee to start the day right. 'What's for breakfast Alma' I would ask. 'Coffee,' would be the short answer. Alma had recently divorced her husband and had the major responsibility for two small children; a boy and a girl. She had to rise early, take them to school, and then come to work. Sometimes she would deliver them to her mother's house in Camarillo, or their father would take them to school. Her son had to wait for a special bus to take him to school. He was hyperactive, she said. I wondered what this meant. Any child who was bored in class and could not keep still was given the label of suffering from ADD – attention deficit disorder. Doctors would prescribe drugs so he could sit still, and he would be forced to survive the pre-planned, artificial system of organised learning. It was the way the system ran. I had never agreed with this program and wondered if there was no other solution. Unfortunately this affected many male students.

Alma complained to me that she hated the job but was just doing it until something better came along. She tried to imitate my Trinidadian accent and was a good actress. 'Oh my Gawd,' she would say, imitating my lyrical song. 'Aay, Aay,' I would reply in surprise when she imitated me. 'You're good Alma.' In return, she'd reply, 'Aay, Aay,' with a musical Trinidadian accent. Alma was on the lookout for a suitable replacement for her husband, and I would sometimes get stories about this man or that. I heard details of how she met up with one during the lunch break had juice and a joint. She then came back to work. 'How can you concentrate?' I asked. 'It's Friday. Don't worry. Nothing much is happening this afternoon,' she said. Alma never ate much; just a juice for lunch … Yet she was not skinny by Hollywood standards.

3
POLLO CON MOLE

Welcome Home Tiffany

As June approached, I looked forward to the return of my little girl. She had been lovingly cared for by Granny in Trinidad and I had prepared her room and a welcome party. I had found a matching wooden headboard to complete the bedroom set. I sanded the furniture which had been stored in one half of my large roll up garage, and painted them white. I then bought stickers of pink ballerina shoes, tiny bunches of yellow flowers with blue bows and stuck these onto the front of drawers and into patterns on the wooden headboard. I then searched the bedroom section of DIY stores for wall paper borders with ballerina shoes to complete the little ballerina's room. I had to get a ballerina bed cover with matching curtains. One day when I called to asked Tiffany what she liked for her bedroom. She said Barbie! I had to search for ballerina Barbie bedding and curtains and of course these were available. It seems many little girls had the same dream. Her bathroom had the same theme with matching curtains and bath mats. Trust the consumer culture in California to provide any and all themes to fulfill the wild fantasies portrayed in the media.

That evening I went to the airport to meet Tiffany. Those were the days when security was relaxed and one could go all the way to the exit gate of the plane, whether travelling or not, to collect friends and relatives. I was waiting with anticipation to see my cute child and my mother as they emerged from the plane. It seemed like an eternity, as people filed out, I waited and waited. They must have been some of the last ones to leave.

Tiffany hopped and skipped down the walkway, hopping towards me, then past me. 'I'm going to meet my mommy in California', she said. I took photographs and she smiled at me. When my daughter Tiffany joined me in California she was three and a half years old. At that time, Tiffany was a slim child with olive coloured skin and large brown eyes with long eye lashes. She had short curly brown hair which my mother would twirl into four curls with a centre part, using baubles to hold the parted hair in place. Tiffany had a happy disposition. She would hop and skip all the time, smiling at complete strangers and engaging them in conversation. 'I'm going to meet my mommy in California!' she told me again.

My child did not even know who I was. My heart dropped for that one spilt second. How could I let her know how much I loved her? How I sacrificed to pave the way for her smooth arrival and settling in California. 'I am your mommy,' I said. 'Look at me. I love you'. As the tears of joy roll down my face, I hugged her and gave her many kisses on her cheeks. Then hugged my mother too, thanking her for taking such good care of my bundle of joy and bringing her home to me. I promised her she would always be with her mommy from then on, through thick and thin, no matter where I had to move. The child hugged her beloved mother whom she had come to see in California! I was told she spoke to everyone one on the plane while travelling to California.

'I'm going to see my mommy who lives in California. My mommy has a house in California you know.' Polite passengers just smiled and said, 'Yes, that's great.'

When we arrived home I took my mother, Gloria, and Tiffany on a grand tour of the little townhouse. They liked the high ceilings and the large bright windows. They loved the little powder room behind the kitchen, the roll up garage doors, and the extended landing with the wall unit and TV. Tiffany was delighted by her baby bathroom and ballerina bedroom. It was fit for a little princess. They ate heartily and were fast asleep in an hour. I imagined the jet lag had caught up with them.

The next day was Saturday and I had planned a lavish welcome home party for Tiffany. I decorated the patio; prepared numerous hors d'hoeuvres for the seven or so guests (I could never cook small quantities). I had decorated the patio with a lovely "Welcome Home" sign and had invited Mary, the organist from choir and her daughter and granddaughter. I also invited Alma from work and asked her to bring her two children and her little niece who were all close to Tiffany's age. I wanted my little girl to meet new friends. Unfortunately, since I barely knew anyone, this was a bit difficult. However, I was thankful for the people we already knew. The children had a good time running around our little patio. The adults had time to gossip and become acquainted. I invited Tarsellia who lived two doors down. She had big granddaughters, but they were a bit too old to play with the children at our party.

One Big Happy Family

George was introduced to my mother and Tiffany and we started having family outings to various sites. George knew a beautiful rose garden in Ventura town, so we took the drive out to Ventura in his car. We looked at roses with Granny and daughter walking ahead while we strolled hand in hand behind. It was almost too good to be true. George was romantic and had delivered roses from his own garden to the house when Granny came to visit.

Next, we all went to his company's summer picnic. This was a big affair with at least five hundred staff members and their families. I had never seen such a large company event in all my life. It was held at event grounds with picnic tables and activities for everyone. There was face painting and games for children and many food stations. The theme was Mardi Gras and we all received beads, masks and hats. My mother watched George and I and winked with approval. 'How long have you known him? He seems like a nice man. Keep your fingers crossed. He might ask you to marry him.' 'Mammy, I don't think I want to get married. After a divorce, who needs to rush into that?' I asked. 'Well, you never know. He might ask you,' she said.

Journey to Baja and Back

While my mother was with us, she took care of Tiffany when my boss and I travelled to visit farms in Mexico for a day. We set out at 5:30 am on a Friday to see contract growers in Baja California. My boss had said to meet him at the company parking lot and I could leave my car in front of the office until we returned that night. It was going to be my introduction to farming operations south of the border in Mexico. The company brought in green onions and a host of other vegetables and herbs across the border to fill the large demand of supermarkets.

I had packed my note books, numerous checklists for food safety, and the ever present clip board. Knowing what to take and what to leave behind was a bit tricky since it was my first out of country journey for the company. I was told we would inspect the farms to see how crop was harvested and packed in boxes immediately. We would also have an opportunity to see the packhouses where some product was washed and packed. Our journey from Oxnard to the first farm in Baja could take us up to four hours, Bob estimated. I was not sure how to dress. I heard news that Baja could be dangerous, so I was surely not wearing any of the gold jewellery that usually adorned my neck and fingers. I had to look like a manager but not be too ostentatious.

There was always a chill in the air. Other people did not feel cold, but I always felt a chill in my bones. After all, I was coming from a life in Florida where it was always warm or extremely hot. I decided on wearing khaki trousers, a long sleeved shirt with a t-shirt underneath for warmth, and a khaki jacket in case I needed it. I wore a decorative little scarf around my neck to add some flair to an otherwise drab outfit. I decided on wearing some makeup to accentuate features and pulled my long hair back into one pony tail.

We literally flew at top speed in Bob's large SUV south on Highway 101. It was so big, one did not feel bumps in the road the way one did in my low-sitting sporty car. There was no traffic early in the morning, even though the highway was full of commuters in and around Los Angeles. I wondered where everyone was going so early in the morning. Californians were always on the go. The long drive gave us an opportunity to chat and learn more about each other from a social standpoint. It was also an opportunity for me to get a better understanding of the fine tuned operations of the company. We passed exits for cities in Orange County, and then eventually entered San Diego County. I wished I could go to visit all the wonderful towns we passed on the way. I was making notes on the drive of places to return for a visit: Long Beach, La Jolla, the city of San Diego; and the list went on.

After passing San Diego, it was just a matter of time before we hit the Mexican border. We stopped to use the bathroom, get some food, and fill up the gas tank at a roadside convenience stop before the border. It was only then I realized I had not packed my passport. All I had was my driver's license in my wallet. As a white or black American, it was usually easy to travel back and forth across the Mexican border. People of Mexican descent were searched or interrogated the most, in case they were illegal immigrants without visas or work permits. I, however, travelled on a Trinidadian passport. I was not American and needed to take my passport which held my H-1B work visa and stamp to show my reason for living in United States.

'Bob, I don't have my passport with me,' I said timidly. 'What? You don't have it? Oh my God. And we're almost at the border.' He stood and took a few seconds to recover from the initial shock. 'We're going anyway,' he announced. 'We'll just wave at them at the border crossing.' I followed his lead. As we stopped at the Mexican border, the immigration inspector asked, 'Americans?'

'Yes,' we chimed in unison. He stared at us and I gulped silently. 'Just going down for the day to Tijuana for shopping,' Bob added. The inspector waved at us and we continued driving. Many Americans went across the border to Tijuana to buy prescription drugs which were cheaper than in the US. They also went for clothing, alcohol, and other consumer goods. It was a brisk business run daily at the border. It was around 8:30 am when we crossed and I even saw Americans walking across the border to do their shopping. On a busy Friday morning, we did not create any suspicion or alarm and we were just part of the daily crossing.

'Whew,' said Bob relieved we were not asked to show anything. 'Jennylynd you're putting us in an awkward position. We'll see what happens when we're driving back into the US. That's going to be interesting.' I was nervous, about re-entering the US. If we met a stickler for details, they could detain me at the border. Oh my God what would happen to me? I had visions of being locked away in a room with other illegal immigrants. They could throw away the key and my family would never hear about me again. However, for the time being, I focused on the day ahead. We drove on the outskirts of Tijuana. The place looked a bit dirty and seedy as we passed and I made a mental note to never to visit for any reason. I was a little afraid of the desolation I saw on the outskirts of the city.

We then continued on a coastal roadway. The terrain was the exact continuation of the desert type conditions of Southern California. In my naivety, I somehow expected to see something different. Of course a border was an artificial line. The weather and terrain on the Pacific coast continued uninterrupted. The arid land with a few grass patches and cacti here and there continued for miles. On the way down the coast, we passed a few big concrete homes. The road was not well travelled and we saw very few vehicles going in either direction. We were going down the coast to a region called Mañeadero.

We passed a few small towns on the way, and then went past Ensenada where I heard some cruise ships from the United States would dock. Many party ships came down to Ensenada to take people binge drinking and shopping. We then took a small roadway heading inland. According to Bob, the owners of our company no longer drove down to Baja California to visit farms, like they did in the past. There was a new fear of kidnappings. However, he said we had nothing to worry about because we were not wealthy land owners. I was still a bit worried about our safety.

There were not many road signs, but Bob knew where to drive. I was glad the company did not send me on this expedition by myself. I would have been lost many times over without proper road signs. As we turned a bend in the dirt road, we came to a road block. A bunch of youths with rifles peered at us and looked around at the back seat of the car. I almost wet myself with fear. Bob however appeared as calm as usual.

'Where are you going?' one of them asked. Bob explained in perfect Spanish that we were visiting the ranch of Jefe Gonzales in Mañeadero. 'Oh really,' said the young man. With that, Bob reached under the car seat and pulled out a wad of US cash and handed it the spokesperson for the group. He smiled showing a few rotten teeth and signalled to his buddies to open the make shift barrier. I could not even speak. The shock of the event which happened in less than a minute, was reeling in my head, and I was shaken.

'But, but ...' I tried to speak as we drove past some of the young men who still stared at our car suspiciously.

'Don't worry Jennylynd. I have things under control,' said Bob, as he tried to calm me down. 'You just have to give them a few dollars and they're fine.' 'But is that some sort of government road block? Were they bandits?' I could not calm down. 'They had big rifles. Oh my God. I was so scared....' The shock took a few minutes to wear off. I still could not understand the situation. 'We may meet a few fellas like that again,' said Bob. 'I have cash under the car seat and a gun. Don't worry,' he said calmly. 'A gun? A gun you said ... and I have nothing to worry about? I've never come close to a gun in my life. I've lived a sheltered life Bob.' I took a few deep breaths and looked out the window as the car sped along.

We had then entered an area where the roads were no longer paved. We crossed one dirt road after another, raising dust behind us. We then came to another barrier where two young men with rifles watched us suspiciously. Again Bob told them where we were going, gave them a tip and we were let through. This time it seemed like a routine with less shock on my part.

We finally reached the farm at 9:30 am. We drove on a dirt roadway which traversed green onion fields. I could see whole families engaged in harvesting the plants and assembling them into bundles. The people were darker than the typical population of Spanish descent. Their almond shaped eyes and long black hair showed they may have been indigenous people of the region; descendants of Aztecs or other first nations people. Small children ran around in the field dressed in basic clothes, some in tatters as their parents worked, their faces dirty from the grime around them. It was a sad sight — child labour. The youngest were assembling green onions and putting them in piles. Some were stringing the stems with blue rubber bands. All of this was taking place so North Americans could get cheap green onions to garnish meals sold at fast food restaurants. The injustice was unbearable to watch. 'Their poor little hands,' I protested to Bob. 'Why are these babies in the fields? Oh how sad!'

Bob explained there was no such thing as daycare. We were in a rural place and the safest location for a small child was with his or her mother in the field. The company had some rudimentary school at another part of the ranch for the older children. Well, I was curious to see the school later on. We drove up to some open packhouses with concrete floors, metal posts and galvanized iron roofs. I saw how simple a packhouse could be, compared to our more sophisticated facilities in California. It felt good to step onto land and walk. The owner greeted us warmly and conversed back and forth in English and Spanish.

We then boarded his jeep for a tour of the farms and went hither and thither as we watched the workers. They stared back at us with curiosity. We then went to one of the packhouses and I took notes. I wanted to make sure if they were washing the vegetables, potable water was used. And also, hand wash stations were needed for staff to wash their hands. At that time in California, portable field toilets had been introduced with hand wash facilities. I did not see any of these when we drove around this growers ranch. It would be my first recommendation. The workers must have been relieving themselves in the fields. Just think of the potential for contamination of the crops.

There I was with my high and mighty recommendations and visiting from the United States. I was sure they would curse me behind my back for increasing overheads for portable toilets in the fields and having to fix the deficient toilets at the packhouse.

We took a break for lunch and were treated to an excellent Mexican meal at a nearby farmhouse restaurant. The owner was friends with the proprietor, so of course we had a superb feast. To start, we had seafood ceviche with freshly fried corn tortilla. Then sizzling chicken fajita was served with rice and beans and corn tortillas, and an assortment of salsas. After the meal, we continued the journey to another farm run by a second grower. This facility had a more sophisticated, enclosed packhouse. The owner asked me to do a hand washing demonstration on the spot. I struggled with my simple Spanish skills to explain hand washing to the packhouse employees. The whole exercise went fine but I was determined to practice my food safety Spanish vocabulary on returning to California. The look on the faces of the staff as I destroyed their language was priceless.

'Crazy American,' the faces seemed to say. This facility had cold storage for some harvested products and in some cases, boxes were loaded onto refrigerated trucks immediately to be shipped north to California. The differences in the growers probably depended on who had deeper pockets to build more sophisticated infrastructure. We thanked our hosts for the tour and I promised to send him a copy of my notes about the visit.

Bob and I started the long journey back to Oxnard, California. We met with equally ominous boy soldiers at the road blocks on the way out of the Mañeadero region. The procedure was the same: give cash with a smile and carry on. I was so relieved to be back on the paved highway heading north to the US border. My relief was short-lived as I remembered I did not have my passport with the H-1B visa to show my purpose in United States. How were we going to get around that hurdle? My boss always looked calm. I wished for half of his attitude.

We drove past Ensenada and flew up the highway. Then again on the outskirts of Tijuana, we passed the wretched ghetto on the outskirts of the city. We then met a line of hopefuls crossing the US border. As predicted, anyone who looked Mexican was questioned thoroughly and asked to show documents. Some had to go across the yard to a special building for further questions. A few had to open the car trunk for inspection. When our turn came, I gulped and put on a nice, fake smile. 'Let me do the talking,' Bob said. 'Of course. I have nothing to say,' I responded. We drove up to the window and rolled down the windows. 'Americans?' the inspector asked. 'Yes. Coming back home,' said Bob. 'OK. Go ahead,' he said and waved us past.

When we drove past and out of ear-shot I screamed 'Woo hoo! What a relief!' 'Next time, don't forget your documents,' Bob warned. 'You put me in an awful position. Wasn't sure what excuse I was going to make.' 'Well you certainly looked calm to me. Ha! Ha! Don't worry. I've learned my lesson.' We drove at top speed through San Diego County and on to Oxnard. I was wondering what next time he was talking about. I did not want to ever have to go through those frightening road blocks in my life time. Little did I know I would have to go to the same farm area the following year. That time it was with one of the sales managers who knew the Mexican roadways. The USDA had found *Salmonella* in samples of our products from Mañeadero sampled at the border. All crops from that grower were Detained Without Physical Examination (DWPE). I had to visit the grower, investigate possible sources of contamination, and put corrective actions in place. On that trip, I was better prepared with all the necessary documents to cross the border back and forth.

Pollo Con Mole

The unofficial social structure of Mexicans in Southern California became evident as the days wore on. The field Mexicans i.e. those who planted and harvested crops, were at the lowest rung of the ladder. Those who worked in the packing houses and warehouses may have been better educated and enjoyed a slightly higher status in their community. The supervisors, of course enjoyed the highest status. If the person actually went to an American school or had a university degree, he or she was close to God.

White skin was also idolized. This was probably a "hangover" from European colonial life in the region. Women were sure to cover their faces while working in the fields. Only the eyes were left exposed as they wore two or three handkerchiefs to cover the whole face. Long sleeves were used to cover the arms regardless of the heat. They did not want to become scorched and wrinkled. This was particularly important in California since the UV rays caused pre-mature wrinkling in the paler sector of the population.

The typical Californian of European descent worshipped the sun and would seek all opportunities to tan. The result of this practice showed up in the skin quality. I'd never seen such leathery brown skin in my life. It was an interesting mix.

When I arrived in Oxnard, I had to learn quickly how the agricultural cycle worked so I could make a worthy contribution to the company. I learned how the growing cycles followed the sun. Planting in the Oxnard plains started mid-winter. This guaranteed a summer harvest. In the spring, planting started in the Salinas Valley further north to ensure a late summer and fall harvest. After this the harvesting took place in the winter months in Yuma Arizona, Baja California and San Luis in Mexico. The company had partnerships with many growers in each region to ensure a year round supply of vegetables and strawberries. It was a big operation to manage. But after decades in business, everything ran seamlessly.

The company planted green leafy vegetables and all manner of lettuce. Strawberry fields abounded. A trip with the field operations manager opened me to a whole new world of growing which I knew nothing about.

During the planting phase, the land was tilled using heavy machinery, seeds were sown, and then hundreds of yards of irrigation pipes were laid out on the land. What an enormous manual task. Some employees were skilled in laying out the pipes and attaching the joints. In Southern California, water was a precious commodity. Water for the early stages in irrigation was pumped from canals in the area. It was called agricultural water. I was horrified to find out that water for crops was being sourced from ditches and canals. However, I was assured this water was applied only to the roots of the crops and primarily during the early phase of growing. Later in the growing phase, if sprinklers were used, then well water would be the source. Using canal water in the early phase was to ensure a cheap source of water for irrigation, and also was supposed to give enough time for disease causing micro-organisms to be reduced in numbers long before harvest time.

I had the 'privilege' to visit a local water treatment plant where sewage water was treated in such a way that the biological oxygen load and pathogen load was reduced significantly so the remaining water could be released into the canals. I studied the whole process carefully to convince myself this would be safe. It was my first introduction to water treatment and there was a lot more to learn.

The Pesticide Applicator, Mark, took me on a tour of the fields to explain how pesticide was applied. We looked at the reports he had to fill to alert the Department of Agriculture about which pesticide was applied and on what fields. We walked the fields to search for the presence of pests. Only if pests were detected, would pesticides be applied. I found it re-assuring that pesticides were not simply applied as a matter of course. There was a specific method employed and at least in California, consumers could be assured their food was not laced with needless pesticides. There was also a required waiting period to harvest time, allowing enough time for the pesticide residues to subside before harvesting.

We would pass in front of a field with young growth and

Mark would know immediately if it was a broccoli field or a carrot field just from the colour of the leaves. This was a skill I would have to master. Harvesting was a time of precision and great activity. The sales team in the main office would take orders from wholesalers around the country. They would in turn call the field operations manager who knew exactly which fields were ready for harvesting. With over fifty different items in the ground and farms all over the Oxnard plains, I wondered how he could keep track of which crops were ready. Sales people could come in as early as 5:00 am to stake orders from vegetable and strawberry wholesalers in Eastern United States. Business started early in the produce industry.

As the summer season in the Oxnard Plains was winding down, the winter season in Salinas Valley was picking up. I had to travel north to Salinas to review the food safety programmes and be sure to implement exactly what I was doing in the rest of the business. I was introduced by telephone and email to the managers in the north, given a beeper and sent on my way. The journey was to take three and a half hours. It in fact took me four and a half hours since I was travelling with Tiffany and did not quite know where I was going.

I had booked an overnight stay at the Best Western hotel that was just off highway 101 and reasonably priced. We could not be extravagant on the company's modest purse. Only inexpensive accommodation and economical meals were allowed. I had pre-arranged with the area manager to have Tiffany play quietly in one of the offices while I poured over the food safety documents and met with staff in another office. He agreed to this arrangement and spoke about having kids of his own. However, I was determined to find a child care provider in the area. The company office was a few miles off the Highway 101 exit and not too difficult to find. Everyone in the office was friendly and I was able to meet many people and learn about the operation in the first two days. Tiffany was set on a large blanket in an empty office with many toys while I went on a tour of the facility.

The corpulent plant manager, Jose, took me for a walk around the plant and I filled out my food safety checklist. We looked at rodent bait stations and the clearing of brush around the facility. Jose could barely walk. He was mestizo with short cropped hair, a moustache, trimmed beard and large round brown eyes. He had a double chin and by all accounts, a double belly which seemed to reach to his knees. He was probably in his early thirty's but because of the heavy weight, he looked older than his years. We started inspecting the interior of the building and observed packing operations. He wheezed and groaned as we walked around. I was worried about his health and wondered why he was so heavy.

'Let's see the packing room, hhhh, hhhh, hhhh,' he wheezed. I followed along nimbly, feeling a little guilty about forcing him to show me everything. 'OK, let's ask the floor supervisor what training she did recently with the staff. Hhhhh, hhhh, hhhh.' The supervisor was Spanish speaking and I tried my best to communicate with her. She was enthusiastic and wanted to be sure she was doing the right thing. I did some training with the staff on hand washing and wearing clean uniforms for work and promised them I would repeat the training on the next visit, following up with a quiz.

During the lunch break, one of the managers took me on a quick tour of the town of Salinas. This town was listed as the largest municipality of Monterey County. The Salinas Valley was inland from the coastline and enjoyed a Mediterranean type climate. Typical daily summer temperatures ranged from 17ºC in the winter to 24ºC in the summer. Salinas was also listed in the top ten American Cities for clean air quality. When I first observed the heavy morning fog in the summer, I thought there was fire in the neighbourhood. A colleague at work explained to me that the marine layer came in from the coast every morning and would burn off by midday.

The town looked like little Mexico. Even though it was historically settled by indigenous people, a wave of populations ranging from Mexican, Chinese, Filipino and Anglo-European Americans populated the area for the purpose of growing crops. Many people came seeking work in the lively agriculture industry. A second wave of Mexican workers populated the area in recent years and so countless Mexican stores and restaurants were visible as we crossed from one street to the next. The most famous inhabitant of Salinas was John Steinbeck who won a Nobel Prize for Literature in 1962. His celebrated books were based on life in the Salinas Valley and the plight of the migrant worker. A special landmark in the town, the National Steinbeck Center had recently opened at that time. It was a museum dedicated to Steinbeck displaying exhibits of his work and philosophy. A great deal of construction could be seen around the area at as roadways and other buildings were being updated. I took mental notes of places for a return visit.

The following day I toured some of the fields with the field manager. I would have been lost trying to find the way on my own, but he knew every back road around Salinas. I also had a short discussion on food safety practices with the field supervisors to find out the best way to disseminate the information to all the field workers. We were supposed to meet the next month at a big restaurant in town for a half day workshop, when I would present food safety training to the regional supervisors. They would then pass on the training to the field hands.

They had planned a big event and I was suitably nervous; especially as everyone expected me to do the presentation in Spanish. I had arranged for a local babysitter to watch Tiffany every time I came up to Salinas. Ms. Terry was recommended by one of the girls in the Salinas Office and we went to visit her one evening. She kept children in her home during working hours. Ms. Terry was a chubby mestizo woman in her early forties. She had a round friendly face and big brown eyes. She looked like a kind hearted, warm soul from the moment I saw her. Her house was clean and she seemed like a level-headed woman. I met her big children and her husband and wondered if Tiffany would be in safe hands. It was always a worry, leaving a small child in the care of strangers. Well, I decided to trust her since I could not take Tiffany around with me while I worked.

I prepared my Spanish training material for the Salinas presentation. Alma reviewed my work for grammatical errors. I also prepared quizzes and assessment procedures. If the supervisors were going to be responsible for passing on information, I had to be sure they understood thoroughly. I practised my Power Point slide presentation until I felt confident enough to stand in front of the discerning crowd.

It was not going to be as casual as my previous experience of impromptu Spanish at a Mexican packhouse.

Soon the big day for my presentation arrived. I drove to Salinas the evening before the event and checked into the Best Western on Highway 101. After a good night's sleep we had the continental breakfast provided at the hotel, bagels, cream cheese and a few fruits and Tiffany was delivered to Ms. Terry's house.

The meeting was an all morning affair hosted at the Chapala Mexican restaurant on Salinas Street. It was a short distance from the main office. I wondered why the company would hire a restaurant for the meeting, then realised it was a grand event hosted by the Human Resources department and many other items were on the agenda. The walls of the restaurant were painted the colour of desert sand and murals simulated the desert cactus on the landscape. The company was assigned a large room on one side of the venue. Many Mexican gauchos came in their finest leather boots and hats for the event. At least fifty men filled the room. Again I felt as if I was on a movie set chairing a meeting of Spanish cowboys. After some HR presentations on occupational safety and salaries, it was my turn to perform.

I presented my power point slides and spoke about the importance of employee hygiene in starting the day with clean clothing, the importance of hand washing when harvesting and other food safety details. A few vocal supervisors challenged my suggestions of wearing clean clothes every day. 'The company does not provide clothing for the field hands. Who's gonna have time to wash clothes so often! They are working in dirt all day. Why do they need clean clothes?!' I gulped at the prospect of answering what was a completely valid question. I did not have the answers and for the most part was working from a list of rules devised for a food processing operation. I trembled a little and then tried to formulate an answer. 'Well, within reason, we need to be sure the worker's clothes would not be a source of contamination,' I said apologetically.

Thankfully my speech passed swiftly and before long, it was lunch-time. The restaurant had the most extensive menu of Mexican food I had ever seen. Most of the dishes I did not recognise so it was like taking a shot in the dark to know what to order. I asked Manuel, the HR manager to recommend his favourite dish for me. 'Their pollo con mole was spectacular!' he said. 'What is mole?' I asked. 'It's a spicy chocolate sauce.' Well, the idea of chocolate and spicy had me intrigued so I had to try this dish. The chocolate was in fact savoury, not sweet. The spices were expertly blended into the sauce and the meat fell from the bones of the chicken. Pollo con mole had become one of my favourite dishes. Many a trip to Salinas in the following years included a visit to Chapala restaurant to consume from their extensive menu and try many other delicious recipes. 'How did the meeting go in Salinas,' Alma asked the following week. 'Well,' I explained, 'the pollo con mole was spectacular!'

Roberto's Granny

I had started a massive food safety training program with short tests after each module. This meant preparing training programs for the packhouse staff, fresh cut vegetable processing, as well as field staff. With Alma's help, I was able to translate some of the slide presentations and practised dutifully to present the information in Spanish. It was an amazing feat for me to accomplish this work and I felt proud of the effort. The challenge was to find a good way to reward employees for their efforts. They had to be encouraged to not only sit through the training which complicated the work day, but their efforts to learn had to be recognized. Some true leaders emerged in terms of highest scores in the tests given.

I decided to prepare certificates of achievement and attendance and have them signed by the company President. The next plan was to have a big party at the end of the year when they would be presented with their certificates. The lunch room in the packing house was full of electric warmers and a few microwave ovens on wooden shelves around the room. When I asked Alma why there were so many warmers, she told me that the staff preferred to eat corn tortilla with refried beans every day for lunch. I asked if they would like some Chinese food for the end of year party. She said they would protest. We had to give them the same Mexican food for the party. Corn tortillas with re-fried beans were staples. But we could add some familiar specialty dishes like radish salsa and barbeque beef so they would feel special.

I gave the President's secretary a stack of certificates for him to sign. He happily obliged at the first fifty. After a while, he realised it was probably not effective use of his valuable time. Jennylynd had gone way too far. He then gave the secretary the job of to signing off for him. I was overjoyed when he came to the award ceremony and luncheon at the end of the year to present the certificates. The employees were shocked to see the big President, El Jefe major, at the party. For some, it must have been their first "big" certificate. Many told me with pride, that they would take their certificate home, frame it and place it on their wall. I was happy to have scored some brownie points while getting the cooperation of staff to participate in food safety programs.

During the course of giving exams to workers at the fresh cut facility, I noticed that one young man who packed boxes at the end of one production line would always get a perfect score. He must have been truly brilliant in his native country of Guatemala. Unfortunately with relocation to the United States, his brilliance was lost in translation and an inability to climb up any career ladder of significance. Whatever his status, I asked Bob if I could promote him to help with lab work. I knew he was bright and would learn the laboratory analyses quickly. My boss agreed to try him out and one day I had the opportunity to speak with him about my plan. He was overjoyed at the idea of going to the main plant to learn a new job and get an increase in salary.

Roberto did not disappoint. He was pint sized with a big brain. He absorbed as much as he could and took over responsibilities in the lab while Miguel was given new and more challenging tasks to alleviate his boredom. I had Miguel sign up for external courses to learn about pest control and sanitation. He earned his certificates after passing tests and was happy with his new role. Within two months, Roberto had mastered his responsibilities in the lab and all the paperwork associated with this job. Roberto's grandmother was visiting from Guatemala on vacation and he told me the news with great excitement. He had not seen her for many years. The following day Roberto presented me with two embroidered cloths. Red threads were woven through many layers of other coloured threads. He said his grandmother brought these gifts for me from Guatemala. She was happy the big boss was willing to give her grandson a chance and remove him from the end of a packing line. He had a very important job in the lab. This was such a touching gift of appreciation and I vowed to keep the cloths forever.

My Birthday Party

In August, George said he was throwing me a birthday party. That was great news for me. It was the first time someone was venturing to throw me a party. I usually jumped in and did everything for myself. George said he had planned a summer barbecue with friends from the office so we could blend the two parties into one. And as a gift, he was going to take Tiffany and me for a weekend to Las Vegas. He had seen a good deal on the internet. Because I knew so few people to invite it wasn't a difficult decision. A friend of my aunt's had a niece in Los Angeles, so I invited her over. And of course I invited Alma and her family. They were considered close friends by this the time.

George grilled burgers on the front patio and I prepared a few side dishes. I spoke casually with his work friends and wondered what they thought about me. Two young ladies and three young men came over. They had varying jobs in the office, both technical and clerical. I could not remember their names, even though George introduced me to everyone. They seemed good natured and easy going which is what one needed in work colleagues. George had a few simple chairs he put in his empty living room, and I brought over a few of my chairs so everyone had somewhere to sit. Music played in the back ground as we exchanged small talk. The conversation was a little disjointed since we were strangers, but the talk became more fluid as time wore on.

When Alma and her family arrived, I took them to see how I had decorated Tiffany's room. Her ex-husband who had dropped them off remarked, 'This place is amazing. I can't believe how well some people are living.' I was a bit surprised at his statement. What did he mean by this? I did not think my little townhouse was fancy. After all, it was tiny with two bedrooms. Where was he living? Then I remembered the reaction of the locksmith. A single woman having her own townhouse was not typical in the traditional Mexican society. One was supposed to be married and the husband was the provider.

Those of us with children decided to leave the party early. 'It's 8:30 pm, time to put them to bed,' I said, motioning to Alma who was just as bored as I was. The children however, were having fun running inside, then outside, making everyone nervous with their exuberance. 'Thanks so much George. It was a wonderful party.' 'Leaving already?' George asked, appearing a bit disappointed. 'Well, we've been here all afternoon, so we're just a little tired.' 'But, but ...' he protested.

'I'll collect the chairs tomorrow. Bye bye everyone!' I said, and left.

As I left, the departures started one by one. People made excuses to go home. When I put Tiffany to bed, I listened intently as the last few guests left George's home. It was a lovely little barbecue party.

Aftermaths of the Birthday

The next day I met with George to re-hash the party and discuss everyone who came. He was proud of himself for hosting a friendly party and was projecting about having another get together for the Christmas holidays. I felt so happy to have him in our lives and looked forward to our time away to Las Vegas the following weekend. We planned to leave as early as possible on Friday after work for the five-hour drive to Los Angeles to Las Vegas. It was going to be us and half of Los Angeles trekking through the desert for a weekend of fun away. George explained he had spotted a good deal for the Circus Circus hotel for the weekend. The hotel featured circus acts all day long and Tiffany would be entertained.

I said it all looked wonderful and would start packing our things so we would be ready for the trip. The Thursday before our trip, I got a telephone call from George that shocked me. 'Lindy, how are you?' he asked. 'Fine thanks. Did you have a good day?' I said. 'Lindy, I don't think it's going to work out between us,' he said. I gasped as if I had the air knocked out of me. Was my hearing failing? Had he just say what I thought I heard? 'I'm just not feeling this relationship. I want out,' said George. Not wanting to appear too shocked or needy, I responded in a matter of fact tone. 'Well, whatever you want,' I said calmly and hung up the phone.

I could not believe this. He was the same man who could not

keep his hands off me; the same one who came over every second day. He threw a party for me the week before. He took my family out a few times and then he wanted to break up? It was an insane moment and I just could not understand his behaviour.

After I hung up the telephone, I cried for at least half an hour. What was I going to do? I was becoming attached to the man. I had no best friend in Oxnard with whom to discuss this problem. I felt alone and betrayed. But I was not alone. I had my little girl to take care of. I decided to give him all the space he needed and I was not going to call him again.

But what about the trip we planned? I called Alma from work and asked her what she thought. She said I should still go on the trip. Everything was planned and even though he changed his mind about the relationship I should not miss out on the opportunity. I was to dress up really pretty and make sure I went on the trip and looked good every day. I was also not to allow him to touch me. 'Men yo-yo back and forth when they think they are losing control and falling for a woman,' she said. I was not to allow him to upset my life. I was going to have to show him that I was in charge of my emotions and could live with or without him.

Circus, Circus, Oh What a Circus

I called George and in a frank tone, asked what time we were planning to drive to Las Vegas. He said we should leave by 5:30 pm. I confirmed we would be ready and would see him at that time. Leaving work half hour early, I collected Tiffany and brought our bags down to the front door. We dressed and were ready exactly at 5:30 pm so we would cause no delay. George spun around doing last minute packing for 15 minutes until he was ready to drive. I did not say much and listened quietly to the music he played on the car stereo. It was a long drive through the desert. As predicted, when we exited Los Angeles and headed north on Highway 15, every Tom, Dick, and Harry was also heading north to Las Vegas.

We passed Victorville and continued driving until the land became more sparse than usual with few trees. I was excited to see the Mojave Desert and actually drive through it. I had heard about this desert and seen it in many movies. Barstow was the next big town on the way through the desert. The air was dry and warm, but we had an air-conditioned car. It was the end of summer, but still hot in the desert compared to the cooler temperatures at the coast in Oxnard. When we opened the door for a rest stop, the desert heat made it difficult to breathe. I had heard so much about Las Vegas and the bright lights for many years, so I was planning to take many photos and enjoy myself, despite not having an amorous companion to share the time with me. We climbed through desert mountains. The expanse of land was both beautiful and frightening. Tiffany took a nap in her booster seat at the back and I had to contend with a quiet George who drove along at top speed.

'So tell me about Las Vegas and what we will see when we get there,' I asked, to break the silence. 'Well, if it's your first time, you have to see Caesar's Palace and the fountain show. All the hotels have free shows.' 'That's interesting,' I said. 'Yes the indoor water fountain comes alive with talking and everything,' he continued. 'What other hotel shows will we see?' I asked. 'Well, the Hotel Bellagio has an amazing outdoor water fountain show at night with lights and music, the MGM Grand has a show with lions and tigers, and Treasure Island has an outdoor Pirate show!'

George became animated as he explained all the shows we were going to see. He was happy again and must have decided he was going to enjoy the trip since he was driving so far for the weekend. 'You also have to do the "Dam Tour"!' he yelled. 'Are you swearing George?' 'No, I mean the tour of the Hoover Dam! Not the darn tour! Hoover Dam is near Boulder City. It's a huge dam and you go down in an elevator to the bottom of the dam. It's real exciting.' Not wanting to be a killjoy, I said I would do the "Dam Tour". The damn must have been a great engineering work to get George so animated. I had seen Hoover Dam advertised on brochures for Las Vegas and Nevada.

We stopped to eat at a Greek restaurant on Highway 15 in the middle of the desert. Why would anyone put a big restaurant in the middle of nowhere? The place, however, was packed to the brim with holiday makers coming and going from Los Angeles. The restaurant had a captive audience at that point in the highway. There was no other food for miles around. I made sure to pay for my meal and Tiffany's in case George became upset for having to spend his money after breaking up with me.

He had already paid for the hotel booking which came with a buffet breakfast the other two days. Perhaps he was upset about having to pay for this. However it was his idea to come to Las Vegas, so I reasoned he should not have been upset. I could not guess what his dilemma was and tried not to analyze him too much. George boasted that Las Vegas had the best buffets and some casinos gave free drinks so people could gamble. Not being a drinker or much of a gambler, I was left out of some of the major Las Vegas activities. However, if Circus Circus and other hotels had family friendly shows, we could certainly find a lot to do on the Saturday, with the Dam tour on the Sunday. I would be back to LA in the afternoon so we could get home at a reasonable hour. Everyone would certainly be driving through the desert with us too.

We arrived late Friday night to the Circus Circus hotel which was at the far end of the Las Vegas Strip. As we entered the hotel, we were bombarded by screams of delight from dozens of children with their parents in the lobby. The whole world had converged on Las Vegas for the last summer weekend away. Children were running in all directions and frazzled parents struggled to keep a rein on them, as clowns and other costumed characters walked around. Tiffany was well rested from her nap and ready to explore the hotel.

George, Tiffany and I shared a hotel room. We put down our bags and walked around the hotel getting our bearings and getting a program for the next day's events. The room had two Queen sized beds. I stayed with Tiffany and he had a bed to himself. We dressed quickly and quietly in the bathroom early next morning and George announced we would be going to a massive breakfast buffet. It was the best in town.

We went down to the main floor and entered a large dining room. Again, dozens of children ran with glee in many directions. The buffet was large and confusing as we tried to think of what to eat and how much to eat. Since lunch and dinner were not included, I vowed to pack in as many calories as possible to last me until afternoon. After breakfast we went upstairs to see a few circus acts. Areas off-limits to children were the slot machines and others forms of gambling. I asked George to hold Tiffany while I gambled away a whopping five dollars on the slot machine. He had a hard time holding her back as the bright lights caught her eyes. 'I wanna pull the handle! I wanna pull the handle,' she screamed, reaching for the handle of the slot machine. 'Ok, you can do it once,' I said. The security guard caught me and announced, 'Ma'am, children are not allowed on the gambling floor. Ma'am, take the child off the gambling floor.'

I won $15 and decided to stop gambling before my luck ran out. We ventured to other hotels through air conditioned tunnels so as to avoid the hot sun outside. Many hotels were linked by small malls and stores that joined each complex. We went from hotel to hotel taking in the sights and the shows. New York New York had a fancy outdoor roller coaster on the side of the building. Caesar's Palace entertained with the talking Italian fountain. MGM Grand was on the furthest side of the strip, and Treasure Island with the big pirates' ships out front hosted a big noisy show. As each one finished and the crowd scattered, a new crowd approached to fill in the gaps for the next show, and the next. It was a never-ending cycle of entertainment.

When the sun went down, the bright, glittery lights were turned on in full force at all hotels and clubs. Patrons filed out to shows around town. However, having a child, I had to retire to the hotel for a rest when it became too late for her. I told George he could go off and have a drink without me. He did not need to have an early night like us. Off he went on his own for a few hours. Since he had broken up with me the day before, I felt no obligation to accompany him. I was too tired and an early rest was the best medicine.

I slept so soundly, that didn't hear when George came back that night. We awoke early Sunday morning to get ready for our trip to the Hoover Dam. We got dressed and went down for the big buffet breakfast and then checked out of the hotel. We then made our way through the desert to Hoover Dam. Getting tickets for the Dam tour was not a problem since we were early, but we saw a trail of cars following us. We knew the site would be crowded by the afternoon. We hoped to get on the highway early in the afternoon to head back to Los Angeles.

We boarded an elevator which took us down to the base of the large dam. There we heard the history of the dam's construction and many other tidbits about the location. I started feeling unwell with an upset stomach and wondered if it was because the elevator had descended too rapidly. As we got into the car to head back to LA in the midday sun, the temperature outside the car was at least 100°F. George cranked up the air-conditioning and I felt even more ill. My head throbbed and I was dizzy. The slightest noise made me even more ill, so we travelled in silence then became stuck in the longest line of traffic through the desert as half of Los Angeles was heading back home.

There was no escape. We could not dare head back to Las Vegas because we both had work the following day. We were stuck in the slow crawl. Tiffany fell asleep in her car seat. I complained about my head and upset stomach and George became more disturbed. I may have had a bout of food poisoning from the enormous, uncontrolled breakfast buffet or I had heat stroke. I was never good at surviving extra hot days. We stopped at a service station to buy cold water and ice, and I kept some ice on my forehead in a rag as we continued the slow crawl through the desert. I drank cold water and tried to stay cool. This did not help and my head continued to pound. The five hour trip took us eight hours. By the time we got back to Oxnard, it was late at night. I thanked George profusely for the trip and his patience driving all the way. He muttered, 'You're welcome'.

I did not see nor hear from him for at least three weeks after that. Life went on without George.

4

THE RULES OF LIFE

Dana and The Rules

One evening after work, I got a call from Dana, my friend who worked at the daycare in Camarillo. It was very exciting to hear my house phone ring just once. I seldom got calls, except the odd telemarketing company. Dana asked if I wanted to go out on Saturday night. I had to control myself from bouncing off the walls and screaming into her ears on the phone. When one relocates to a new town, any new friend is a blessing. 'Of course I want to go out! When? Where? What time? Let me find a babysitter first and I'll get back.' I called my work colleague Trudy who said her daughter would be available to babysit for me that evening. Trudy had to bring her then come to collect her whatever time I got home. It seemed like a big inconvenience for Trudy, but she did not mind.

Dana suggested we meet at The Whale's Tale restaurant and bar in Channel Islands Harbour for drinks. This was an exciting turn of events. I had wondered for a few weeks if I could ever find someone to come out with me on the weekend, and finally it happened. Dana suggested meeting just after 9:00 pm so we would not have to be seated for dinner. She timed the outing to the minute to have the most economic evening out, yet have a good time. If we arrived before 10:00 pm, we would not have to pay a cover charge. That was good for me since I already had too many bills to pay. She informed me about the men we might see at the bar and said the music would be great for dancing. The crowd was usually a mix of people from the neighbourhoods in the district.

I arrived at Channel Islands Harbour early so I could locate the bar and find the best parking. I waited in my car until it was 9:00 pm. The idea of showing up to a bar alone was a bit disconcerting. However, I had to remind myself that I moved to California alone, so going to a restaurant/bar alone was not a big feat of endurance. I walked in and ordered a ginger ale at the outdoor counter. The Whale's Tale had an indoor restaurant and a covered outdoor deck which faced the waterfront. Dana had mentioned meeting on the outdoor deck. I ran to the nearest free table for two and sat shyly nursing my glass of ginger ale. The DJ played loud music but the space was sparsely populated up to that point. Eventually she showed up in a mini dress with high heeled sandals and flair. I would have to dress like that the next time. My jeans and simple blouse would not attract a mob of eager suitors.

We gossiped non-stop and danced when the crowd piled in. Dana had become my resource for everything Californian. She knew about most of the schools, shops, and social places in Camarillo and Oxnard. She was able to give advice on where to go and what to do. Dana said Camarillo had a more prestigious reputation than Oxnard. That was why she was renting a one bedroom apartment in Camarillo. It was supposedly expensive for her but she did not mind. Dana was obsessed with status and appearing wealthy, as were most Californians. Her salary was barely over minimum wage. She complained that her last job paid just $8.50 per hour, but the present one was paying $9.25 per hour. It was better for her. I could not fathom the difference between the few cents and thought the wages were outrageously low. This was especially true for someone who was trying to appear rich!

She told me numerous stories about how she saved for months to buy a diamond tennis bracelet. All wealthy women sported a diamond tennis bracelet. 'Dana, do you play tennis?' I asked innocently. 'Not at all. You don't have to go near a tennis court to have a tennis bracelet! It's just for pointing at objects in public places so people can see you have diamonds!' I listened attentively and learned what was required to become Californian. I was a long way behind on this knowledge and absorbed like a sponge.

'If a man were to ever propose, you would have to get a diamond engagement ring of at least one carat. It would have to be set in platinum.' 'OK. Got it,' I said, agreeing blindly. 'Gold is cheaper than platinum you know. And the carat of the diamond is very important.' Dana also told me about the time she went into an Ethan Allen store to get her grown son a gift. Her son was turning 21 and she wanted to buy him a keepsake from an expensive store. She had walked around the store and finally spied a keepsake box. It was offered at $200. 'Well you know how snobbish their sales people are. When I walked in the store and asked to look at the box, they thought I was too poor to buy it.' 'Oh did they?' I said, wondering how she handled the staff. 'Yes, that bitch looked down her nose at me and said the box cost $200. I had to ask her twice to look at it!' Dana continued, 'She didn't want to take it out of the showcase. Well, I decided I would give my son the box for his twenty-first birthday.'

Dana's adult son was from an old relationship, and he lived somewhere in the Valley. 'I went back the next day and bought the box with cash!' She seemed quite proud of her accomplishment whilst I was wondering why the box was necessary. A twenty-one year old man would have little or no use for this and would probably tell her to keep it for him. 'You did what?' I asked surprised. 'Yes. I sure showed her!' Dana explained. 'Yes you did,' I sympathized with her. 'Do you know how long it took me to catch up on bills because I bought that box?' By this time, Dana's voice was wild and I was wondering what insanity I was witnessing. Why buy a box if you could not afford it? Showing a sales clerk you can buy an expensive item would not change her warped opinion of you. Dana was just barely surviving over minimum wage.

'What else do you think I should have Dana?' I asked calmly. 'Well a single strand of pearls would be nice and a complete tea service. Typically Royal Doulton is a good brand. There's a Royal Dalton outlet store in Camarillo. You could go and buy one piece at a time. You also need crystal glasses and a complete matching set of cutlery to serve at least eight.' I had only just recently started a mortgage loan and could not fathom adding extra fluff to my expenses, to impress some unknown people I had not yet met. I felt the Friday night auctions held the key to success, however. One could find just about anything at the auction. I was determined to return so I could fill the list of Californian necessities.

So, the lesson learned from Dana was to live outside your means just to show the staff you can buy expensive goods; especially if they ignore you in the store. Creating impressions was part and parcel of the Southern California way. Well, I despised shopping and would rather stay out of the stores, than face the wrath of snobbish sales clerks and cashiers.

I examined the men at the bar. Many came with partners. The place became packed by 11:30 pm. It was not easy to move around. We walked around the crowd a few times to see who was there. The few single men in the crowd chatted amongst themselves and did not ask us to dance. I wondered if they shy or just not interested. I would have to see what happened at another night-on-the-town.

Dana was an expert on men. She advised me how I should approach them, what I should tell them, and where I should meet them. I listened attentively. As a divorced woman, I was willing to take all the advice I could get. I told her I had a short fling with my tall neighbour and even though I was not enamoured by him, he might have made an interesting long term partner. After describing the relationship between George and me, she shook her head in disapproval. 'What's wrong?' I screamed over the music. 'You did not follow the rules!' she said. 'What rules? What are you talking about?' I asked puzzled by her description of these all important rules that I missed. 'If you'd followed The Rules properly, this man would've been eating out of the palm of your hand. He sounds like a decent fella too. You messed it up!' I was so distressed about messing it up. Suppose the man was to be my soulmate. Did I just throw away my chance for true happiness?

It was too noisy for a serious conversation so we promised to talk the following day so she could explain The Rules. I could not wait to learn. Like a good student, I wanted to know everything possible to find a good husband in California. We drove off just after midnight in our separate cars. I had to run back home to the babysitter who promised to watch Tiffany until 12:30 am. A night out would always cost in babysitting fees: minimum wage times the hours. I must have appeared stingy because I never tipped.

Dana called the following evening after Tiffany had gone to bed. For the next three hours, I learned all her likes and dislikes in men. She enjoyed one who would spend his money. He had to be a gentleman and open the door for her. Manners and chivalry were very important. She said she was on a permanent diet and trying to shed some weight. She felt the need to be skinnier to meet Californian standards. It seemed like everyone in California was on a diet. Everyone wanted to be very skinny like the movie stars. Everyone wanted to be tan with blonde hair. Despite being skinny, however, everyone wanted to have large upright breasts. This led to a lot of breast implants being performed. Dana remarked she did not need such enhancements. The next time we were out, she would point out the fake breasts.

Dana was on the Scarsdale diet at the time. She said she had to fight fat all her life. I couldn't believe this because she looked skinny to me. 'What's the Scarsdale diet?' I asked, baffled by the title. 'You mean you don't know what the Scarsdale diet is?' she said in disbelief. 'No. Tell me,' I answered. 'It's where you eat only protein. You have to cut out carbohydrates. They just go straight to your stomach.' Yikes I thought. I ate bread every day. How was I going to do that? 'I have eggs for breakfast. They must be hard eggs. I do not like runny eggs,' said Dana. 'And I only have the leanest steak for dinner. Do you know how much lean steak costs?' She went off on a tangent about the price of lean steak and I wondered if it was so expensive why she would bother. Fish had just as much protein and I did not even like beef.

'I don't eat bread, she said. 'I'm a celiac. I'm allergic to it.' 'What happens when you eat bread?' I asked. 'A lot of mucus comes up. I can't be bothered with it.' I was still waiting to learn about The Rules, but had to sit through one full hour of Dana's preaching about how being skinny was the only way to attract the right man. Her life sounded really sober without the joys of good hefty meals. I was not sure if I could keep up with the skinny rule requirements for women in California. The elusive male never bothered with being skinny from what I had seen.

When we finally got to the topic of The Rules, it was quite late. 'I have to lend you my book called The Rules,' she said with great superiority. 'In fact, you must call up the Barnes and Noble store on Telegraph Road in Ventura and see if they have it. Buy your own damn copy.' I was being ordered to buy a book I knew nothing about. It must have been an extra important document. I didn't mind getting the book if it would help me. 'This book is the bible for relationships. It was written by these two women who wrote down all the time tested rules to trap a man! Ha! Ha!' She laughed hysterically at the thought of trapping a man. I was about to ask her why she was single if she knew The Rules so well. She must have been reading my mind because then she went on to describe all the characters she had "worked The Rules on".

She explained how I had to dress up and look beautiful at all times, even when going to the supermarket. Speaking to a man first or staring at him was forbidden; even if I liked him. I was NEVER to pay on a date. 'But suppose the man asks me to split the bill?' 'Never do it,' she said. 'He should be paying for the pleasure of your company. And never see him too often when you first start dating.' 'Oh my gosh! I saw George almost every day when we had our little relationship,' I confessed. 'You see?! That was the problem!' she shouted. 'What?' I asked. 'He got tired of you,' she explained. 'If you had taken the relationship slowly and played your cards right, you would be married in eight weeks! You would still have him. He would have asked you to marry him!'

Oh my God! I felt like crying at that point for my folly in not knowing The Rules. I had let George slip out of the palm of my hand. Did she ever stop to think that George had attachment issues, not just with me, but with anyone? For Dana, being married was very important. She expressed this idea repeatedly to me; so much so, that I was beginning to believe it. I was slowly being transformed into a believer of The Rules. If a woman was not married, she was nothing!

'Never accept a last minute invitation for a date. If a man is serious, he will ask you well in advance to go out with him on the weekend,' she explained. 'Yikes, how late is late Dana?' I asked. 'Girl, you will really have to get your copy of The Rules and study very well! You don't know anything! I've read mine at least 20 times!' she boasted. 'You have to find some men and practice The Rules on them,' she said. It was a big challenge for me to find some men and practice The Rules on them. How was I going to do that?

The following evening, I went to Barnes and Noble after work. I was frantic to get my hands on a copy of the dating bible! I ran to the associate at the front desk. 'Hello. Do you sell The Rules?' I asked. He looked calmly at the deranged woman in front of him. 'Ma'am, I'm not sure what you're talking about. Do you know the name of the author?' Of course not ... Why would I know the name of the author? It had never entered my head to verify this with my "dating advisor". 'Just look in the catalogue on your computer,' I said. 'It's all about dating.' He looked for a few moments as I inhaled deeply and tried to maintain my composure. 'Yes I found them. Which do you want; The Rules or The Rules II?' he asked. 'You mean there's a part two? Yah gotta be kidding right? Dana didn't mentioned two books,' I said. 'Yes ma'am; two versions,' he said. 'Gimme both of them! A girl can't be too prepared!' I shouted.

He led me to the shelf and we found the original book and the follow up guide. It was my lucky day. Hallelujah! I would be ready for those men. World look out! I bought my books and rushed home to start reading. I had to tear myself away to get some sleep before work the next day. The following evening I studied and studied. It was a lot to learn. I had been doing everything wrong according to the first book. Many would have considered the ideas old fashioned, like waiting constantly for the man to take the lead.

However, I imagined if a man thought he was in charge, a relationship would run smoothly. This might have saved my old marriage. I studied the book and read it again. Then I started on book two. Preparation for dating was a science requiring more skill than a job interview.

Red Car Long Legs

How was I going to meet eligible bachelors? I called Dana the following weekend. I had been studying The Rules and wanted more suggestions as to where to meet eligible bachelors. 'Leave it to me,' she said. 'I know all the best places.' I trusted her completely at that point. I was going to listen intently and try my best to have a meaningful "Rules relationship". 'How am I going to meet guys?' I asked. The last group at Whales Tail didn't even ask us to dance. 'Well,' she said. 'You have to get out more and dress up so men will notice you. I might introduce you to some people, but I don't like making introductions.' 'Why's that?' I asked. 'I don't want to be blamed if a relationship doesn't work out. Can't be bothered with that responsibility,' Dana admitted. 'We have to go to Westlake Village to party. It's a rich town on the way south to Los Angeles,' she said. 'Why would we drive all that way to go to a bar in Westlake?' I asked. 'Well, if you want to meet good men, you have to go to the Friday night after work parties at the bars in Westlake Village.'

I listened in disbelief as I imagined having to drive at least thirty minutes south and over the hill when our neighbourhood had dozens of bars and restaurants. 'You would meet a better calibre of man over there. In any case, this bar I know gives free appetizers on a Friday evening up to 8:00 pm. I don't have to cook dinner on Fridays,' she said. 'I just go over there and eat whatever they have.' I thought she was on a serious Scarsdale diet. I guessed Fridays were not diet days. In addition, when she was on a date, she also ate heartily and kicked the diet to the curb. I wondered if I should trust this woman with my project to meet Mr. Right.

One Saturday afternoon at a mall, she introduced me to Keith. He was a friendly black man with a large head and skinny limbs. He had a medium sized afro and a lisp. He was enamoured by Dana, but she seemed to be channelling him in my direction. 'Keith is a great friend to have,' she said. 'He's from Belize.' I had heard many people from Belize lived in Los Angeles and a few bad seeds had tarnished their reputation. Since I was not attracted to Keith, I decided there and then he would be my buddy for sight seeing and wandering around the area. I would not be working any rules on him. Keith turned out to be a great resource. One day he met Tiffany and me to go to a neighbouring ranch for an Indian pow wow. We watched people dance, we ate food, and I learned about Chumash Indians and different types of dream catchers. Keith was an amazing source of information for everything practical in the Ventura County and surrounding areas.

When I needed a mechanic for my red Mitsubishi Eclipse with the sun roof, Keith knew just the person. He recommended Perry's Auto Repair in the Valley. In calling to make an appointment, I realized Mr. Perry had a Caribbean accent. In fact Caribbean people were scattered all around California and I was slowly meeting them. Because of California's proximity to Central America, Mexico, and Asia across the Pacific, many new immigrants settled where they entered the first major US port of Los Angeles. Thus, black Caribbean people came from Belize, Honduras, and Panama. I had only begun to learn the significance of history and the movement of African populations to the new world, when I started working in California.

Two weeks passed and Dana invited me to Happy Hour at a

restaurant and bar in Westlake Village after work on the Friday. The place was packed with office people, professionals, casual people, and others. They seemed like ordinary middle class people who enjoyed the free appetisers, charging hungrily at the tables. The bar served chips and dips, vegetables and dip, wings and dip, bread and dip, and dip and dip. It was a dipping frenzy and everyone took part. Dana and I had dressed up and walked around aimlessly from one side of the bar to the next. 'Don't stay in one location too long,' Dana advised. 'You don't want to look desperate.' We then walked casually to the other side of the room. I felt desperate, however, waiting for the elusive, fabulous man to approach and chat. The Rules had said a woman should never talk to a man first. As we waited patiently, a young skinny man finally approached. 'How are you girls doing?' he asked, bobbing to the music. 'Just great,' we chimed in unison. 'OK, that's great,' he said, and moved on. He was completely drunk and was just walking around the venue.

I felt very desperate and wondered if there wasn't a better way to meet men. Driving such a long distance to munch on a few appetizers and walk around was fine for socializing. However, after three hours of aimless wandering and fake smiles, we gave up the chase and went home. I planned to return another day; but I was not sure if this would yield the desired response; especially since we were acting coy and pretending to ignore all the guys who buzzed around. It was a delicate balance of psychology, bordering on insanity.

It was 1999 and the internet was expanding exponentially. This included internet dating. Dana suggested I go online and see who I could meet. I promptly signed on to the popular internet site called Date-Maker.com. I decided on a profile name of "Red Car Long Legs". I thought this handle would certainly create interest or shock, as the case might be. I started my search for potential dates in Ventura County and Thousand Oaks. I also signed up on a website aimed at Ivy League university graduates. The website promised sophisticated matches and more successful dating experiences. At the time the website manager had to get a hard copy of one's photograph in order to upload it online. This was promoted at an extra cost. In general, profiles were descriptive and no photos were seen. The face of a potential date was usually a mystery. Within a week of posting my profile, I was in conversation with a few men. I re-read The Rules to be sure I was focused in my efforts and set up some dates to practice. These men would either like me or it was their loss. That was my attitude.

The first gentleman I met was Scott. He said he lived on a boat in the Channel Islands Harbour at Oxnard. The idea of living day and night on a boat was fascinating, even though I thought something was a bit odd about this. How was it possible? How could he cook, get his mail, sleep, or even have a family? This was possibly a bachelor's life. Would the boat be heated in the winter? I went to a local bar to meet the boat dweller. Scott was stout and tall, with a beard and moustache. We spoke about life and sweet nothings. This man was extremely boring and it was cold outside. I could not see myself living on a boat! Next!

I had to find someone at least reasonably well educated with the potential of making a good husband in order to practice The Rules. I then met Jeff, a gentleman who advertised decent qualities and asked me out to dinner. Well, I thought, this was a good start. If he could meet and pay for dinner, he must be focused and serious. We arranged to meet at the Embassy Suites Mandalay Bay on the coast in Oxnard. I had seen this hotel in one of my numerous drives around the area and was delighted to be going there for dinner. He offered to pick me up at home, but I declined. He could have been a deranged murderer and I was not taking any chances. In any case, driving my own car gave me the option to run away after two hours. The Rules book for dating said to limit the first date to two to four hours so the man did not get too much information out of the girl and become bored too fast.

I parked in the underground parking and went upstairs to the restaurant. I had looked at the menu online to decide in advance what to order. The meal must not be too expensive, but not too cheap. As I waited in the lobby, I tried not to look too anxious. This was not easy. Even though I saw my date's photo online, he had no distinguishing features so I could not easily recognize him in a crowd of other middle aged white men. Eventually, a man came up to me. 'Hello, are you Lindy?' a man with a pepper and salt moustache asked. 'Yes I am,' I said shyly. 'Good to see you. I'm Jeff.' 'Nice to meet you too,' he said.

Jeff and I made our way to the restaurant and took our seats. I looked at him and tried to imagine him as a husband. He had salt and pepper hair, spectacles, and was of medium height. He was slim and trim with no paunch. He had decent manners and opened the door for me, scoring brownie points in my book for that. We looked at the menu and I ordered a simple meal and tried to act coy all the while not saying too much about myself. This was very difficult for someone who loved to babble non-stop. I gave him all the time he needed to chat about himself. I had been looking at my watch and remembering. The first date should not last more than two hours. We had just finished eating the main course when I looked at my watch and saw the time was up.

What should I do? Poor old Jeff was considering dessert. I hated desserts. I was a salt addict, sometimes going for three or four servings at a Chinese buffet. I breathed in slowly and decided to leave Jeff right there and then. The time was up and that was it. 'Well thanks for a nice night Jeff. Gotta run. Early day tomorrow,' I said. 'But ... But ...' He struggled to say something gesturing with his hands. The man looked at me in disbelief. The waitress had not even removed our dinner plates. He must have thought he was a bad date. He did not realize I was practicing The Rules and I was trying to be a good student. That was all. I was only mildly interested in him and there was little spark to encourage me to break The Rules. 'Take care,' I said, and I was off.

As I drove home, I wondered if I had done the right thing. Well, Jeff never called back and that was fine with me. I consoled myself in thinking if he was really interested he would call. I would have to move on to the next target. Two weeks later I was shopping at Vons supermarket on South Ventura Road, and who should I bump into? It was Jeff. I hung my head down in shame and pretended not to see him. I was too embarrassed. My goodness, what would he think of me? I had walked off on him abruptly on a date! I had to learn some finesse in performing The Rules next time. I promised myself things would get better and nodded at Jeff then moved speedily to the checkout counter.

Another evening I arranged to meet Peter who said he lived

in Montecito, by the beach. We were supposed to meet at the Elephant Bar and Restaurant in Ventura. I had spied the Elephant Bar a few times while flying up Highway 101 through Ventura, so I was curious to know what the place looked like inside. Peter advertised himself as a tall, handsome male in his 40's. Even though I was in my thirties, and looked a great deal younger with a childlike face, I decided to have an open mind and go out with an older man. I arrived on time and stood inside the main door of the restaurant waiting to be recognized. He did not have a photo so it was a guessing game until someone approached me. Eventually, a medium height man who looked a bit wrinkled, possibly in his late fifties approached me.

'Hello, are you Lindy?' he asked. 'Yes I am,' I said, as I held out my hand to shake his. He shook my hand and we entered the main restaurant to be seated by the hostess. 'Would you like to sit inside or outside?' she asked. Well, it was a typical foggy and chilly summer's evening, so I said I would rather sit inside. Peter looked at the menu right away. He must have been hungry. 'Do you want an appetizer? Let's have an appetizer,' he said without waiting for an answer. 'That's fine with me,' I said. I had eaten dinner before coming out since in our email exchange, we said we would meet for drinks. Peter said he liked the potato skins with cheese at Elephant Bar. Why would anyone eat potato skins? I was still trying to assess his wrinkled skin. He was not old, yet he was not young. Perhaps his skin was weather beaten from too much exposure to the sun. Peter proceeded to mention all the wealthy people he knew in Montecito. I was not impressed because I had no idea who he was talking about. The most I could do was say, 'That's amazing,' and listen to his exaggerations and stories.

The moment the potato skins came, he dove right in. The potato skins were topped with cheddar cheese, bacon and green onions, and served with sour cream. They looked delicious so I picked up one to bite. As I looked at Peter biting into a skin, I thought I saw a plate of false teeth shift. Oh my God! What was this? Was I just seeing things or was this real? Not only did he lie about his age, but the man had false teeth! How was I going to kiss a man with false teeth? He said he was house-sitting for some friends in Montecito. Did this mean he did not have a home of his own? How was I going to last another hour on the first date with Peter? I decided to look away every time he bit into his food so I would not have to look at his teeth. I tried to observe the other guests, think pleasant thoughts and count down to the end of the hour so I would not be too rude and leave early. As the bill came he paid and continued yapping. 'Well Peter, it was nice meeting you. So long,' I said. 'OK, OK ... We'll keep in touch right?' He called after me as I made a mad dash to my car. 'Sure!' I lied as I started the engine. Next!

The next weekend, I went off to a late evening date to meet Terry in Newbury Park. We had met once at a bar in Oxnard, and there was a bit of chemistry on both sides. He invited me to his place for a barbecue. Against my better judgement, I agreed to go, deciding to have my car keys ready in case there was any monkey business. Explaining my date to the babysitter, Ms. Cheryl who was a 'God-fearing' woman was difficult. She would never understand the concept of internet dating with unknown people. "Blasphemy against the Lord!"

'Where are you going?' she asked when I dropped Tiffany off. 'Who are you going with? What time will you be back?'

As a grown woman, I felt like a guilty teenager playing hooky from school. Holy people may have felt women with children should not go on a date. I had to hide my story from her at all costs. When I was able to peel myself away from the interrogation, I made my way South on Highway 101 and over the hill to Newbury Park. Terry gave me detailed directions to his house. When I got there, he had the tiniest grill set up in the dirt next to the driveway with a few coals set in it. He was trying to get the coals started. Was this what the man called a barbecue? He was stooping over the little grill in the dirt when I showed up wearing my cutest casual party outfit, in my red sports car!

I had to take a deep breath, calm down and keep an open mind. Our conversations were cordial on the phone during the week, so he may have been a good man. Terry was tall and muscular. He had a neat moustache and a nice crop of dark brown hair. I could see myself possibly having a relationship with him but would have to overlook the primitive barbecue.

'Great to see you Lindy. Thanks for coming over,' he said. 'Great to see you too,' I said as I surveyed the yard, the house, his car, his body and everything else in one quick swoop. The sun had started to set so I had to get a good view before it got dark. 'So how was your week?' I asked. 'Well, same as usual. Hard work and glad for the weekend,' he answered. I listened to his conversation as we entered the kitchen. 'Would you like a beer?' he asked. 'Sorry, I don't drink beer. Do you have soda?' I asked. 'No, I don't,' he apologized. 'Well, water is fine for me.' He opened the tap and filled a glass with water.

'Cheers,' I said nervously as he held up his bottle of beer. Terry gave me a tour of his little bungalow. It was a basic two bedroom concrete home that was certainly in need of a paint job. He spoke about his divorce and putting money away to start his life over again. 'Hmm, that's good,' I said and listened attentively. 'This is the living room, this is the bathroom. I have an extra bedroom and this is the main bedroom.' As I looked around the little house, I decided it was basic but neat. Could I see myself in the little bed in his main bedroom? I didn't think so. Terry did not have much furniture and what little he had was used, functional gear. It was definitely the home of a bachelor. He then decided it was time to start the barbecue grill before it got too late.

'Are yah hungry?' he asked. 'Sure. Let me know if you need any help,' I said, very curious to see what was on the menu. 'We're having steak and potatoes!' he boasted. 'Yah like steak?' 'Sure,' I lied. I was not fond of beef and sometimes found it hard to digest. I would have to eat it if there was no choice. I should have known. What else would a basic bachelor cook? I watched as he played with the tiny grill on the gravel in the front yard. He did not use a table or anything to lift it off the ground. There we were stooping on the ground over the little grill. Was it camping season in the front yard? He stuck some more coals into the tiny gadget and tried to light them with starter fuel and a cigarette lighter. 'Too primitive; just too primitive' I kept saying to myself. How open-minded could I possibly be? He took two huge slabs of beef steaks out of the refrigerator and slapped them onto the grill when the coals were lit. There was no seasoning, no marinating, nor tenderizing. It was from the fridge to the grill. In good cave man fashion, the steaks were removed rare from the grill.

'Hey Terry, would you mind cooking my steak a bit longer,' I asked as I stood from the driveway observing the scene. Even if I had to eat a jumbo steak, I did not want to see any blood! 'No problem bud,' he said. I'm sure he and his buddies ate steak and drank beer on a Saturday night, but I was a fine lady. I deserved more than the buddy offering. Despite my open mindedness, I could not see myself fitting into Terry's world. We sat at the counter top in the kitchen with our steaks, some sauce and the potatoes that were baked in the oven. 'Hmm good,' I said, observing how he attacked his rare steak with relish as I played with mine cutting it into smaller and smaller cubes.

After chewing on this meat for a long half hour, I stretched and yawned. 'Don't know why I'm so tired. Looks like I'll have to call it a night,' I said dreamily. We had been eating and making small talk and it was a bit boring. I wondered too if he expected me to spend the night. The thought had crossed my mind as he gave me the grand tour of the little bedroom. I had to find a way to escape swiftly and seamlessly. 'Already?' he protested. The childcare clock was also ticking away. He did not know I had a child who was at the babysitter's house. I was being charged by the hour and had to get back before the bill was too high for me. 'Thanks so much for having me over Terry. Will keep in touch,' I said, as I stood up in the kitchen and gathered my things. He gave me a big bear hug and I dodged his beefy lips as he tried to kiss me. The kiss was planted firmly on my cheek. 'See you next time,' I said as I entered my red Mitsubishi Eclipse with the sun roof, and drove away. Next!

Was I being too picky? There had to be more to life. I vowed to continue the search for Mr. Right. So, the following week,

I planned a date with Alex in Ventura. His online advertisement said he was in his late 30's, six feet tall and muscular. I hoped this description was true and not wishful thinking. One could never be too sure when reading stories online. After exchanging telephone numbers, we spoke a few times and Alex asked me out to dinner. He asked what food I liked best. Being quite flexible, I suggested a Thai restaurant on Main Street in Ventura. We were to meet at the main entrance to the restaurant. I had a hard time finding parking and came running in just in time, and out of breath.

'Hello, you must be Lindy,' said a good looking man near the entrance. 'Hello,' I said, 'and you must be Nicholas Cage. Has anyone told you that you look just like him?' I asked. 'Well yes, I've heard that all the time. Can be a bit annoying sometimes,' He admitted. 'That's amazing,' I said as I stared at the marvellous specimen of a man in front of me. 'Should we get seated?' he asked. 'Yes certainly,' I embarrassed myself with the useless staring at this good looking man. We sat and chatted for a good while. I had to pinch myself to stop breaking The Rules and appear nonchalant. I was supposed to be evaluating his character and not his looks. But, his looks were definitely distracting. I explained that I recently moved to California from Florida and how I was learning about the terrain slowly. He volunteered to be my tour guide. That was an amazing suggestion in my books.

When the bill came, he looked at it with wide open eyes. He took out his credit card and seemed to be suffering from a slap in the face. How much could it have been? I wondered about his distress, but tried to keep a nonchalant facial expression. We had ordered two appetizers and two main dishes. I never drank alcohol or ate desserts. In my mind the bill should have been manageable. 'So what do you usually do Alex?' I asked. 'Well, I've been working on my acting career and hoping for a lucky break,' He said. It was the typical California hopeful story. Every second person was working on his acting career and hoping for a lucky break. This usually meant "I have no money!' The would-be movie star couldn't, however, disclose this information openly. We walked down the street toward the parking lot so I could get to my car. 'So you women love shopping, huh?' he said. I wondered what prompted his question. 'Quite frankly, I don't like shopping,' I said. 'I only go to the store if it's absolutely necessary. The only thing I buy every week is groceries. Other than that I stay out of the stores.' He looked at me in disbelief. I was a woman who did not like shopping; a rare species.

'Well, thanks for a lovely night out,' I chirped. 'Yah, and next time you will pay for dinner,' he said. 'What?' I asked in disbelief. He repeated, 'Next time you will pay for the dinner.' I smiled at what I was hearing. The bloody cheapskate! Was this a threat? Why had he asked me out to dinner when we planned to meet? He could have said, 'Let's meet for coffee or a drink. But no; he had said 'Let's go out to dinner!' I looked at the man who appeared so attractive ten minutes before and suddenly he wasn't so pretty after all. 'Sure,' I said.

According to "The Rules", a woman should not go Dutch on the first date. Only when a relationship or clear interest was established should she return in kind. It was one of the ultimate tests of a man's interest. Did he want to please the woman of his dreams or was I just a time-filler? 'See yah,' I said. Next!

Single Parents

I had been trying to find ways to make new friends with people who had common interests. One day while combing the Classified advertisement section in the Ventura Star, I found a notice for Parents Without Partners (PWP). This group promoted itself as a social club for single parents of all ages. That seemed perfect for me. If I joined, I would be able to meet other people who had similar stories of divorce to mine. I called the number of the organizer that night and friendly John, asked me to attend the next monthly meeting with my child. It was a pizza night and they were admitting new members.

The prospect of meeting other single parents and making new friends was very exciting. The membership was based in Conejo Valley. Most people came from Thousand Oaks, Newbury Park, Agoura Hills, Westlake, and Moorpark for events. The evening of the meeting, I collected Tiffany from childcare, changed out of my work clothes into casual gear and we made our way South over the hill on Highway 101 to the Pizza place in Thousand Oaks. I waited a little in the parking lot to scope out the scene and have a look at any others who may have been going to the PWP event. I saw a number of men and women enter the restaurant with small children.

I wondered if they would be friendly. How many would be new members? Would the children know each other from school already? Would Tiffany be able to make friends? We entered the restaurant about five minutes after the starting time just to be sure other members were there. I asked the waitress where the PWP group met, and she directed me to the back of the restaurant. As we walked back, I saw many children running helter-skelter and a number of parents huddled in conference at two big tables.

'Hello. I'm Lindy and this is my daughter Tiffany,' I said. 'Hello Lindy,' said a tall man with glasses. He stood and welcomed us to the clan. 'Tiff, would you like to go and play with the other children?' I asked. Tiffany looked at the children shyly then looked at me. One mother introduced her little daughter to Tiffany and the girls immediately made friends and went off to play. John welcomed the group of mostly new members to the PWP and told us about membership dues, the monthly dance, subsidized pizza nights and other group activities. He mentioned the Father's Day brunch when moms cooked, and the Mother's day brunch at a park in Thousand Oaks, when the dads cooked. I thought right away, if I stayed with PWP, my social life would be set for the year. They seemed to have many activities for parents and children all the time. A friendly young woman, Joanie, who also served on the committee chimed in, 'And the next parents' potluck is at my place and everybody has to come.' 'What's the parents' potluck?' I asked. 'That's when you get a babysitter so you can have a night off for yourself to socialize with people your own age,' she explained. 'We even trade babysitting sometimes, cuz some members have big kids; woo hoo!' This woman sounded like a lively one. I was determined to get to know her.

The following week, I was sure to hire a babysitter on Saturday night. I made a big salad and followed the directions to Joanie's house in Thousand Oaks. On the Boulevard I passed row after row of townhouses. They all looked the same. In addition, it was difficult to see the house numbers at night. Eventually I located the townhouse and parked some distance away. When I arrived, I saw many people were already there talking and laughing.

'Hi Lindy!' Joanie shouted. 'Come on in and meet everybody. Everybody, this is Lindy. She's new!' There was no hiding in a corner with Joanie. She was loud and open and made sure everyone felt welcome. I walked around and introduced myself and tried to learn people's names. There was John and John, Gary, Liz, Yvonne, and too many names to memorize. 'You'll have to take the name quiz at the end,' one person joked. I studied the faces closely. Everyone was of European descent and had a story of why their parents or grandparents moved to California. The stories were quite varied, but many had parents who either moved to California after the Second World War or in the 1960's.

Gary was a tall handsome man of Irish descent. He had his way with the ladies who swooned over him because of his height and good looks. I overheard him telling two men, 'I love blondes with big tah tahs. I just can't help myself man. It's a natural thing man. I'm a hot blooded male.' His male audience smiled and listened attentively. He was a bit mad, but I loved that. I wondered if he would be my buddy. As I walked across the room, Joanie was explaining how she got her place for a steal of a price at $120,000 and she was doing all the repairs herself. 'I know how to use a drill. I'm changing all these old cupboard doors. I painted all the walls myself. I'm very handy. Why wait for a man when you can do it yourself!' she shouted.

'Men listen up! Women can be self sufficient! We have

muscles too!' Joanie screamed at the top of her lungs. The guys in the party just laughed. She was loud and they did not take her seriously. 'Drink some beer everybody. I'm not half German for nothin'!' We had a feast for dinner and there were new dishes I never tasted before. One favourite was baked brie in filo pastry. Liz said she brought this for every potluck. It was her signature dish. One woman made seaweed noodles with vegetables. It was another strange but tasty side dish. Joanie was so open with everyone, that we learned her life history of marriage, divorce, her parents' story, and her siblings' stories, all in the space of two hours. She had a young daughter and was recently divorced from a husband who also had a daughter from a previous marriage. Joanie was in her late 30's and sported tan skin with blonde hair and highlights. It was the typical California look.

'You see these red roots? Do you see these red roots? I have to do something about them. Nobody must know I'm a red head!' She had no concept of privacy with a full house and a few beers. She openly accepted step sisters, former in-laws and their siblings, previous and future married couples and their children and children's children. Everyone was family in her life. She winked at me saying, 'I only kiss a man who has perfect teeth. I can't stand crooked teeth. I'm very picky,' said Joanie. 'That's funny,' I said, not knowing why that gem of wisdom was uttered randomly. She continued, 'I'm looking for a good husband and I'm holding out. Nobody's going to jump into bed with me unless he's serious. Only serious contenders!' She shouted to the wind and everyone laughed. Joanie would go to a local tanning salon every few weeks to use the tanning beds. A tan made her feel better, she admitted. With my dark skin which seemed to be getter darker every day in the California sun, I could not imagine why tanning salons would even be necessary. But, however, the general white population loved to have a tan and blonde hair. That was the norm.

I danced just as wildly as those who were drinking alcohol, even though I only had my usual ginger ale. 'Hey Lindy, you have to come out partying with my gang. You look like you love a good dance,' said Joanie. 'Oh yes. I love dancing,' I confirmed. We danced for a few hours, ate and drank until it was time for me to go back to Oxnard. The babysitter was going to be waiting for me. I wished I lived in the Thousand Oaks. It seemed like all the best parties and friends were over the hill. 'Yah gotta move closer Lindy. You're leaving too early,' pleaded Joanie. 'Will see what I can do,' I said.

The next week, I went over the hill to meet the gang for Friday evening drinks after work at a bar and restaurant on Westlake Boulevard. More PWP friends came to hang out like Mona, Drew, George, and others. Everyone had a story and we talked for hours. When the DJ pumped up the music after 8:00 pm, the after-work drinks turned into an all night dance party for those who did not have to go home right away. I was really enjoying my new friends and could see unions were forming. Liz had fallen for one of the Johns and Tammy had her eye on the other John.

John and John were single dads with shared custody of their kids. They also shared a big house with a swimming pool and would sometimes host pool parties and back yard picnics for the PWP clan. These parties were the most enjoyable events, since the parents could sit and chat on one side of the yard while the children played happily in the pool. We were invited to our first pool party and potluck that summer and enjoyed the event immensely. Tiffany made new friends and I had a steady flow of new friends too. I started enquiring about property prices and schools in the area. I had to know what would be the best choice if we were to move. Property prices were on the rise in the year 2000, so I would have to think seriously about a move over the hill.

My first monthly PWP dance was a curiosity. The hall was rented at a local school and one of the men in the group performed the role of disc jockey (DJ). The DJ played a mix of rock and roll and 70's funk. The crowd was also a mix of all ages, from men and women in their late 20's to people in their 60's. I guessed there was no age discrimination. A single parent was a single parent. 'We know where we can party when we get old!' Joanie shouted, as we admired an elderly couple on the dance floor. 'I'm not dancing with any geriatrics. I can tell you that,' said Joanie loudly over the music. 'I don't like their skin. I can feel the difference to young skin.' 'OK, you're right,' I agreed. The music blared and we did not have to worry about babysitting that night. Laurie's daughter, a teenager, was watching our girls for us.

When the PWP Easter dinner and dance approached, Joanie said we had to dress up for the party. She managed to hook up with one of the PWP men and they planned a date for the night. I did not find him particularly attractive, but Joanie was temporarily happy and contemplated marriage. Everyone in PWP was contemplating re-marrying. It was a general theme in the group. Nobody seriously wanted to remain single. We boasted about having more freedom than married couples. We could go out every weekend while married people tended to stay at home, watching television.

However, PWP members were forever on the lookout for Mr. Right or Ms. Right. Joanie was no exception.

'That one has potential,' she would say. 'He owns a big house. He bought the house after his divorce. That means he has a great job and the ex-wife didn't get everything. He's good marriage material.' I listened and learned. She was another teacher I was eager to follow. 'That's Norm over there. I have my eye on him you know.' She winked and nudged as she pointed out Norm on the dance floor. 'But he's huge and he looks like Fred Flintstone,' I said. 'A bit scary!' 'It doesn't matter,' said Joanie. 'His wife died some time ago. They say he's retired. Imagine he's friggin' retired and he's only in his 40's. That means he has shit loads of money! I'm in.'

'But … but …' I protested as I looked at the giant dancing with a small woman. Did Joanie not hear he had three small children too? That would be a lot of work for an incoming step-mother. 'You have to check out his zip code,' she explained. 'If he lives in 91362, that's Westlake, so even better,' she said. 'What?' I needed clarification. 'Well, the Thousand Oaks schools are ok, but Westlake schools are the best in Conejo Valley. You have to see what the guy's zip code is. Then you know if it's worth the effort.' My wise teacher had the answers. 'That's one way of looking at it,' I agreed.

'Larry drives a big car. It's a Lexus SUV. Look at the size of that car. The bigger the better, but you have to check out the brand. All the high profile car dealers camped out on Thousand Oaks Boulevard,' said Joanie. 'Hmmm, that makes sense to me,' I agreed blindly to all the coaching. 'Brian is a pilot. I don't know what he does with his money. He's not dating anyone now. Maybe you should make a move on him,' urged Joanie. 'I would have to see,' I said. I was not even vaguely interested in Brian. He spoke about his daughter a lot and one could tell he adored her. Other than that, he did not harass any women in PWP. The following week, Joanie called to tell me about her date. He was an older man she met through PWP. They were going to a dinner-dance and she would see if she could fix me up with someone. Yikes, I wondered who Joanie would find for me. I hoped at least he had a decent face. Some of her past choices had frightened me.

The Shiny Shoes

I got a call next day from Joanie saying her friend George who would sometimes hang out with the PWP gang, had a friend he wanted to "fix me up with". This was a European man who adored black women. Well, I thought I would meet him and give him a chance. One never knew as far as these things went. We would have to see if he was marriage material. We were to meet at a backyard party in Thousand Oaks and sit at the same table. 'Wear something colourful!' said Joanie. 'It's a Luau!' I had no shortage of colourful clothing, so I found a beautiful Hawaiian skirt, with matching blouse. I fixed curls in my hair and put flowers for added effect. On entering the host's backyard, I heard Joanie call out my name. The yard was well decorated with lanterns, flowers and a number of tables were scattered around with colourfully dressed party goers.

'Over here Lindy! Over here!' I heard Joanie's voice from across the yard. 'I'm coming,' I said, as I hustled over to the group's table. 'You look great,' said George who was seated at the table next to Joanie and Carl, her date. Next to George was a wide eyed man with a neat crop of reddish brownish hair that hung a little over his right eye. He had a boyish yet mature look. The wrinkles on his neck told me he may have been in his 40's. George and his friend immediately jumped to attention as I came to the table.

'Lindy this is Alan,' said George. 'Ooo lah lah,' the man said as I outstretched my hand for a hand shake. I smiled shyly but could not retrieve my hand as he pulled it to his lips for a delicate kiss. 'What have we here … hmm?' he asked with a strong Eastern European accent. He stared into my eyes then ogled me from head to toe, TWICE. I was shocked and amused by his reaction and great show of affection. At a loss for words at first, I needed a few seconds to regain my composure. Then I asked, 'Where am I sitting?' 'Next to Alan of course,' said George. This fact was obvious to everyone except me, since it was the only spot left at the table. Everyone went off babbling with each other about the party and the buffet that would be ready in a few minutes. This left me no choice but to converse with Staring Alan.

'You are as beautiful as a flower,' he teased. I enjoyed all the attention and compliments, even though it may have been a bit excessive. 'Why thank you. You're not so bad yourself,' I teased. I looked at his bright red shirt, his well ironed cream trousers with a definite crease, and his shiny brown leather shoes. He was better dressed than most of the men at the party and was definitely an elegant European with expensive taste in clothing. His perfume was intoxicating. I was immediately 'in like' with Alan. What a fine man with good taste. My mind wandered as I dreamt hazily of trips to

Europe to visit family and friends. 'So Alan, tell me about yourself. Where are you from? When did you move to California?'

He was an engineer from Croatia. He fled during the war in former Yugoslavia in the early 1990's. After serving a mandatory term in the Croatian military for a year, he had found a way to leave and moved to California. His stories were drawing me in as he tried to learn more about me too. He was a man with an interesting history. 'I was captured and beaten during the war,' he said. I could not believe what I was hearing. It was an eye-opening and educational moment for me. I was intrigued by his anecdote and wanted to hear more. We ate dinner and then danced together non-stop. It was as if the rest of the gang disappeared as Alan and I conversed.

'I had to leave. They beat me,' he said with his heavy accent. 'Now I have a good life in California.' I was going to have to ask Joanie to ask George for more details about this man. I suspected I wouldn't get his whole story and was too polite to question him a lot. The dandy Alan asked for my phone number. He said he was going to call me to arrange for a future date. That sounded promising and I looked forward to his call. Alan called several times a day and I took his call every time. I completely abandoned my lessons from The Rules book and responded to every request to go out to dinner or a show. My head was abuzz with Alan and his accent. I allowed my infatuation for him to take the place of all common sense. Before I knew it, I invited Alan to my house for dinner, and he asked to spend the night. I did not hesitate. He was very charming and I wondered what he would be like in bed with all his poems and beautiful words.

It turned out however, he had trouble performing. He said however it would be better next time. I saw his crooked blue-black leg that was always hidden under the immaculately ironed trousers. 'What's wrong with your leg?' I asked. 'I told you I was beaten when I was captured in the war,' he answered. I felt so sorry for Alan that I completely forgot about the disappointing night and was again infatuated. The poor war hero had fought for his nation. That week, he sent me several email messages with sexual content. He was sending this material in the middle of the day judging from the times of the email. If he was a serious engineer at work, how could he have time to send those crazy videos?

For my birthday, I invited a few favourite new friends including Alan and George and cooked a big feast for everyone. We played music and danced in the front patio. A good time was had by all. As I opened birthday gifts, I saved Alan's for last. He had given me a bunch of beautiful red roses. However, a small box was attached to the roses. I could not wait to open the little blue velvet box. My heart was a flutter. What could it be? Was it a ring? Was he proposing? But I had just met the man a few weeks before. I know I did not do The Rules, and if anything, I had moved too quickly. I had never been invited to his home. Where did he live? I had so many questions which he carefully fielded with romantic statements.

Carefully opening the blue velvet box, I found a pair of gorgeous gold earrings. They were medium sized with an elegant design and stoppers at the back. 'Here. Let me put them on dah beautiful woman,' He suggested. I yielded to his wish with the eyes of a young puppy… I was madly in love, at that point. 'Oh, thank you. They're amazing!' I said. When everyone left, Alan stayed to help me clear up. It was evident he had no concept of what to do around a house. He was too dandy to get his elegant clothing dirty. Instead of getting annoyed with him, I told him to relax and I would clear up everything. I had truly lost my mind.

Again that night, we had sex but he admitted to be best at oral pleasure and not so good at "dah other stuff". I accepted this story and tried to keep my disappointment to myself.

Two days later, Joanie left a message on my answering machine sounding extremely animated. She had some gossip for me and I was to call back as soon as possible. I could not wait to hear the news and called back immediately. 'You would not believe what I found out,' she teased. 'Found out about what? About whom? Tell me! Tell me! Don't keep me in suspense,' I said. 'About your man, Alan,' she said. 'What about him?' I asked. 'Well George said, that a friend of his who met Alan first, said that he thinks Alan is living with a black girl in the Valley.'

'How could that be,' I asked. 'He's at my place a lot these days,' I said. 'Well, that's what George said he heard. And he heard Alan is just living off the girl and not even paying rent,' Joanie continued. 'I don't want to believe that. It's just crazy gossip,' I said. 'Well, I'm just passing on the news,' said Joanie. I was shocked and just did not want to accept this story. Maybe they were jealous that things worked out between Alan and me. One could never tell. I decided to ignore the news. However, after a few weeks I became suspicious when Alan cancelled a date unexpectedly saying he had to work that day. I even arranged to meet him at work the following day to discuss the matter and went to his office in Agoura Hills. This was partly out of curiosity to see where he worked and partly out of disappointment of not seeing him for a few days. I was acting desperate and should have recognized this. He was able to gloss over my fears and misgivings with flowery language, which I accepted.

When Thanksgiving weekend came, Alan said he would be busy with work all weekend. He had deadlines to meet, so we could not get together. In my head I was going to have Thanksgiving Day with Alan and Tiffany like a happy little family. I was disappointed it was not going to work out that way. Joanie had invited Tiffany and me to her family gathering and I was grateful to have somewhere to go. I resisted calling Alan to find out how his "work" was going and a few days later found a voice message left hastily on my answering machine. 'Loving you much and talk to you next week.' It was the voice of someone who had stolen a chance to make hasty phone call and had to hang up quickly.

I called Joanie to discuss the situation and she told me that George said, that his friend said, that he also heard that Alan had lived off a lonely older woman in the Valley too. She suggested I dump him and find somebody else. I had invested about three months in the relationship, which seemed like an eternity. What if I did not find anyone else? What if he was going to turn over a new leaf? What if … what if … I had heard the gossip and still wondered if to believe it.

When he called me the following week, I informed him I would be looking to buy a house in Westlake in zip code

91362 so I could be closer to all my friends. 'You cannot afford a house in that neighbourhood,' he said confidently. 'That's why you bought a house in Oxnard.' I could not believe the man who was reportedly living off women in The Valley, was telling me what I could and could not afford. Even though he looked fine and dandy with shiny shoes and neatly ironed shirts and trousers, he never once suggested I come to his place for a visit! I became angry at this statement, even more than any of the gossip I'd heard about him. 'What do you mean by that? Get out of my life! I never want to see you again!' I slammed down the phone and ran off to find something to do to drown my sorrows. The rumours and gossip must have been true. The house phone rang and rang repeatedly. Eventually I took it off the hook so I would not be bothered by the noise. The next day I called Joanie with the update. I vowed I would not invite him to my house warming party whenever we moved to Westlake 91362.

'There are many fish in the sea girl! Don't bother with idiots,' said Joanie … Next!

Networking and Conferences

Mabel had suggested I attend all the Industry conferences and sit on food safety committees. It was good for the company's profile and also good for me to network. This was one way to keep up to date with what was happening in industry, and I could always call on people in my network to assist with work issues. I was already a professional member of the Institute of Food Technologists (IFT) from my university days. Sitting on their Fruit and Vegetables Council would help in networking with targeted members. I also joined the International Association of Milk Food and

Environmental Sanitarians (IAMFES) which changed its name to International Association for Food Protection (IAFP).

I registered for meetings with the United Fresh Fruit and Vegetable Association (UFFVA), The Produce Marketing Agency (PMA), and the Grower Shipper Association of Central California, sitting on every food safety committee. I was a professional committee member.

There were so many acronyms to remember, it was confusing. In addition, when attending meetings, I was introduced to a number of food safety professionals from agriculture, food manufacturing, food service, government agencies, trade associations, and special interests groups. If truth be told, they all looked the same. I was going to have to become skilled and remember names and affiliations to network effectively. I wondered how they knew each others' names. They would call out to each other across a room with ease. Mabel suggested joining sub-committees, so I did this right away, being completely overwhelmed by the subject matter in meetings. During my first few months at meetings, I listened to discussions of recent legislation in the industry. All I could do was sit quietly and take copious notes, hoping nobody would ask my opinion on anything. I had no opinion. In that learning phase, I felt so stupid. Trying to fade into the background, while sitting at a round table with ten or so professionals was not easy. Added to that, I was usually the only black woman in the group. I could never hide!

The best time to learn names however was at the social gatherings that followed the serious meetings. Organizations would have numerous cocktail parties and dinners sponsored by various large food companies. All one had to do was show up and gossip with whoever was in attendance. Eventually I made a few close colleagues who would come with me to these events. They introduced me to people they knew and so my network expanded. One short but vocal manager, Lucia, worked with a big company and claimed she had a huge entertainment budget. It seemed to be a mile long. A group of ten or more food safety professionals would go out dining at upscale restaurants after a day at the conference at Lucia's expense.

'Order anything you want,' she would say. 'Are you sure?' we would ask in disbelief. I knew I never had that luxury with my company. Meals had to be cheap and cheerful. Members of our group would order the best appetizers and main dishes. For those who liked desserts, they really pigged out. When the bill came, she would say 'Let me handle it!' This was much to the amazement of the waiters who probably received good tips. Everyone would gush and thank her profusely. 'Don't worry! If I don't spend this entertainment allowance, it goes right back to the company! Gotta spend it all!' Most of us worked at companies that would never put up with such extravagance.

I was put in my place during one trip with my first employer. The sales team took out two managers from a potential fancy client out to dinner. The sales people always wanted me around in case the client had a food safety or Science query. Jennylynd would know the answer. And I hoped I did. We were going to wine and dine the client at Ruth's Chris, one of the premier steakhouses in the city where the conference was held. I did not like beef and made a mental note to myself to order an alternative from the menu. As the guys spoke with the terribly important people, I looked around for fish on the menu. At that time, I was not used to ordering from such complicated menus and it was very confusing. I saw lobster (Market Price) and thought it sounded fine. It was coming from a market. At the end of the dinner, one of the salesmen from our company put the bill on his credit card, and we were off.

The following week I was summoned to the CEO's office. I wondered out loud as I entered, 'Oops. Called to the principal's office ... What have I done?' The CEO was not amused. 'Jennylynd, when we took the clients out last week, you ordered the most expensive dish on the menu!' His face was red with rage. 'I did?' I said sheepishly not knowing how much our final bill totalled. 'It was $75 for that lobster! This kind of meal is reserved for our big clients only. We take the big hit for them!' Gulp. I was shocked by his reaction, plus doubly shocked that market price actually meant the restaurant could charge whatever the market was demanding on the day, plus a huge profit. What was I to say? I couldn't regurgitate the lobster and get a refund. The man was fuming mad and I was a little afraid; but not too much. I had to stop myself from laughing at his rage over the lobster.

I put on my best pious face and said, 'It was not my intention to break the bank. I do apologize. I had no idea what "Market Price" meant.' I genuinely didn't know. 'The next time I will be sure to order a reasonably priced meal.' I'd learned my lesson. It would have to be fast food most of the time when on the road with this company, and mooching along to fancy dinners when the big spending Lucia invited food safety professionals out to dine.

After a year of attending conferences and socializing with everyone I met, I was being asked to moderate sessions for student papers and other seminars. A big role was serving as chair for the Food Safety Committee of the Grower Shipper Association of Central California (GSA). I was terrified at the first meeting, but realized the chair just kept the meeting rolling along, getting others to do most of the talking. It was a skill I had to learn fast. The company's management was adamant that I keep this role. It was good for their profile in the industry in Salinas. I wondered what I had gotten my self into, but rose to the challenge and honed my skills as a good leader. I was asked to speak on a TV production filmed at one of the company's farms. I had to give a speech at an early morning breakfast for the Pacific Business Alliance in the Oxnard area. After sweating through my one hour speech with questions and answers, only then could I partake in the sumptuous breakfast with the attendees. My network kept growing over the years.

Yes Madam President

Since university days, I loved to serve on committees getting to know countless people in a short time. In California, I continued in the same vein looking for organizations I could join and quickly get onto the management committee. One of my passions was being in charge. I did not mind the responsibility and no one else wanted to do it. I wrote my Alma Mater's alumni office in Montreal, and found out that McGill University had an alumni branch in Southern California. They sent me the contact email and telephone number for the president and I got in touch with her. She responded right away giving me a list of activities in the coming weeks. The group had a big summer event at a fancy venue in Los Angeles every year. I reserved a ticket and with great excitement showed up for the luncheon. The venue was near the waterfront and dozens of people were in attendance. The organization was made up of young and old graduates. I looked at the demographics. Many members were retired Jewish doctors and lawyers. They were wealthy and enjoying life in Southern California. I looked around to find people closer to my age and eventually saw one tall, young executive who was on the committee.

I sat at a table with a mixed crowd of older couples and one young couple. The young couple said hello and made conversation. The event was a blur with speeches and a nice lunch then everyone went his separate way. An email went out to the membership from Brenda who said she and the

Vice President were retiring from the committee after running the organization for many years. They were looking for new people to take over the reins. Brenda was hosting a meeting at her house in Beverley Hills. I was extra curious to see the inside of a home in Beverley Hills so I wrote back immediately and said I would attend. She lived close to the Beverly Hotel and I found the street easily. She lived in a simple bungalow and in fact I saw other bungalows on this street. It was no doubt worth a fortune. The neighbouring properties would have been super-inflated because of the Beverley hills zip code.

The tall, young executive, Julian came to the meeting and also the young couple I had seen at the luncheon. That was amazing. The group was going to have young leadership. We could plan more than the one fancy luncheon per year. Julian volunteered to be the new president and I said I would help with events. I planned a Christmas dinner at the Magic Castle and we were hosted by one of the Magician members at the Castle. He was a McGill alumnus. The following year I stepped forward as President of the organization, planning a Christmas luncheon on the Queen Mary and several picnics. Julian offered his home to host a meeting when the Dean of Medicine visited. It was a packed event and our chapter was bestowed the Charles Peters Branch Award for the most active branch that year. We always received T-shirts, pens, and other McGill souvenirs when I asked the head office for event door prizes.

My quest to be the leader was also satisfied when I joined with a jovial food scientist from San Diego to form the Southern California Association for Food Protection. Marg and I had met at the national event for food protection professionals and observed how active regional chapters from other States seemed to be. We planned workshops, lectures and site visits for our members, as well as hosting the national meeting in San Diego one year. I would sometimes take Tiffany to our committee meetings after work in Anaheim or some other venue. 'What would you like to be when you grow up little girl?' Some of the attendees would ask her with great amusement, after seeing how focused she looked during the meetings. 'I want to be a food scientist just like my mommy,' was always the answer.

Juggling two presidencies, my job, and being a single mother did not frighten me. I managed everything with great precision. My friends in PWP used to say, 'If you want to get anything done, give it to a busy, single mother!'

5

SINGING THROUGH THE MILLENNIUM

Neighbourhood Church

I really loved to sing and looked forward to rehearsals with the church choir in Camarillo on Thursday nights. I would also take Tiffany with me to save on child care costs. The choir members were good-natured and did not mind as she sat quietly colouring with crayons or playing with toys until she fell asleep. At most, twenty singers came to rehearsals: six men who split into basses and tenors and the rest were ladies. Poor Mary had to hammer out the notes for each section so people could learn their parts. She was very patient. She had moved to California from the mid west during the sixties. It seemed many people had moved to California from the Midwest. It must have been the thing to do, gravitating to life in the sunshine. The Californian accent thus tended to be non-distinct and very mild compared to other parts of the United States. One of the middle aged ladies asked me if I was married. I mentioned my recent divorce and she showed me one gentleman in the bass section who was also divorced and available. She smiled broadly and winked at me with anticipation of the match.

Trying to keep an open mind, I looked at him closely. He was a middle aged man with a stern face, grey hair dyed brown, and of medium build and height. He seemed ordinary. For a few seconds I day-dreamed about what life would be like with him at the house. 'Pass the potatoes dear,' he would probably say in a monotone. 'OK honey,' I would respond in a monotone. How would I cope with a boring middle-aged white man, in a middle-class suburb, while he held down a quiet job? My heart skipped a beat. I would surely get bored really fast. No way, not this time; I decided he was not for me without further investigation. 'Thanks so much for pointing him out,' I reassured her with a slight smile, as I let that opportunity pass me by.

When I told the choir members of the Camarillo Church I lived in Oxnard, they shuddered with apprehension. 'Be careful, OK …' 'Take care of yourself and the child!' 'Lock all your doors at night!'

Such were the comments of people who knew nothing about Oxnard and never ventured there. The routine of choir rehearsals and services sunk in after a while. We went through the mass for Sunday: the hymns, the singing of the liturgy and any recital pieces the choir would perform at the Sunday mass, and then we parted. 'Take care on the way home,' they warned me. For the life of me, I could not understand what the fuss was about. Since we moved to Oxnard there was not one shooting, or robbery, or murder. People worked hard and went about their daily lives. Oxnard, however, had a higher concentration of Mexicans and black people. Oxnard also had large pockets of Filipinos. What I came to realise was that any area with a predominantly coloured population was considered BAD. Oxnard may have had a period with a spike in crime in the past. At the time we moved in, there had been an expansion of construction with new housing developments. Little, if any crime was ever announced.

I asked a new acquaintance, Melissa in the choir if she had ever been to Oxnard. She was one of the most vociferous in criticizing the town. She admitted that in all her years living in Camarillo, she never had any reason to go there. I decided to invite her over for lunch at my home just for the experience. I had an hour off and she could always drive over to meet me since she was a stay-at-home mom. She agreed to take the high risk journey out to the other side of the planet for lunch.

When she got to my gated community of California Lighthouse just off Ventura Road, I had given her the instructions to buzz me at the gate. When people buzzed at the gate, the home phone rang and we could find out who was there by speaking to them at the gate. I pressed the buzzer to open the automatic gates so she could drive in. From her wide eyed look as she parked and walked under my jasmine archway out front and through the patio, I knew she was impressed. Who would not be impressed by the beautifully manicured gardens, swimming pools, peach coloured buildings and lovely patios throughout the townhouse complex? Even the security gates at the entrance were impressive. As Melissa entered my front door and stared up at the vaulted ceiling and the sweeping staircase going up to the loft, her eyes widened.

'Is this Oxnard? Wow,' she said in disbelief. 'Yes. Let's have lunch. I'm starving.' I treated her to some homemade wraps and salad with fresh juice. We gossiped for a short while before it was time for me to go back to work. I had hoped to change her unfounded bias by showing how beautiful and civilized life in Oxnard could be. Her imagination was fraught with misconceptions of another era. Melissa invited me to her Camarillo home one day too. It was not impressive in any way and I felt justified with my pretty townhouse at

California Lighthouse.

In Full Voice

Dana introduced me to her friend Stanley who heard I liked classical music. As our first date, he took me to a performance of Mozart's Requiem at a beautiful Church in Camarillo. The choir was the Ventura Master Chorale and Opera Society. As they performed, I sang along quietly at the back of the church. Mozart's Requiem was one of my favourites and I could not help myself. I was not physically attracted to Stanley, but thanked him profusely for inviting me to the concert.

I could have kicked myself for acting too shy to approach the conductor at the end of the program. I really wanted to find out about joining the ensemble. The director was a stocky, older man with grey sideburns, and a serious face. He had an important air about him and was surrounded by well wishers at the end of the show. I did not dare approach him, but smiled profusely at the choir members as they processed through the church at the end of the performance. I secretly wished and hoped to find a way to be part of the group one day. Only one black woman sang in the choir, but she did not notice me as she left the church. I was not sure how to become part of the group. I searched the concert program and found a summary of the musical director's career. It also said he was a professor at Ventura College. After hesitating for days, I gained the courage to call Ventura College to speak with him and ask for an audition. It took me half an hour to dial the important number. The person at the main switchboard transferred me to the music department and someone gave me a time to call when the director would be in the office.

I called back within a few hours and was very excited when he answered. 'Hello, my name is Jennylynd. I was quite impressed with your choir's rendition of Mozart's Requiem.' 'Why thank you dear,' he said in a cheerful tone. 'I have a soprano voice and I've sung with several choirs in the past. I would love to audition for the choir. Are you accepting new members?' I asked with hope. His voice was kind and calm as he responded. 'Yes we usually have auditions early in September. I'll give you the number for the choir secretary. You can call her to set up an appointment.' 'Thanks so much!' I screamed with delight. 'Thank you. Thank you.'

The telephone call was not as difficult as I had imagined. Within a day my appointment for an audition was arranged. I just had to wait through the rest of the summer for the big audition day in September to come. Auditions are always a nervous time for performing artists hoping to join any big group. The expectations were standard. It was usually to sing a piece, sing some scales, and then the dreaded sight singing. I knew auditioning for the Ventura Master Chorale would definitely be more extensive than the church choir. My nerves played havoc with my brain all day before the evening audition. I could barely concentrate at work. I just wanted to get it over and done with. Would they like me? How many people would be present during the audition? How many sopranos would be auditioning? Suppose he said no. I would be devastated. My nerves had gotten the best of me by the time I arrived at Ventura College that evening. Finding parking early, I was able to locate the large rehearsal room with the stage up front.

'Hello, my name's Linda,' said a middle aged woman with a clip board. Everyone here for auditions can stand outside or sit inside if you like. Choir members won't come for another hour. In the big room with at least 100 seats, the accompanist sat on the stage and the director sat in the front row of seats. We could hear the other hopefuls singing through the walls, but would not dare go in to see them. That would be too much. By the time my turn came, a few regular choir members had arrived and quietly went into the hall to sit and observe. That was no fun. I would actually have a small audience. 'Don't worry. It'll be just fine,' said one woman as she entered the hall and winked at me. Did this woman know how my knees were knocking and I could barely breathe.

When my name was called, I entered the room and went up on stage. I gave the accompanist a copy of Ave Verum, my favourite audition piece and the director said we could start whenever I was ready. I could still feel my knees knocking, but decided to focus on the chairs at the back at the hall and sing to them. I managed to take some deep breaths and sing out. The Ave Verum went OK but I did not breathe in the best places for phrasing. In fact I felt as if I had not breathed at all through the piece. He then asked the accompanist to lead me through a few scales to check my voice range. This was followed by the dreaded sight singing. I was given a piece of music I had never seen before and fumbled my way through it with some prompting by the accompanist. In my mind it was dreadful. 'That was fine,' said the director. You're a soprano. Thank you.' He appeared calm as usual. Did that mean I was in? I was not sure. I said thanks and walked out the room taking deep breaths. As I left the room, the next hopeful was called in. The coordinator told me I was accepted to the choir and could start rehearsal with everyone that very night!

I was so happy after all the preparation and anguish! I had become a full-fledged member of the Ventura Master Chorale. After the last two auditions were completed, all the choir members stormed the room with loud conversations and greetings. I observed all the characters as they arrived for rehearsal and found the soprano section to sit with them. As the weeks went on, we prepared for an up-coming fall concert, then a Christmas concert. I started making new friends in the soprano section and conversed profusely with everyone possible during the breaks. The choir hierarchy and politics were also interesting to watch. One woman, Anne, was responsible for putting out the treats at break. Each section took turns in bringing snacks: sopranos, altos, tenors, and bases. It was a democratic way to distribute the responsibility. I asked Anne one evening if she wanted help in managing the tea break. She looked me over and said, 'No thank you.' I must have created the perception of a stranger trying to take over well guarded territory. It was no problem for me. Everyone had his or her perspective of what was important. She obviously enjoyed taking care of the tea break and did not want to relinquish any bit of this role. Her behaviour was amusing for me.

Choir members came from many locations: Ventura town, North Oxnard, Santa Barbara, and even towns in the Conejo Valley. The black woman in the choir told me she drove all the way from Los Angeles for rehearsals because she really enjoyed singing with this choir. One soprano, Trish, hailed from Santa Barbara. She looked like an old doll in young woman's clothing. Her hair was dyed blonde and her face did not move. As she spoke her mouth did not move much. She wore tight leather pants and a fashionably short leather jacket. Her neck however was wrinkled. I asked another woman sitting next to me why Trish's face did not move when she spoke or sang. The woman winked at me and said, 'Plastic surgery my dear'. I had heard about movie stars doing plastic surgery to continue looking youthful, but it was the first time I encountered anyone who was the product of plastic surgery. I then became obsessed as I went around town the following weeks, looking for other people who had the plastic surgery face.

Alma at the office informed me that many people in California had plastic surgery done. In addition I would see boob jobs with implants and many other enhancements. It was a rude awakening for me. The lengths people would go to look glamorous were baffling. A middle aged woman in the choir called Noreen complained to me about her father's new young girlfriend who was planning to take all their inheritance money. 'If she thinks she's going to get his money, she can think again!' She spoke to me as if I knew the people involved. I kept a neutral and concerned look on my face. Looking at Noreen who had a lot of grey hair herself, I wondered how old her father could be. Maybe he was in his seventies or eighties and his money had attracted a young bride. 'We have to set up a prenuptial agreement! There's no way she's getting his money!' exclaimed Noreen. 'No way!' I chimed in.

Then there was Kaitie, a plump and pleasant woman with a large soprano voice. The director seemed to like her voice and gave her most of the soprano solo parts in concerts. This did not please some of the other sopranos who were waiting to also get a soprano role. I observed the politics that played out. It was the same in every choir. An older Danish couple, Caja and Bendt lived in North Oxnard and came to every rehearsal. They were very friendly and attracted a lot of praise when they prepared tasty treats for the tea breaks. They were famous for catering big dinners.

One of the younger members in the choir, a red head with gaps in her teeth told me she had sneaked out of her mother's house one night to see her boyfriend. 'And when did you do this, pray tell,' I asked. 'While I was in high school,' she said proudly. I always thought she looked quiet as a mouse. I could hardly imagine her doing anything so daring. But, it was the quiet ones who would always create surprises. Roland, the judge, was a tall white haired gentleman in the bass section. The choir had its share of prominent people from the Ventura community so I was in good company. We sometimes divided into sections for separate rehearsals led by section leaders, and then met at the end to put everything together. The rehearsal technique was instrumental in learning the music thoroughly and I really enjoyed singing and performing with the choir over the years.

New Millennium Party

The approach of the year 2000 caused a flurry of activity in the media. Prophets of doom and gloom were convincing many people to stay indoors with predictions of the end of the world and computer glitches.

The main debate with the approach of the year 2000 was whether the beginning of this year should be called the beginning of the new millennium, or whether it should be the start of 2001. The Y2K bug, Y2K problem, or the Millennium bug was described by technology pundits as the time when computers would not understand the move from 1999 to 2000 since the last two digits of the year were commonly used to describe the year. Thus the year 2000 may not have been recognized or distinguished in computer systems from the year 1900.

What if all the computers were to shut down? What if we lost all data stored? What if all the traffic lights shut down? What if all the computers in automatic cars shut down at midnight? What if? What if? There would be chaos in the cities! People would lose all their money if bank systems failed! There would be weeping and gnashing of teeth! Companies worldwide tried checking and double checking computer systems to ensure they would work as they moved from 1999 to 2000.

Tiffany and I had been invited to a New Years Eve party at the house of the Danish friends, Caja and Bendt from the choir. I looked forward to their dinner party and gift exchange since it was a nice opportunity to get out on New Year's Eve and be able take Tiffany with me. I considered myself lucky to get an invitation.

Some members of the public were paranoid and caught up in the hype. 'I'm not going on the street that night,' said one local friend. 'Well, I'm going to a party,' I said casually. 'I always go out on New Year's Eve.' She looked at me as if I were crazy, and shook her head vigorously. 'You'll regret it. You'll regret it! New Year's Eve is always crazy on the highway,' she said. 'Well if everyone's like you, then the highway should be empty!' I reasoned. 'It would be the best night to drive to and from a party!' The woman gave up on me. She was off to stock up on food and prepare for her imaginary 'Millennium War'.

When New Year's Eve arrived, Tiffany and I dressed in our finest velvet dresses and I donned a shiny corsage. The party was listed as a dinner and gift exchange. The couple said we were to bring a gift valued at no more than $15 for the gift stealing game. I had no idea what this meant, but imagined it was some type of mischievous affair. Caja and Bendt lived in north Oxnard near the golf course. The other two couples invited also lived in the neighbourhood. One other single woman like me was invited so I did not feel like a left foot at a couples' event. Everyone was beautifully dressed and the dining room and living room sported ornate decorations and a sparkling Christmas tree. We dined on one course after the other as the couple brought treats from the kitchen to stuff us.

At dessert, we took a break to have a sing along. Since we were all experienced vocalists, except for some partners who were not in the choir, a party was not a party without a sing along. Caja brought out copies of music and we took turns leading. After some delicious chocolate mousse and rich cakes for dessert, they announced the gift stealing game and we moved to the living room. I had brought a simple chopping board which was nicely wrapped for the gift exchange. We took turns in order around the room un-wrapping a random gift from the pool and announcing whether we would keep the gift or steal a previous gift from another person who had a nice one.

Deborah brought a plastic flower pot with some singing poinsettia flowers. The flowers twirled and bobbed up and down as they sang. 'Rocking around the Christmas tree … la la la ….' People seemed annoyed by the singing plant. Tiffany, however, was enchanted by the gadget and did a little dance every time someone pressed the button. As the game went around the room, anyone stuck with the little plant was sure to give it away and grab a more interesting gift. When my turn came, the gift collected from the pile was a pair of oven mitts and a kitchen towel. They were beautiful, but I saw how much Tiffany wanted the singing plant. I decided to grab the poinsettias from the last "victim" and claim them as my own. Everyone was delighted not to have to bother with the noisy gadget and I was happy to have a new toy for Tiffany. A few seconds before midnight, we counted down joyfully while popping fire crackers. Tiffany screamed every time someone released a cracker. She was terrified at the noise. One man in the group released a cracker near to her on purpose and the poor child bawled with fear. He obviously did not have a clue about dealing with small children since he had none. The poor child ran to the nearest bed and within ten minutes she was fast asleep.

We watched millennium celebrations on television around the globe. There was no power outage; no breakdown in the media; no weeping and gnashing of teeth! I started my car easily as we set off for our home nearby.' Miraculously' there was no problem in starting the car. Systems worked as usual and there was no Millennium bug to fight. All the hype about disaster at the start of 2000 was an elaborate unfulfilled story when no disaster occurred. Happy New Year!

Lady with the Nose Tattoo

The choir had its fair share of hippies and artistic types as did the town of Ventura. It was interesting to note that some hippies also sang classical music. I guessed that an artist should be free spirited enough to enjoy all types of music.

The Chorale had planned the Western Wynde Tour in summer 2000 to travel up the coast from Ventura to San Francisco, singing at various Catholic Mission churches. The three-day concert tour looked like a wonderful trip and I signed up with my deposit of $50 as soon as it was announced. We had options to pay to share a hotel room or reserve an independent room in Buelton and in San Francisco. Since I was on a very tight budget with more than I could handle, I checked the option of Tiffany and me sharing a room with someone. Who would be willing to share a room with a young mother and a four year old child? It would have to be another mother who understood children and didn't mind.

We had to pay weeks in advance for the bus, the dinner in Buelton, the breakfast in San Francisco, and hotel costs. All other meals would have to be paid out of pocket. I finally teamed up with a friendly soul called Karen in the alto section. I did not know her but she always said hello at rehearsals. I was particularly intrigued by the tattoos near her nose. She had two card symbols; a spade and a heart. Why would anyone get tattoos on the nose? I was determined to find out from her while we were on tour.

We rehearsed our music for the tour during the spring and finally June came for our departure. The first concert was at our local Mission, the old San Buenaventura Mission. Music by John Taverner: Sanctus Benedictus and Lauridsen: O Magnum Mysterium started the Western Wynde Mass. This was followed by a series of Madrigals. The audience was appreciative and we went away excited that evening to rise next day for the drive up the coast. Some of us boarded the bus while others chose to drive their cars on the tour. Our next evening concert was at the Old Mission, Santa Inez in Solvang. Solvang and Buelton were Danish towns north of Santa Barbara. It was surprising to me to see a collection of windmills and Danish buildings in the middle of nowhere. As we drove into Solvang, I felt we were being transported into Denmark. Some performers in costume roamed the streets and one could see them dancing in colourful gear in front of pastry shops. One pastry shop after the other lined the streets. Unfortunately for our group, we had a rehearsal planned and this was quickly followed by the concert.

Everything was programmed to the minute. We were going to be whisked away on the bus for dinner at the Best Western Buellton, better known as Pea Soup Andersen's Inn. The restaurant was famous for miles around for its pea soup. We stayed overnight before continuing up the coast to San Francisco. I vowed to return at a later date to explore Solvang very slowly and absorb the Danish atmosphere. My roommate was a curiosity with various protocols as she got ready for the night. I was a bit cautious and hoped Tiffany would not cry or scream to disturb the roommate. We had to stay awake for the concert and a late dinner. This finished long after Tiffany's typical bedtime of 7:30 pm. She was extra tired.

After a quick shower she went to sleep without protest. It

was 11:00 pm. Karen and I had a short moment to speak and then we went to bed. I knew I snored at night and hoped the roommate would not be too disturbed by this. She was such a pleasant soul. Even if the noise disturbed her, she would not complain. 'Had a good sleep,' she sang in a musical sleeping voice next morning. 'I have to iron my clothes before we leave.' I got Tiffany dressed first, then dressed myself. I should have done it the other way around because I had very little time left. We all checked out of the room and went to the lobby to board the bus. We had brought snacks to munch on the way if we got hungry. There was no time for breakfast. Tiffany was the choir mascot on the bus. Everyone wanted to speak with the little girl and hear her sing. She grew tired of all the attention and memorising everyone's first names. She had a solid memory which was admirable. Eventually she fell fast asleep until the next rest stop.

Bus transport was slower than by car. When we finally got to San Francisco, the driver could not find Grosvenor Suites on Pine Street. We went around in circles for a while until he finally located the place. Some members who were driving their own cars arrived long before the bus. They had changed, and were on their way out to explore San Francisco. I asked Karen if she would walk around the town with us. I had never been to San Francisco and was a bit apprehensive about walking around at night on the first trip there. We had to find dinner too and I had no idea where to go. She mentioned she had lived in San Francisco many years before.

When we deposited our belongings in the room, we set off to explore Chinatown and other places. We saw a sushi restaurant that had a narrow channel of water built into the bar which carried boats with morsels of sushi. The channel twisted and turned in front of seats at the sushi bar. This was one of the most interesting places I had seen. Karen knew where we could get a reasonably priced meal, so that was where we ate. She kept coins to give out to homeless people as we walked around the city. 'Why are you giving so many street people money,' I asked her?

That was when she opened up saying that she was once homeless on the streets of San Francisco. Her family, including her own children did not speak to her at that time. She said she knew what it was like to be homeless and she felt an affinity to the street people. I also asked her why she got tattoos on her nose. She said it was at a wild time in her youth. I wondered if it was during her homeless phase or before. At any rate I was very disturbed with what I had heard. I wondered whether she was safe as a roommate. My bias stretched even further to wonder if she had suffered from mental illness. My state of paranoia heightened. Was I normal and she wasn't? When pairing up with a random roommate from a group, one never knows who will be sharing the room.

The following day we performed at the Shrine of St. Francis of Assisi in the north Beach area. After this we had our second night in San Francisco and explored another part of the city. One more night with the lady with the tattooed nose and I had heard many other weird and amazing tales about life on the street. We checked out of the hotel early and headed south to sing at the Carmel Mission near the coast. This was a morning concert, on a Monday, and we wondered if anybody would be around to hear us. The church was ancient with the typical large stone slab floors and white washed concrete walls as built by Mexican priests and labourers. The audience was sparse and included a few tourists who were visiting Carmel for the day.

When we were done we headed south for the long drive back to Ventura. Tiffany entertained choir members as a true mascot could, until she finally fell asleep from exhaustion. The tour was a wonderful way to bring choir members closer together. We had many days to get acquainted on the bus and over meals. I looked forward to more events with the choir in future.

The Choir Boy

We met while singing at one of the big concerts at the Thousand Oaks Performing Arts Center. The choir had prepared for an exciting recital with the Los Robles Master Chorale from Simi Valley. Our guest conductor was Paul Salamunovich, Music Director of the Los Angeles Master Chorale and we were performing with the Los Angeles Philharmonic Orchestra. He kept staring at me backstage and then smiled. I said hello and was flattered by the attention. 'Hi, I'm Sam. And you are …?' he asked, waiting for a response. 'Hi, I'm Jennylynd,' I said. 'Just joined the choir this year.' 'Welcome to the choir,' he replied in a matter of fact way. 'Hope you enjoy the music.' 'Thanks,' I said. It was great to meet a friendly soul in the group. I was a little shy and smiled at a few people, but did not dare strike up a conversation unless I was sure someone would speak with me. Sam was about 5ft 10 inches tall, of medium build with a receding hairline of blonde hair. He had piercing blue eyes, a sensible nose and round forehead. Sam was a baritone and a strong addition to the small numbers of male members in the choir. I looked out for Sam the following week at rehearsal and wondered if he'd also looked out for me. During our coffee break, I felt a little tap on my shoulder and turned around to see it was Sam.

'Coffee Time,' he said. 'I'm not really a coffee drinker, but I'll try the snacks and have some lemonade,' I said. Sam told me a little about his background. He was of German descent and grew up in Minnesota. Most of his family and friends followed the Lutheran faith. I also learned about the strong Lutheran contingent in the Conejo Valley as well as the California Lutheran University. After exchanging some pleasantries, we were called back to sing and my heart was a flutter from speaking with Sam. Did he have a romantic interest in me? Would he ask me on a date? Was he married or single? Did we have many single men in the choir? My questions were endless. I wondered who I could trust in the choir to provide me with answers.

The following week, I asked an acquaintance in the soprano section if she knew about most of the people in the group. She said she had sung with the choir a few years and knew almost all the members. I then took the opportunity to ask her if she knew anything about Sam. 'He's a nice friendly guy,' she said. 'Do you know if he's married? He spoke with me once and seemed really nice.' 'I'm not sure,' she admitted. 'Why? Do you like him?' 'Well,' I said without admitting guilt, 'Perhaps.' 'OK,' she said, 'I'll ask around and get back to you next week with what I find out.' I watched Sam's receding hairline out of the corner of my eye as rehearsal ended. I was conversing with some of my neighbours in the soprano section and he left for home quietly. Why was I attracted to this man? Was it because he said hello and made conversation? Anyone could do that?

I waited anxiously for the following Thursday when we would have rehearsal. I had scoped out the concert program to see Sam's full name. He had a long German surname that was hard to pronounce. During the break, I was sure to meet with my private investigator to find out what news she had gathered for me. Sam was not at rehearsal that day which made me a bit sad and anxious. It meant I had to wait another week to actually see him and strike up a conversation. 'He's single from what I gathered. And he lives over the hill in the Thousand Oaks area,' my informant told me. 'Well, that's good news. Now I just have to figure if he's really interested without driving him off with my anxiousness,' I said. 'Just feed him,' she suggested. 'Invite him over for dinner and feed him!' 'What? Are you kidding me?' I smiled at her advice, but realised it would not work if I was being a true Rules Girl. We were never supposed to open up to a man too quickly until well into the relationship. That included not inviting him over to the home on a first date. The following week, I planted myself next to the refreshments during the break. The guys always went for a treat and sure enough Sam approached the table.

'Hello Jennylynd,' he chimed as I tried to maintain my composure. 'Hi Sam. How are you this evening? I love this music. It's always fun to sing Mozart.' I managed to blurt out several statements in one breath. We spoke about the music and the weather for a short time and then moved onto another topic. 'Say, I was wondering, would you like to meet up sometime later in the week?' asked Sam. He was reading my mind. Of course I wanted to meet up. I was hoping he would ask me out. What was taking him so long? 'Yes, sure,' I said shyly. 'Give me your phone number. I'll call you sometime,' he said.

I gave Sam my number. By that time, we were being called back to rehearsal. The breaks always seemed too short when a good conversation was going. I could barely sing during the second half of rehearsal. The prospect of a date was so distracting. If I dated him, we would make a good couple, I reasoned. We were both interested in classical music. That would be common ground and we would have things to talk about. My mind raced uncontrollably. Everyday when I came home from work, I looked at the answering machine to see if it was flashing with messages. Nothing showed up. This was a time when messages had to be left on your home phone or your beeper. I did not give him my beeper number or my work number. By day two I wondered if he would ever call. As I put Tiffany to sleep and got lost in reading a book, I heard the phone ring. Could it be Sam?

I let the phone ring three times so as not to sound too eager, and also to steady my breath. 'Hello, good evening,' I said calmly. 'Hello. This is Sam,' he sang joyfully, as he spoke. 'How are you?' 'Oh, just fine. Relaxing for the evening,' I replied. 'So, I was wondering if you like Korean food. Where do you live?' he asked. 'I live in North Oxnard,' I said, wondering if he knew the difference between the North Oxnard connotation and the South part of Oxnard. 'Good. There's a really nice place on N. Oxnard Boulevard called Korean Swan Restaurant. I've been there a few times. We can meet one evening for dinner. That way you won't have to drive too far,' he explained. 'Sounds great,' I said.

'What day's good for you?' he asked. I knew very well my calendar was blank and I was waiting to go on a date with someone. According to The Rules, it was best to wait three to four days before scheduling a date. That would create the illusion of being extremely busy with other suitors. 'How about Saturday evening?' I asked. 'Oh, that's perfect,' he said. 'Will meet you at six o'clock.' 'That's great. See you then,' I said. As I hung up the phone, I did a little dance and song. 'Ah got me a date. Friday night at eight. And I can't be late.' It was a little song Alma at the office used to sing every time she had a date.

I promptly arranged babysitting so everything could fall into place and waded through the work week anxiously waiting for my date with Sam. I even passed by the restaurant a few days early so I could see where to find parking and check out the food samples in their showcase. Some dishes were perched in the window. I was not sure if it was real food or rubber replicas. I saw raw beef with a raw egg on top. I also saw many different pickles and unfamiliar products in the window. As I peeped through the window I saw patrons cooking their food at the table in what seemed like a deep pot. What are they doing, I wondered? Sam was going to have the job of educating me on Korean food. I didn't know much.

When the Saturday evening came, I wore a pretty dress with light make up and left in good time for my date. Sam was pulling into the parking lot the same time as me. 'My you look lovely,' he said when we met in front of the restaurant. He was all charm and I was lapping it up. 'Thanks,' I said blushing and moving towards the entrance. We got seated and the waitress brought out about ten small plates containing different types of vegetable pickles. Sam explained the various pickles and which were spicy. I looked at the menu which was a puzzle to me. I then asked him to recommend what he thought I should order since I had no idea which dishes were good. He said the sizzling eel was good, and we could also order beef and noodles to cook in the hot pot.

'What? Cook?' I asked in disbelief. 'Yes, they put a delicious broth in the pot and you can put pieces of meat and vegetables to cook in there'. The eel came into the room on a sizzling skillet with great pomp and ceremony. As I bit into a small piece, it was such a delicate flavour and texture; I could not imagine having missed out on such a meal all my life. The pieces of meat and vegetables cooked swiftly in the hot pot and we feasted and talked for a while. I ate all the little bits of pickles on the tiny plates. They were tasty and tangy. If Sam did not want anymore, I cleaned up one bit at a time. After all they were low calorie and good food could not go to waste.

The whole experience and the company made me lose track of time. I was 'in like' with Sam right away and hoped he would ask me out again. When we parted for our respective cars, I was hoping Sam would give me a kiss, but all he did was say, 'Will see ya at the next rehearsal. Bye!' And he took off. Was that it? Was I the only one "In Like"? Well, I had to be grateful for the wonderful dinner experience and looked forward to future outings with Sam. The following week he invited me to a play at the Thousand Oaks Civic Arts Centre. That was an exciting opportunity and great for me to learn about a new venue. The same situation took place at the end of the date. Sam gave me the old buddy punch on the arm and said, 'See yah next week'. I was languishing and wondering if I had done something wrong. I had tried to follow The Rules to the letter, no calling up unnecessarily just to hear his voice, or lingering too long when he did call me. I appeared interested in all his stories and behaved like a beautiful angel. But Sam did not kiss me.

6

PLANNING A MOVE

The Wedding Dress

I was invited to Dana's apartment finally, after having her over to my place quite a few times for dinner and to hang out. I supposed she was cautious with anyone she met and did not care to open up too swiftly. She showed me around the tiny one bedroom apartment in Camarillo and proceeded to show me some of her treasures. 'This is my diamond tennis bracelet. It's at least one carat in diamonds and valued at hundreds of dollars.' She boasted as I examined the little bracelet that was so important. 'Every fine woman in California should have a diamond tennis bracelet.' She knew I did not have a diamond tennis bracelet and had no intention of getting one. I must not have been a fine woman and quite frankly I didn't care. 'Do you know how many meals I had to miss to pay for that?' she screamed at me and I wondered what I had done wrong. The woman must have been mad to miss meals to pay for the foolish bracelet. I had heard that story some months before.

Then she showed me her faux fur coat. 'Every woman must have a fur coat,' she said. 'Isn't that excessive for California winters? We never get any snow here, except in the mountains. What the hell would I be doing with a fur coat?' 'Well you need to have one just in case!' She was losing her patience with me since I did not subscribe to the program of objects a fine woman should have. Dana then quibbled over the fact she was making fifty cents less per hour than another employee at the childcare centre. She felt it was unfair, but she would have to work another year in order to make the bigger salary. 'They are full of shit over there. I hate the owner of the place. Does she know who I am? I work really hard cleaning up after those little monsters,' she said. 'I'm sure you do,' I said in sympathy. 'I hate cleaning up all the mess those children make,' she continued. 'Their parents are no better. They just drop them off and we have to deal with the mess. I hate my job,' Dana confided. 'OK.' All I could do was nod and listen. This was a monologue requiring no input.

We then looked at some more of her treasures and I gave the appropriate 'Ooos and ahs' of approval of some of her favourite outfits. It was then she showed me her wedding dress. It was a cream coloured, shiny silk gown with a halter back. The neckline had delicate embroidery and the dress was cut to fit a slim and trim figure. 'Why do you have this wedding dress hanging in your bedroom? I thought you were never married,' I asked innocently. 'No silly. That is the dress I will use when I get married. I have to make sure I stay skinny to fit into it,' Dana explained. 'But you are not seeing anyone seriously at the moment. Why would you buy a dress?' I asked. 'I don't want to have a mad scramble when I trap a man and work The Rules on him,' she said. 'He will ask me to marry him and I have to be ready,' she explained.

I had never heard about advance planning for a wedding without having a man. This was the craziest thing I had heard in all my life. Surely if a boyfriend was on the scene and a conversation about marriage was in the air, then I could understand the need to purchase a dress. However, the whole idea was bizarre for me. 'I put that dress up in the corner over there and look at it everyday. Let me tell you about the wedding plans,' said Dana.

'Oh you have wedding plans too?' The plot seemed to thicken as I listened attentively to the wedding plans. 'I love Las Vegas, so that's where the wedding is going to be,' she said. 'OK. Sounds interesting,' I agreed. 'I've already called the Bellagio Hotel to find out the prices for their wedding packages. We must have a bridal suite,' Dana confirmed. 'If you insist,' I chirped. 'Do you know how expensive it is to rent the bridal suite up on the top floor? I've already started saving for this,' said Dana.

'Call me old-fashioned, but don't you think you should meet the guy first?' I asked. 'Shut up. I know what I'm doing!' she said. She certainly knew what she wanted. The Wedding package was selected from a host of packages offered by Bellagio. The Sunday to Thursday packages were the least expensive and the ceremony room was reserved for one hour. Las Vegas was notorious for assembly line weddings. No doubt, another bridal party would be waiting in the wings for Dana, the groom and guests to vacate the room for the next party! Dana already had her guest list. 'I'm only inviting people who are important to me. In fact, I will invite everybody who thought I could never have a proper wedding,' she continued. It seemed to me the wedding was going to be an opportunity to show off to her enemies.

'After we leave the ceremony room, we'll all go up to the bridal suite to hang out.' Dana already decided she would get a bridal suite for two nights, the night before and the night of the wedding. Any more than that, and it would cost too much. She would show the guests she could have a fancy bridal suite. 'Wouldn't you want some privacy with your husband after the ceremony? Why have everybody invading your room?' I asked. 'Well the ceremony is only one hour, so people will want to hang out and eat and dance, so we can do that in the room. The groom would have the rest of his life to spend time with me,' she said. They would check out the day after the wedding. Well, everything seemed logical. Dana just had the small task of finding a willing subject.

'I can sing the Ave Maria at your wedding,' I volunteered. 'I've sung at all my friends' weddings. That way you won't have to pay for a singer.' 'That's a great idea,' she said. 'I'll put you down on the program.' And so that was how I made it onto the guest list. I was being presumptuous that a brand new friend like me was going to be invited to the wedding to be. 'If you do The Rules really well, a man could be driven to insanity. He would have to marry you to be able to sleep with you,' said Dana.

I left her apartment with my head spinning. Her ideas seemed insane! How could anyone plan a wedding before meeting a man? Why would she buy a dress? How bizarre and unique these ideas were to me. I did not know if to agree with the ideas or laugh at them. Maybe this was what made sense in the old days before women's liberation.

Wedding in Vegas

Dana and I continued to go out to various upscale bars on weekends, keeping a watchful eye for potential husbands. It was easy to eliminate undesirables based on their behaviour. All the while, I was under the tutelage of a crazy woman. 'He's too cheap. Couldn't even buy me a drink and wants to speak with me for hours. Go away, go away. Next!' 'That one over there is a keeper. He's looking in our direction. Don't look at him too hard, you'll scare him off,' she advised. 'OK, OK. But how would he know I'm interested if I don't look at him? He'll go somewhere else,' I said. Dana's friend, Diane joined us in the hunting expeditions. Diane was in her mid 40's with large breasts that made her look stouter than she really was. She had short brown hair styled like the average middle aged woman and piercing green eyes. Her lips curled up as she spoke with a very strong accent which I could not place. She assumed I was in my mid 40's since I was hanging out with them.

I never told anyone my age. But I was tempted to correct her when she looked at my sporty red Mitsubishi Eclipse with the sun roof and said, 'Don't you think that's more for a young woman?' I was a young woman in the prime of my life. I had seen many an old, grey man in sports cars since we moved to California. I wondered what she thought about them. I decided to bite my tongue and just responded, 'Hmm. I like my car.' Diane had one daughter who, she claimed, would never know her father. She was the result of a passionate moment in time. The child was bright and beautiful and made a lovely playmate for Tiffany. Diane spoke at length about the Jacuzzi with the twenty-five jets which would be installed in her back yard. We heard about the purchase, then about the time leading up to the fateful installation.

'It will raise the value of my home you know. I don't think other people on the street have a Jacuzzi with 25 jets. I will be the envy of all my neighbours.' She made such a big commotion about this, that even I wanted a chance to bathe in her Jacuzzi with 25 jets. I had my own pool and hot tub at our community club house, so there was really no need to drive miles away to use Dianne's. However, she made it sound very important.

One day, Dana announced she had met a man through a friend of a friend in Los Angeles. He was a tall salesman. She decided since he had the potential to make money, he would be a fine husband. 'When will we meet him? When will we meet him?' Diane and I asked with excitement. 'You're not going to meet him,' she said. 'The Rules say a man should not be introduced to your friends and family until you're sure about him. He has to beg to meet my friends!' With that statement, she laughed hysterically. I knew the chase had begun and the mysterious man was the chosen groom for the pre-planned wedding. 'I'll just say he's a black guy from Los Angeles,' explained Dana. 'You're not giving us much to go on. There are many black men in Los Angeles!' I said.

Over a month, Dana called with snippets about how they went out for lunch or they went to an event. She hesitated to bring him to her apartment. 'I can't open up too soon. In any case, I've decided he can't have me until we're married,' she said. 'How are you going to manage that Dana? These are modern times. He will start making demands,' I said. 'Well, I will let him kiss me in two weeks' time, and that's it,' she said. I listened with amusement at the strategy knowing very well I could never resist for such a long time. One evening she called me triumphantly. 'He mentioned the 'M' word. He actually said it. I would never say it. That would scare them off you know,' she said. 'Sure, I know that,' I agreed. 'He really wants to get to know me better, so he realized he would have to marry me to make it happen,' Dana confirmed.

'But you only met this man six weeks ago. Do you know anything about him? Have you met his family and friends?' I asked. 'I know enough. I'm ready to get married,' she shouted. 'Well, has he bought you a diamond engagement ring?' I knew how much value the Californian woman placed on the diamond ring. Its meaning transcended the value of the relationship. 'Well he promised when business picked up, he would be able to buy me a big ring. For now we will just exchange gold wedding bands.' It seemed to me she had lowered her standards just to get married. The same woman who bought herself a diamond tennis bracelet was going into a marriage without a one carat diamond engagement ring!

It was already autumn and even though it was not too cold by California standards, things were a bit grey. 'I've planned the wedding in November,' Dana proudly announced. 'That's only a month and a half away. Wouldn't you want to plan a summer wedding next year?' I asked. 'No, the prices in Vegas are cheaper at this time of year, so I better take advantage of that. In any case, I don't know how long I can hold this man off.'

As she made final reservations for the wedding and invited guests, we had to make a mad scramble for hotel reservations and gifts. I was on a very tight budget with more than a dozen bills to pay each month. I wondered what practical gift I could buy to fit into the total wedding budget. Since I would have to pay for a hotel, meals, and gas to drive to and from Las Vegas, the gift budget went down really low. I thought about Dana's small apartment. She said they were going to live at her place until sales picked up and they could buy a house. In my mind, it was another set of excuses the mystery man gave for not having money. I wondered why she would go through with the marriage. Her determination to stage a wedding was more important than the reality of the situation. I decided to buy them a practical laundry sorter which could fit easily into a corner of the bedroom. I was at my wits end having to balance my own budget, while trying to add another person's crazy wedding plans to the list.

As the time came closer, Dana had booked a block of rooms at a reasonably priced motel for anyone who wanted to stay in Las Vegas. I doubted if any of her friends planned to stay at the Bellagio. Who could afford it? Diane said she would drive up the day before with her daughter. I said I would leave early the morning of the wedding and return to Los Angeles the following day. This way I would only have to pay for one hotel night. 'Do you know how much this wedding is costing me?' asked Dana. 'I will have to work overtime the next couple weeks to make up the difference. The hotel is waiting for the money,' she said. 'Hmm,' I said, trying to be supportive in the middle of the mayhem. 'Yes, I can well imagine.'

She ordered a few appetizers and some sparkling wine juice. The package deal did not include food. Dana decided to also order some fast food to consume later when people gathered in the honeymoon suite. The time passed swiftly and before we knew it, guests were driving across the Mojave Desert to Las Vegas, Nevada. Tiffany and I left very early in the morning so we were able to get there at lunch time. We checked into our motel room, ate some food we had bought on the way, and then changed into our fancy wedding clothes. We walked a few blocks away to the Bellagio Hotel and tried to find the correct Wedding Ceremony Room. There were many brides and grooms walking all around the hotel. It was like a scene from a strange movie. In addition, wedding guests were well-dressed and running in many different directions to find their respective bridal parties. I confirmed the ceremony room number on the invitation and walked with Tiffany toward the area.

When we got outside the room, many of Dana's friends were standing around in the hallway. We were all early. In fact, another wedding was taking place in the room and we had to wait a while for them to finish. We were on the assembly line of a wedding factory! As the wedding was completed, they danced and celebrated for the one hour allotted then they had to leave. A cleaning crew came in, fixed the room and assembled everything for the next wedding. As the bride and groom filed out with their wedding party, I stared in disbelief. All that pomp and splendour for one hour seemed a bit contrived. I heard from one woman Dana was in a nearby room fixing her dress and getting her makeup done. Diane and her daughter appeared with gift in hand and we traded stories about the journey through the desert.

When the room coordinators had finished, they invited us to come in and find seats. I decided to sit near the front since I was part of the program. The room was beautifully decorated with flowers and smartly dressed soft chairs with cream chair covers. They must have put out about fifty chairs. The fanciest chairs facing a make shift alter were for the bride and groom. I saw a tall black man with an afro and glasses walk in with two buddies. He spoke with them for a while, gave us all a quick hello, and then walked to the front.

He was the groom. We were finally seeing the groom. He fiddled with the chairs up front, sat down in one chair, then got up and walked over to one side of the room. A man who looked as if he would be performing the ceremony had walked in. He had programs for us and the hotel's photographer also came in. 'Randall Grant', it said on the program. I guessed that was the groom's name. When he came back to his seat, I decided to go up to introduce myself. 'Hi Randall,' I said as I held out my hand to shake his. 'My name is Lindy. I'm one of Dana's friends. I'll be singing the Ave Maria for the ceremony.' He shook my hand and stared saying it was good to meet me. I had a chance to study his face and mannerisms closely. He had a pleasant face but he was not good looking. His height was one saving grace. I know Dana liked them tall. Randall's voice was deep. He was a manly man. I wondered how Dana was able to coerce him into the whole marriage game without his knowing he was part of an elaborate plan staged years in advance. After a few pleasantries we all took our seats and waited for the ceremony to begin.

The music started and the bride strolled regally into the room. Someone played a recording of the Wedding March. Dana looked beautiful in her ivory silk dress with halter back and embroidered plunging neckline. It was a sexy dress and fit her very well. She managed to lose a few extra pounds before the wedding to be sure no bumps showed under the delicate dress. Her hair was beautifully coiffed into a bun with curls around the hair line. Her make up was light and complemented her skin tone. She carried a bunch of long stemmed white lilies. Randall stood and smiled admirably to greet his bride. She just looked at him and then looked away as she stood in front of the chair next to him. The celebrant went through the motions of the ceremony he probably performed six to eight times that day. It was a job, but he looked the part. He must have been a good actor to pretend to be interested in the welfare of every couple who came through the door. I could not help but be cynical of the day's proceedings. It all seemed artificial; too contrived.

When my turn came in the program, I was invited to stand in front of the bride and groom to sing to them. I brought my own cassette recording of accompaniment for the Bach Gounod version of Ave Maria. As I sang, I looked at Dana's face. She was not glowing. She just looked a bit bothered. I assumed she was very nervous from all the work of planning the wedding. I sang my heart out and when I was done, the guests clapped happily in appreciation. Randall and Dana clapped too. I then went back to my seat and studied the body language of the couple. Randall wanted to hug and cuddle, but Dana wanted no part of this. She was formal throughout the wedding.

'I now pronounce you man and wife. You may now kiss the bride.'

Randall planted a big kiss on Dana's lips and she pulled away ever so slightly. I wondered if this was the first time he had the opportunity to kiss her. She had boasted to me that she was holding out until the wedding for everything. The celebrant then invited everyone to enjoy the festivities. We had drinks and appetizers to enjoy for the rest of our allotted time in the room. This however was just about 40 minutes after the short ceremony. We had to party hearty and then get out for the next wedding. Dana led a conga line around the room as the dance music blared. Everyone was truly enjoying the party. After all, we drove all the way from Los Angeles so we all made the most of it. Randall was babbling with his buddies who came to support him. They were standing on one side of the room and Dana was conversing with her friends on the other side of the room. I didn't think I noticed the happy couple walk around the room greeting guests as one unit.

Eventually I saw the bride sitting by herself in the corner as guests danced and gossiped amongst themselves. Her eyebrows formed a furrow and her lips were pouted as she sat sulking near one of the decorated tables. This was supposed to be a happy occasion. The least happy person that afternoon, however, was the bride. 'What's wrong with you?' I asked as the music blasted in the background. Some of her friends danced frenetically and guzzled punch and wine. The waiter passed with another tray of appetizers. We had to make the most of it, since the hour was almost up. 'What's wrong with you? Why don't you go have a dance with Randall?' I asked. 'I don't like him!' she exclaimed, then pouted. I could not believe what I was hearing. There had been so much plotting, scheming and planning; such a huge expense for someone who had very little money or resources. The dress had been purchased years before. However, booking the Bellagio Hotel in Las Vegas, the honeymoon suite, and the food and drinks cost her a fortune. I had driven all that way to sing the Ave Maria! Had I just wasted my time and my money? That was all I could think of.

As the organizers hustled our wedding party out, Dana announced we could all go up to the honeymoon suite to hang out. It was on the top floor. I wondered how thirty or more people could squeeze into the suite. It must have been a big one. The suite had a set of sofas and chairs, a kitchenette, a very large bedroom with more arm chairs, and coffee tables. It was ample space for everyone to find a corner. Someone turned on a boom box and people gossiped in groups. Dana may have ordered pizza, because food was delivered to the door. Everyone was whispering about the bride and groom. It was obvious she was ignoring the poor man and he reluctantly stuck with his buddies while she stayed at the other end of the room conversing with her own friends. I felt sorry for poor Randall. It was a cruel blow to his ego. He was used as a pawn in her game. I made a decision not to speak to Dana after the Las Vegas charade. She was a master manipulator.

Little Tiffany

'I'm a kid and I can't sleep,' said Tiffany early one morning, waking me out of my sleep. 'What are you saying?' I asked as I emerged from a deep slumber. She was talking to someone on the phone as she sat on my bed. 'I said … I'm a kid and I can't sleep.' She stressed her point to someone on the other end of the line and spoke even louder. Her tiny voice was very cheerful but insistent. The person on the phone asked her a few times to give the phone to her mother. As I snapped into action, I took away the receiver. 'Hello, who is this?' I asked. 'This is the emergency line 911. Please tell your child not to call this number. It's only for emergencies.' Tiffany had woken early and took it upon herself to call 911 for her own emergency. 'Oh I'm so sorry. I didn't know what she was doing. Sorry about that.'

When I hung up, I scolded Tiffany for calling 911. 'But … but …' she protested and then started to cry. I had told her a number of times if mommy fell on the ground or could not move, she was to call 911 to say we had an emergency. In her little mind, I was asleep and not moving so she felt she had to call them. The situation was cute, but I could not laugh. I had to show her it was not serious enough to make that call. Poor little girl; it was one of the misadventures of our mommy daughter relationship.

Every night I put Tiffany to bed at 7:30 pm sharp. She was quiet and did not protest. The only requirement was for me to read her some bedtime stories. She never grew tired of Good Night Moon, or the series of Dr. Seuss bedtime stories. She also had a few Disney favourites from her book of fairy tales. It was amazing how the same stories could entertain over and over again. No matter what was happening, I upheld this time strictly and she did not protest. All I had to do was read her favourite bedtime stories for about twenty minutes and the lights went out. This was a godsend since I had a few hours to work or relax after she went to bed.

We had settled into a routine during the work week with school and after school care. This was followed by homework and getting ready for the next day. She always wanted to help. She would fight me for the broom or mop. 'Let Tiffany do it! Let me do it!' She had said this since she could speak and continued to be a very helpful child. On weekends I tried to squeeze in as many activities as possible. I searched for a ballet school in Oxnard but could not find one. However in the Yellow Pages, I discovered the Ballet Academy Ventura, located on East Main Street, Ventura. Tiffany was enrolled in Creative Movement, the first class designed for toddlers. They said when she completed one term in this class, she could move on to Pre-ballet which was for ages three and a half to five. Tiffany's whole bedroom had the Barbie ballerina theme, complete with bed spread, curtains, wall paper border, and furniture with ballerina stickers. She was very excited when I revealed she was going to be a ballerina.

We started at the Ballet Academy Ventura and quickly made some new friends in her class. All the parents were proud of their little children dancing in the class. Only one boy attended with all the little girls. Very soon Tiff was being invited to friends' birthday parties. It was a wonderful way to meet some new people in another town. I also found a very good ice skating program at the Oxnard Ice Skating Center on Wagon Wheel Road. This center was advertised as the training center for World Champion and Olympic Gold medalist, Scott Hamilton. People brought their children for lessons at this Center from many neighbouring towns so they could possibly rub shoulders with Scott. We met him one morning and took photos with him. At three and a half, Tiffany barely qualified for the Tiny Tot Ice Skating class. I was pushing her, but knew she would be up for the challenge. During the first day of class the Tiny Tots put on their rented ice skates, and helmets, and frowned or cried as the eager parents encouraged them to skate. Tiffany was unsure of her footing and started to cry. The kids were allowed to hang onto a square brace and push it along as they moved from one side of the rink to the next. I was busy filming the episode like many other parents. We wanted to capture our children's every move for posterity.

Would she ever gain confidence on the ice? After six tries back and forth across the ice, the class came to an end. 'I don't like this mommy. I don't like ice skating,' she said at the verge of tears. 'That's ok Baby Doll. You'll be better next time,' I reassured her. We sat and watched as the older children pranced around on the ice during the free skating session. 'You'll be just like them in a while,' I encouraged her. Tiffany's instructor, Chandra was very patient with all the little ones. After a few weeks, they gained confidence and started moving without helmets and square braces. It was wonderful to watch the progress. Tiffany moved from the Little Folks class to the Tot Beginner, Tot Intermediate, Pre Alpha, Alpha, Beta, gaining badges and ribbons. She was also enrolled in the Ice Skating Institute of America. I had visions of my figure skating champion taking part in shows as her proud mother sat on the sidelines cheering her on.

After Ice Skating class we would go nearby to In-And-Out

Burger on Wagon Wheel Road for lunch. It was the once a week burger and fries treat. In-And-Out boasted of grill beef burgers and fries from freshly cut potatoes. This fast food was her reward for being a good girl all week. I trained Tiffany not to watch television. However, on weekends we would go to the local Oxnard library and borrow videos of interest. Tiffany enjoyed watching the Nutcracker Ballet, Giselle and Swan Lake. Swan Lake however made her afraid when dark images appeared on the screen. 'I like the LIBRAIRWY mommy,' she would say, to the amusement of passers-by.

I decided one year to take Tiffany to a live performance of the Nutcracker Ballet at the Oxnard Performing Arts Centre. She sat at the edge of her seat through the whole performance even though it was quite lengthy. She was intrigued by all the dancers. It never ceased to amaze me how much she enjoyed ballet and classical music. She never slept through any of my choir's recitals. One of her favourite Disney movies was Cinderella performed by Brandy. She also had a Brandy doll. At that age, Tiffany imagined her dolls were alive. She broke into tears when her favourite Polish doll in traditional costume, developed a droopy eye. 'Pamela, open eye! Open your eye!' She bawled at poor plastic Pamela becoming quite distressed.

After Kindergarten, Tiffany went up one level to the pre-school class. Her teacher was an older Filipina woman who could not pronounce the letter 'f'. It was not a letter in the Filipino language of Tagalog. Ms. Alfonso called her "Tippany". Ms. Alfonso seldom smiled and the children were afraid of her. It was the school's practice to honour one student of every class each month during a planned assembly. The Student of the Month award was given for good marks and good behaviour. The prize recipient was given a certificate and a McDonald's Happy Meal; the ultimate prize for any small child. Tiffany came home cross every month because she had not received an award.

'When can I get an award mommy?' she asked on the verge of tears. 'Don't worry. One day you will get your award.' I had hoped the teacher gave each child in the class a chance to feel important, otherwise, there would be many unhappy people in the room; not to mention ambitious parents! One day, Tiffany was extra quiet when she came home. I asked what had happened at school and she said she was accused of eating a boy's Happy Meal. I could not believe they would accuse my Tiffany of this. She may have been sad not to win the Student of the month Award, but she would never take another child's food. I went into the school the following day ready to challenge Ms. Alfonso. I had challenged the previous teacher for stuffing my child with candy for Easter, Valentine's Day, Christmas, Halloween, and other celebrations. I never bought candy but could not win in the fight against sugar given to students. But this was a different fight.

Tiffany said she felt forced to admit eating the Happy Meal because Ms. Alfonso threatened to cut open her stomach to see if the food was in there. Poor Tiffany actually believed the teacher would cut her open, so she admitted to the crime. Tiff assured me she would never take anyone's food though, because she had her own. I believed her.

'How dare you accuse my child of stealing the Happy Meal?' I attacked Ms. Alfonso the following morning in the corridor. 'Ms. James she said she took it.' 'Well she didn't. Don't accuse my child again without proof. I would appreciate if you did some investigation to figure out who really ate the food.' I looked at the fat little boy who said he lost his happy meal, and was sure he ate it all himself. He might have hoped to get a second meal in the process. I was probably labelled as "The fussy parent", but I didn't mind. Ms. Alfonso had told the students she did not care if they said she was mean. 'When I die another mean teacher will come after me.' This statement frightened the living daylights out of my Tiffany. She came home terrified of the mean teacher and other mean teachers to come. It was education through fear. She learned everything that was taught, making an extra effort. So much so, that the following month she received the Student of the Month Award!

Moving to 91362

'I need to sell my house and move to Conejo Valley,' I told Pam my real estate agent. Pam's daughter was in class with Tiffany at Mary Law Private School. We had become good friends because of the girls. Pam was of solid build and medium height. She had a round jovial face, almond shaped eyes, dark skin, a broad nose and a broad smile. Her short straightened hair was neatly coiffed at all times. We were both single mothers working hard to take care of our girls.

'Conejo Valley has a reputation for great schools, so I would not have to pay for private school,' I told Pam. 'Well, the houses are also very expensive and property taxes are higher,' she warned. 'I imagine it will work out to be the same in the end. I'll have to pay a higher mortgage, and that would replace the monthly private school payments.' 'Hope you're sure about what you're doing,' she said. 'Yes I'm very sure. I have some friends in that neighbourhood too and I always go there to party. Just think I won't have to drive too far after going out!'

Imagine using party plans as a reason to move house. I must have appeared insane to the average person. I visited the county school board and got a map of the area and school zones. I also did some research online to see school ratings for the Conejo Valley and got an idea for the public and private schools. The choices were great and serious decisions had to be made. I was leaning towards Westlake Village since my new friends and acquaintances seemed to think this area was better for schools and socializing. However, I wanted to keep all options open with the move.

Pam put my property up for sale and explained all the paper work involved. Selling a house involved the same amount of paper work as buying. It was a bit confusing with the safe box for the keys, the timing of accepting offers, and of course having to clean and decorate every time someone came to look at the property. Since my purchase and moving into the townhouse in February 1999, property prices were on the rise in 2001 and nothing was stopping them. Pam explained I could make at least $50,000 profit if we priced the house correctly and found a good buyer. I had to learn new terminology and facts about selling.

Bake some bread and let the smell fill the house. Psychologically buyers liked the smell of baking. I had to buy fresh flowers and put them throughout the house. All photos had to be removed so buyers would not see who lived there. 'Why is that? It's a crazy idea. Why should it matter?' 'This is United States my dear. Some people would not buy a house from a black family.' I had never heard such a concept. 'You have to conceal your identity. All they will see is your name,' she explained. It took two weeks for me to clean the house thoroughly and put all traces of identity in boxes in the garage. It was also an opportunity to start packing.

Pam arranged with a few potential buyers to visit the home. When we got a call, Tiffany and I were required to tidy the place, heat up some bread, and then disappear for about two hours until called back. Pam mentioned a couple who wanted to make an offer. She felt sorry for them because they were selling their family home and downsizing. 'How could you feel sorry for them Pam?' I asked. I was a bit annoyed with her. 'Who are you working for? Me or these people?' Pam was too kind and soft hearted and I wondered if I would really get the best price for the house after all. My nerves were completely on edge from packing and fixing and I became annoyed easily.

All appointments were arranged during my lunch hour so I had to rush out of the office and rush back without alerting anyone at work about what I was doing. It was a little frightening doing all this wheeling and dealing, but it was also exciting. If I made a sizeable profit from the sale of my house, then I would have money to use as a down payment and for closing costs of the new home. I would not be stranded like the first time, buying a house with nothing to deposit. Pam advised that I did not want buyers who were in a chain. 'What is a chain?' I asked. 'That's when they have to wait for someone to buy their home in order to get a down payment to buy yours. If something goes wrong in the chain, it all falls apart.'

How were we going to find buyers who were not in a chain? Only some retired people would have cash to pay for a house. Others could be first time buyers, in which case as soon as they got a loan, they would be ready to buy. I hoped and prayed for a chain free buyer; even though I knew I would not be attractive to the next person who was selling the house I wanted to buy. In the meantime, I also had to find a real estate agent who could help me buy a house in Conejo Valley. I asked Pam if she knew anyone there. She called her company's office in Conejo Valley and they suggested an agent who handled that district. When I got the agent's number, I called to set an appointment. At the end of the receiver, I heard a thick French accent.

'Oui? Allo? Zees ees Odette.' 'Hello, my name is Jennylynd. I was given your number by someone from your office. Can we meet to search for homes in Conejo Valley?' 'Boot oof cooorse. When can you come?' We arranged to meet during my lunch hour the next day in Thousand Oaks. Odette asked for my price range and I gave a wide and optimistic range. I still had to go back to the mortgage broker for a final estimate of what I could afford with the promised deposit and current salary.

Odette was short and skinny with a large round head, large round blue eyes and a boyish hair cut of dyed blonde hair. She had a broad mouth with thin lips with a permanent French pout. She seemed extra fussy in her large black Mercedes Benz. 'You park here and we drive in my car,' she said. 'That's fine with me,' I said. We drove around

Thousand Oaks looking at townhouses and even passed near to Joanie's townhouse complex. Some of the places we saw were acceptable, but others were a bit ugly. I thought I had to narrow the search or else one would spend many days looking at random places. I had to cut the tour short and return to work. However, Odette and I planned to meet two days later after I spoke to my mortgage broker and determined the loan amount I pre-qualified for.

I finally got word from Mike that I would qualify for $250,000 if I came with a deposit of $50. Armed with this information, I was delighted my allowance had jumped significantly since my first purchase of $120,000 in 1999. Things were looking up for me. Of course in Oxnard, I would have been able to buy a nice little bungalow at the time for that price. However, I wanted to live in Conejo Valley, and more specifically in Westlake 91362. I looked online to find directions for the elementary school in Westlake and drove over the hill after work that evening to find the place. Tiffany and I looked at the school and the neighbourhood. It had two main concrete building and a series of prefabricated buildings painted in beige and friendly cream. The school had large grassy fields and looked like it was part of a central park in the general neighbourhood. I drove around the streets surrounding the school. The houses were all bungalows of varying sizes. From what I had seen online, prices ranged in the high 300's to 400's and I could not afford any of them at the time. What were we going to do?

'One day you will be going to that school Tiffany,' I told her. 'It's a big school mommy,' she said with her eyes wide open. She may have been a little afraid. 'Don't worry,' I tried to reassure her. 'I heard it's a very nice school.' I called Odette with the news of my prequalification and we planned to meet at her office to review the options. When I got there, I told her I wanted to narrow the search to only the Westlake Village 91362 area.

'Dat ees not for you!' she said loudly.

'What!' I said in shock. Was she working for me or herself? She was certainly very rude to say such a thing. 'Dat ees not for you! You can find something in Thousand Oaks or Moorpark.' 'No, I want to live in Westlake!' I confirmed. 'There will be nothing on the computer,' she said, without even looking.' 'Oh really,' I said, trying to stay calm and avoid strangling her. 'Let me see your computer. Show me the listings. I'm sure there must be something in my price range.' 'Oh you will find nothing,' she stated with conviction. 'Let me see your computer,' I insisted. The woman was so unpleasant. I could not believe I was continuing business with her. However, I had invested time in the process and wanted to get it over and done with.

I sat boldly at her desk and combed through the listings on her computer since she was reluctant to do so. Eventually I spied four townhouses in 91362 within my price range. One was a one bedroom place. It would be too small. The others had potential. I showed her the listings and asked if we could to pass to visit these places right away before other buyers grabbed them. 'You see, I told you I would find something.' I triumphed in my initial success. I had to drag her to the location reluctantly in her own car. She was not a hard working agent. The rising property prices had made some agents wealthy very quickly and with minimal effort on their part. Every Tom, Dick and Harry was a real estate agent. He just had to pass a test and get the license. Common decency was not a requirement.

We went to see a townhouse complex on the south side of Highway 101 and spotted the unit for sale. The area looked fine, however not many amenities were included. We then carried on visiting the next townhouse complex on Via Colinas just north of Highway 101 and off Thousand Oaks Boulevard in Westlake. The listing said "Pools and hot tubs". That sounded quite appealing; after all, Moby Dick Lane had a beautiful pool and hot tub. I never had time to use it except on a rare occasion with Mr. Shiny Shoes. However, I was determined to change this at the next home.

As we drove into the complex, I saw it was not gated like California Lighthouse. That was fine for me. Who needs gates? The neighbourhood was supposed to be safe anyway. The beautiful flowers along the roadway and manicured lawns in front of the townhouses showed the area was well kept. The townhouses were constructed in the 1980's and the buildings were all a light brown colour with some wooden trim and blue painted concrete trim. Everything looked the same as if made from a cookie cutter. Town homes of varying sizes came off the main Street of Via Colinas with tiny laneways leading to rows of roll up garages. Walkways with beautiful flowers adorned the front of the homes. The place was very quiet and nobody was seen walking in the neighbourhood.

The first stop was a two bedroom townhouse right in front of the pool at the beginning of the complex near Thousand Oaks Boulevard. Via Colinas then continued up the hill to more and more townhouses. The house was smaller in square footage than my Oxnard house and cost $100,000 more. How could this be possible? As the old saying went, "Location, Location, Location"; I would be paying for the location. The vaulted ceiling and simple white walls with beige carpets was a standard throughout Southern California for townhouses. One flattering feature was a tiny wrap around patio on the outside and another small private patio open to the sky and coming off the kitchen area. The first house we saw was in front of a big pool. Would it be noisy in the summer? Being close to the main thoroughfare on the edge of the complex could have been a disadvantage. We were not sure.

The next townhouse was a little way up the street. The model was the same as the other we saw near the pool at the main street. I walked a little way up the street and saw another pool and hot tub just a few steps away. So we would be close to the pool but not right next to it. This location was definitely more agreeable from the standpoint of being quiet but close to amenities.

The place was listed at $251,000. 'Odette, let's make an offer for $250,000,' I said. 'I'm approved for $250,000'. 'No. Just offer the $251000. Eet ees nothing,' she responded without emotion.' It was easy for her to say this. She did not have to pay out the interest that would be accumulated on an extra $1000 on a mortgage loan. 'Just take eet,' she insisted. 'I will prepare zee papers.' I was the one now trying to stall as the woman would not take my suggestion of bidding just below the asking price. She was the same one who said I would not find anything in the neighbourhood. She was now rushing me to sign papers to submit an offer. Working with real estate agents required great patience and perseverance, and I had little. I signed the documents and went away.

Later that night, I got a call saying the seller accepted my offer. 'That's great I said. 'We're waiting on final word from the buyers of my Oxnard house. They should come back any day now.' I hoped they would answer soon or the seller of my Westlake house could back out. I had given a large deposit when signing with the offer, so I prayed there would be no monkey business. Timing the selling of one home and the buying of another was testing my nerves to the limit. I could barely focus at work. In fact, I had not told anyone about my decision to move. I did not want any possible negative energy coming my way and so kept it all to myself. I decided to only reveal my new address after moving.

One day passed and the potential buyers of my Moby Dick Lane property backed out. Pam gave them back their deposit cheque and the house went back on the market. 'How could you give them back their cheque? I thought the point of having the cheque was to prevent a default?' I was hysterical. 'Oh, I can't do that to them.' She was being sympathetic to the poor couple and I was losing my mind. We then had another flurry of visits that week requiring the house be cleaned and fixed for viewing. It was annoying having to show the home again to new potential buyers. However, we had no choice.

The following week, a buyer made an offer at the asking price. It was the happiest day indeed when Pam came over with the paperwork for me to sign accepting the offer. The next stage was nail-biting as the escrow company organized collection of the buyer's funds. Escrow had to work with my mortgage broker to pay off the old mortgage and collect the profit. This was then applied to the new mortgage loan so I could buy the new home. Many lunch hours were spent signing documents and running back and forth with legal issues. Eventually I got a call from the Escrow Company indicating which day I should vacate my premises and collect keys to the new house. I had the keys to the new house two days before I was required to move out.

I had to figure out how to move everything out quickly and clean the house to give the new buyers their space to move in. I was not prepared to paint the house as some would do. Pam suggested I clean the carpet as a courtesy. I hired a moving company from the Valley to move us on the Saturday. They charged by the hour and I kept a sharp eye on those men as they walked around casually picking up one odd lamp or the other. They did not seem to have a system in place. 'I'll take all the small stuff in my car,' I urged. 'Just take the heavy furniture!' I felt like I was pushing them. However, they made the job a two trip affair saying they would have to come back for the second load.

I drove back and forth taking small boxes and anything that could fit in my car. It was too much for Tiffany and I asked Ms. Cheryl to keep her until I had finished emptying the house and cleaning. The carpet cleaners came to steam the carpet promptly, late in the evening. At last, I was ready for them. They did their best on the staircase which was dirty from all the trampling and moving. I was weak and tired from the day's ordeal when I collected Tiffany and some fast food to go over the hill to our new house in Westlake Village 91362. I was fortunate to find sheets, and fixed my bed so Tiffany and I could sleep that night. We saved the unpacking for the following day and the weeks to come.

The next week Odette sent an email message. 'Hope you like your new house. Now write a recommendation letter for me.' The same one who would not lift a finger to ensure I got to live in the neighbourhood I wanted was demanding I write a glowing recommendation for her! It was laughable.

A New School

I had given notice for Tiffany at Mary Law Private School and got her registered at Westlake Hills Elementary School when the house deeds were firmly in hand. It required skill in planning and timing to get everything to fall into place neatly. Another very important point was after school care. Since I was still working up to 5:00 pm in Oxnard and driving over the hill on Highway 101 to get home, I needed to find reliable after school care. My PWP friends suggested the names of many after school programs in Conejo Valley. The large Calvary Church further down the street off Via Colinas offered an after-school collection and child care service. Mini buses would collect children from all over the Valley after school, take them to the church buildings, and there they would be given a snack and an opportunity to do homework. After this, they were allowed to play until parents collected them. Another such service was offered in Newbury Park. That facility had swimming lessons for an extra fee. Hundreds of parents in the area worked so these services were a vital part of life. We could not function without them.

On Tiffany's first day at school that September, many other parents arrived with their children and took photographs.

The first graders looked hopeful but a little afraid of the new environment and the new children around them. I met one Chinese woman dropping off her daughter, Jennifer. We said hello to each other and spoke briefly. We then introduced the girls and asked them to look out for each other. I also had to show Tiffany where to stand for the Calvary bus at the end of the day. It was a frightening prospect leaving her that day and hoping things would run smoothly. The teacher, Ms. Dayton spoke to all the parents briefly then bid us farewell. We had to leave our babies so they could grow up.

I cried all the way to work that morning. How was my daughter going to cope in the new prefab building? Would she be able to find the bathroom? Would she find the correct bus at the end of the day? There were buses going to Calvary in Westlake Village, as well as other buses going to other places. I know the drivers would have all the names of students they were responsible for, but I still had doubts. What if she ended up in the wrong place? What if? What if? It was a mother's nightmare. I could barely concentrate at work all day and I was tempted to call the school to find out if everything was OK. I had never done that before, but I was working in Oxnard and Tiffany was over the hill in Westlake Village!

At 5:00 pm sharp, I left the office and rushed over the hill to the After School program. Parents had to collect children by 6:00 pm or pay fees for overtime. I was frustrated sitting in rush hour traffic and watching the time tick away. It was bad for my nerves. When I finally got to the Lindero Canyon Exit off Highway 101 and turned into Calvary, I breathed a sigh of relief. Many children had been picked up already.

There was Tiffany waiting for her mother. She hopped and skipped towards me. 'Bye Lorraine. Bye Tony!' she said. I had to sign out for her and was happy they had such a strict policy of signing out for children. Tiffany was happy and excited by her first day at school. She wasn't half as worried as me. We drove a few minutes to our house up the hill and settled down for dinner and stories.

The following week I looked at my list of bills since moving to the more posh neighbourhood of zip code 91362. I would be putting out significantly more money and sending out more checks in the mail than ever before. I had the mortgage, home insurance, home owners' association (HOA) dues, the car loan, car insurance, life insurance, electricity, gas, water bill and an additional bill for sewage which I had not paid before. I paid the telephone bill, the after school program. In addition, cell phones were just becoming popular and I rented my first cell phone. I refused to add cable television to the mix since I did not watch TV and could not afford another bill. How much would be left for groceries and gas for the car? Only time would tell. Would we even have money to go out once in a while or buy basic clothing? It became evident that I would have to make more money to support the life style I had decided to embark upon. I was going to have to find a higher paying job since I did not think my company would likely increase my salary.

The search for a new job had begun.

7

CHANGING HOUSES, CHANGING JOBS

September 11th 2001

I sent out a few applications and started consulting with colleagues I'd met at conferences to see if they knew of job opportunities. An associate asked me if I would be interested in a position at a frozen food plant based in Columbus, Ohio. According to him, it was worth checking out their facility and the city of Columbus in general. I knew nothing about Columbus, Ohio. Researching the town online showed it was not as exciting as Southern California. However, they wanted to hire a Quality Assurance Manager right away. They promised a great salary and a lot of autonomy. After going through the massive move to California and then moving house to Westlake Village, I was not looking forward to changing States again. However, making new contacts and getting interview experience were worthwhile activities. In addition, I was contemplating doing part time consulting work. In the midst of unpacking and mayhem, I booked a vacation day from my job the following week. Then I contacted the new company's director and made arrangements to visit for an interview.

I had almost finished unpacking our belongings and planned to use the extra space in the two car garage for storage. It was great that the past owner had mounted shelves. This gave me ready storage space for boxes and items I could not place quickly. I promised myself to go through the boxes and discard anything that would never be used again. However, the time for sorting did not come easily. A major project was painting the walls in the garage after work, doing a small piece at a time to make the space more liveable, even if it was just a garage.

On September 11th, we awoke early as usual; packed lunches and I took Tiffany to school. Playing music all the way to work helped me pep up for a day in the office. 'Hello Bob; hi Mel,' I said cheerfully as I walked into my office and put down my bags.

Mel was in Bob's office and the television was turned up to full volume. The plant engineer and two others were also in the office and they were standing and staring at the television with shoulders slouched. Few words were exchanged. What were they looking at? What could keep a loud mouth like Mel so quiet? My boss called from his office. 'Jennylynd did you see the news? Did you hear about the bombing?' he asked. 'Bombing? What bombing?' I said as I ran into the office. I saw what was causing such great trepidation. There on the television, repeated over and over was a video of a plane crashing into a World Trade Centre building. Then another video was played showing another plane crashing into the second building. These were places I had visited as a child. I remembered how excited we were to ride the tourist elevator tour up to the top floor and look down at the tiny cars and people below.

We watched the news in disbelief. Buildings were crashing down. People were jumping out of windows. The injured were walking from the wreckage covered in blood and dust. It was unbelievable how much pain was caused in such a short time. Because we were on Pacific Time, Californians were just waking up to the news of what was taking place in

New York City. 'All subway lines in Manhattan are down. Do not, I repeat, do not come to the city if you don't have to,' announced the reporter from the scene of the disaster. I stood numb for a full minute taking in the scene. Then, as my brain cleared, I tried to remember the friends and family who lived in New York. Were they safe? Were they anywhere near the disaster zone?

I knew of one childhood friend who worked in Manhattan's financial district. My initial response was to call friends and family and find out if they were ok. My sister, Colette had lived in New York for many years and had kept in touch with many cousins and old family friends. I ran back to my office and called her right away to get phone numbers. She was able to give me a quick synopsis of all the people she had spoken to. She lived on the East Coast and had heard about the disaster in real time. There was no delayed reaction as mine. Colette told me about our friend Charmaine who worked downtown Manhattan at a bank.

'The place is raining ashes! It's dark from all that smoke,' said Colette. 'What else? Well, what else? How's she going to get back home to Brooklyn?' I asked. 'She's trying to walk home. The trains and buses aren't running. She'll have to walk over the Brooklyn Bridge to get home,' Colette explained. 'What about her sister. Did she get trapped too?' I asked. 'Alicia was going in to work late this morning so she hadn't even left home yet,' said Colette. 'She's so lucky. It would have been a disaster,' I said. 'Charmaine was inside the bank and they wouldn't let the staff leave. Then I heard they were told them to get out and walk home quickly,' said Colette.

I hoped people knew where to walk. It was one thing to take public transit everyday to and from work. Walking out of the city was not a familiar activity for many commuters who generally lived outside the city. I called as many people as I could on the East Coast, crying uncontrollably as I tried to find them and make sure they were OK. I don't know what this information could have done for me, but I needed to know. My thoughts then shifted to my daughter's safety. I was being irrational at that point. What would happen to my child if we were to have a disaster in Oxnard, California? After all, it was in the earthquake fault. Everyone used to talk about "The BIG ONE". People were predicting the "Mother of All Earthquakes" would come one day and California would sink into the ocean. I called the school immediately and demanded to speak to her grade 1 teacher. 'Ms. James, Ms. Dayton is busy teaching the class at the moment,' said the school secretary. 'Do you know what happened in New York City this morning? Huh? Do you? I demand to know that my child is safe,' I shouted. 'Yes ma'am, everyone is safe at the school. There's nothing to worry about,' she said. 'Nothing to worry about? Are you kidding me? Suppose terrorists were to come to California, then what would we do?' I was hysterical.

I couldn't help myself. My behaviour and fear were beyond reason. I wanted to get onto Highway 101 to collect my child and make sure she was safe. I told this to Mel who tried to calm me down. 'Don't worry. She'll be fine. You can go for her after school,' he said. I could barely concentrate all day at work. It was the worst feeling of panic I had experienced in years. There was no way to relax. I called my aunt in Florida to find out what she heard about her friends. She had worked on Wall Street for many years before retiring and moving to Florida. She still had friends working in the area. People she contacted were fine and were not in the office when the disaster struck.

Leaving promptly at 5:00 pm, I drove to the after-school care to collect Tiffany. I sped like a mad woman on the 101, over the hill and directly to the Lindero Canyon Exit. I was the happiest mother when my child was delivered to me safely that evening. I hugged her and squeezed her and asked if she was OK. 'What's wrong mommy?' She looked at my red eyes. 'Are you OK?' 'Yes, I'm fine.' I lied and tried to maintain my composure. That day I had cried tears of anguish for the death and destruction in New York and for the souls of people I didn't even know.

When Tiffany was safely tucked into bed I continued listening to the radio news. They described the chaos in New York as people tried to walk away from the disaster zone. The casualties and chaos were described repeatedly. I migrated to the garage to continue painting walls and crying. Playing happy music to get into a cheerful mood would have helped. However, I could not do it. I just cried and painted; and cried and painted some more; trying to make sense of what had happened. Later that night, I went to my computer and wrote a long letter to Tiffany's teacher telling her I wanted to pull my child out of the school for her safety. The feeling was that Tiffany would be better off in a school physically close to my job. However, I never sent this letter.

Jittery Travel

My interview in Columbus, Ohio was scheduled three days

after the collapse of the World Trade Centre and the disaster in New York City. With thousands dead and the airspace only just re-opening, warnings were issued to travellers within the United States to be prepared for extra security checks. We no longer had the luxury of running last minute to a closing airline door, hoping to get in. I had done this many times, just making it onto the airline in the last two minutes. Everyone was going to be checked thoroughly for explosives. Friends and well wishers were not going to be allowed into the departure lounge as in the past. New security measures were going to be enforced to combat terrorism. Air travel security measures would change forever.

I had pre-arranged childcare for Tiffany with Joanie, not mentioning this trip was a job hunting expedition. Joanie would have probably told everyone she knew if I had told her. My travel description was kept to a minimum; an important work trip. I had my doubts of whether to still proceed with the visit to Ohio. After all, I could still carry on at my job in Oxnard, even though it was getting a little repetitive. However, the salary could barely sustain my new lifestyle. Taking the risk of travelling that day was based on the assumption that extra security measures would be in place to make sure travel was more secure than it was before.

In the Yellow Pages, I found the Road Runner Airport Shuttle bus that took passengers door to door, from their homes in the Conejo and San Fernando Valleys, directly to Los Angeles Airport. I was not prepared to drive my car to LAX and I did not mind sharing a shuttle bus with other travellers. It seemed like the sensible thing to do. I packed

Tiffany's bags for school and a stay-over, and delivered her to Joanie's. I heaved a sigh as watching my innocent little girl run off to play with Joanie's daughter. Returning to the house, I packed my things and waited for the shuttle to LAX. We needed to check in three hours in advance of our flights according to revised instructions for security screening. That meant leaving home four hours in advance.

When I got there, the questions were extensive. 'Ma'am did you pack all your bags yourself? Are you carrying any weapons?' asked the stone faced travel attendant at the counter while supervised by armed security. I had never seen so many armed security guards at the airport before. I wanted to ask if I looked like someone who could actually fire a gun, but had to remain calm and answer all the questions. 'Why are you travelling at this time?' he asked. 'I have a job interview,' I said. 'Do you have a job now?' he asked. 'Yes,' I said. 'So why are you travelling?' he asked again. 'To interview for a new job,' I said. As a matter of fact, since it was my business and not his, the process was bordering on being too intrusive. 'Please go over there to have your bags checked,' he said.

It was the first time all bags, including hand luggage were searched thoroughly. The only thing passengers did not have to do was strip completely. Even though the procedure was more extensive than in the past, many flights may have been cancelled or people were afraid to fly. The airport was sparsely populated, so everything went quickly. I then had two and a half hours to sit around and wait for my flight to Columbus. That was not a good thing. Too much idle time in a jittery airport seemed more frightening than jumping on a plane after the bombing. Nobody spoke, even though people would normally have exchanged a greeting or made eye contact.

People eyed each other with great suspicion. Every move and every noise startled my neighbours. If someone threw an empty soda can in the bin, everyone jumped out of fear. Two hours of this made me even more nervous. I was overjoyed when an announcement was finally made to board the late night flight to Ohio. When I arrived, everything was cold, dark and grey so there was nothing to see. I was staying at a basic airport hotel and I went directly to bed. I just hoped to remember everything from rehearsing interview material the previous week.

The next day we went around the frozen food plant. I wondered about their menu selection and how I would cope in the boring factory environment. I could not see myself staying for a long time in one factory setting. However, the owner promised some travel to their other factories in the Southern States. At least that was going to make it worthwhile working for the company. I answered all the questions correctly and offered suggestions for improving their operation. I knew enough about food processing plants and food safety documentation to give advice to anyone who asked. I was thankful to leave Ohio that night, returning to California to be with my daughter.

'Where did you go mommy?' she asked. 'Oh just had to travel for work,' I said. I told Joanie about all the extra security measures at the airport and she was happy she didn't have to fly anywhere soon.

The following week I heard back from the company. They

were interested in hiring me; that was until I asked if they were willing to apply for a work permit for me. The manager seemed confused. Work permit? He probably assumed I was a US citizen with a foreign accent. This was possible, but it was not my story. The way he faltered, I knew he was not prepared to find out what was involved in getting a work permit. I thanked him and made up my mind to continue searching elsewhere since the salary offered was too low to entice me to leave sunny Southern California for cold Columbus.

Interview and a Job Offer

One colleague, Ravinder from my food safety network mentioned that he had heard about a new position for a Corporate Quality Assurance (QA) manager to oversee tropical fruit production in Latin America. Ravinder worked for a big company and the prospect of working at the main office was exciting indeed. He promised to get back to me and was true to his word. Within a few days, an interview was lined up with the head of the QA department at the main office. This man, Tom was relatively new with the company. Tom and Ravinder were to meet me at the main office for an interview at 9:00 am. I had studied the company's products thoroughly in the days leading up to the interview and rehearsed what I would say about my academics, my work background, and all the benefits I could offer the company. The good news was that the office was only a few minutes from my new house. Driving through the gate of the big company's world head quarters, I was struck by the sight of the beautiful building. It was made of red brick, concrete and glass. It was no more than three stories high, but still had an air of wealth and grandeur. I found parking around to the left of the building marked for visitors and crossed the path through the neatly manicured gardens.

I enjoyed watching rows and rows of shrubs and rosebushes neatly pruned back for the winter season. It was already October, but I imagined that in the summer the gardens would look beautiful. Everything was neat and in its place. On entering the main lobby, I paused to take in the grandeur of the hallway. A glass ceiling let in the daylight and the main foyer seemed to stretch all the way up to the sky. A tall mural of fruits decorated one wall panel and several glass cases of photos and miniature structures displayed the history of the company over the decades. A large vase of flowers stood on a broad pedestal table in the middle of the foyer and plush sofas decorated this area around the flowers.

I approached the broad desk to the right of the foyer where two security guards and a receptionist sat. 'Hello, I'm here to see Tom the Vice President of Quality Assurance,' I told a security guard. I had to sign in and was given a security tag to enter the building. It was such a grand entrance to the company, and I tried to imagine myself working in that environment. As staff members passed by, I noticed they we all dressed for business. Men wore shirts and ties and many women wore skirt suits or business dresses with jackets. I was going to have to pull out all my conference suits to work at that office, but I was prepared. It was not casual like my current office where jeans and cowboy boots were the order of the day. There were no offices in temporary trailers or warehouses. It was a big difference working in operations close to the farm, as opposed to working in corporate

America. Only time would tell if I was ready for this gig.

Tom came to meet me in the foyer, introduced himself, and we walked through what seemed like a maze of corridors to get to his office. Tom was a tall stocky man with a bald head, glasses and a broad nose. A few salt and pepper hair strands formed a crown and extended to the back of his head. His generous stomach, bushy grey moustache, and wrinkles around the eyes and mouth showed someone in his sixties, probably close to retirement. He was cheerful and bouncy and I followed his energy.

'Right this way Jennylynd. Ravinder is in my office.' As we entered his office, Ravinder stood up and shook my hand. 'Good to see you again Jennylynd,' he said. 'Thanks so much. Good to see you too and thanks for arranging the interview,' I said. Ravinder was dark brown and of East Indian descent. He wore glasses and had black hair that was beginning to recede at the hairline. He had an academic air; however, his ready smile was infectious. Ravinder worked in another division of the company close to the Salinas area, so I was grateful he had taken time out of his schedule to come for my interview.

As I sat before them I felt my heart beating heavily in my chest. Great concentration was needed to smile and form clear sentences to create a good impression. Tom cracked a few jokes to set everyone at ease, but I may not have bitten the bait. I was a nervous wreck with a "corporate smile". All my previous years of networking helped me to function effectively in this situation. I was taking the floor eventually with explanations of farm situations and audits. It happened so quickly and so easily. Within a few minutes Tom said he had heard great things about me and I had the job. 'What? That's it?' I looked at him in disbelief.

'Let's take a look at your new office and meet some folks in the department.' All my cold sweating, rehearsal of facts, and the sleepless night had not been needed. When a friend offers to get you a job, you actually have the job. That was a new revelation for me. Five people worked in the department at that time. It was situated on the ground floor of one corner of the building. Four offices with windows were situated at the corner. They framed a central desk manned by a middle-aged woman who took calls and recorded information. She stopped a few seconds to say hello, then continued with her discourse on the phone. A young woman who worked in the office on one side of Tom said hello. He then showed me the office of another QA Manager who was out of town that day. I met a forty-something year old food scientist with large spectacles who was pouring over notes for a big meeting. He said hello and continued his work. A larger central office without windows was pointed out as a possibility for me if I were to start with the company. With that, the interview was over.

I thanked them profusely and promised not to disappoint when I started the job. I was prepared to do the best job possible for such a big company. The best news was the proximity to my new home. I was going to be close to home and close to Tiffany's school. I did not have to remove her from Westlake Hills Elementary again. The new job was going to require a great deal of international travel to Central and South America, but I was willing to travel. I would just have to figure out the small matter of child care. I did not reveal this major detail to my eager interviewers when they asked if I had any concerns. 'When can you start?' asked Tom. 'Well, I'll have to give a few weeks' notice at my current job. When can the company apply for a work permit for me?' I demanded. 'Well let's start the ball a-rolling,' said Tom confidently. 'That could take two weeks.' I started my new job in November and got ready for the next chapter in my life.

The New Job

'In the valley of the blind the one-eyed man is king!' Those were the cautionary words of Mark, the super active seventy-year old food scientist on the Senior Quality Assurance team. In three weeks' time, the big company managed to secure my work permit and I was ready to start. It was difficult leaving my first job. Staff was kind-hearted and my boss was so easy-going. I knew I was going to miss everyone. However, the quest for more money and power was overwhelming. I wanted to move up in the world and would not let sentimentality get in my way. Moving over the hill for house, work, and play were steps up in my mind. 'Money makes the world go round,' they say and I was moving for more of it.

I had a meeting with Renata, the HR manager, to discuss my salary and benefits. The company offered some of the best benefits in terms of a retirement plan, as well as health, dental and vision plans. They paid the full cost for a lawyer to prepare the work permit as a rush job. I was given 17 days' leave which included sick leave. By US standards, this was considered better than the two weeks the average person received. I was oblivious that other countries offered more rest days to staff as a legal requirement … "Ignorance is bliss."

'What salary do you expect?' asked Renata. I had no idea what to say since I did not know what the other QA Managers were making. Three of us had Ph.D.s in the department and another Ph.D. was being hired to manage Quality Assurance of different products. 'Well, I would want to make more than I'm making now,' I said with a nervous giggle. She did not laugh. She was serious. 'Well, tell me a figure,' she said. Having no idea what to say, I fumbled. 'Ah … well, I'm making 65k now, so I would be happy with 80k,' I said. That was when she smiled. 'Are you sure that's what you want?' she asked. 'Yes that's fine,' I confirmed. 'OK, that's what you'll get,' she said. I wondered what made her smile. However, with that salary, I could afford to pay all my bills and have a little left over, so I was as happy as a lark!

Renata took me around to meet the HR team as well as key people in the tropical fruits group. The building was a series of corridors opening up to offices with glass windows overlooking gardens and parking lots. The floors were tiled with granite and the ladies' room was lavish with granite tiles and granite counter tops. I imagined no expense was spared in out-fitting the office space. The company had grounds with a man-made waterfall and a pond crossed by a wooden bridge. This could be viewed from the large lunch room which was staffed and run by a well-known hotel catering company. I was impressed with the opulence and grandeur of the building. I could not wait for the lunch break to run across the bridge for fun. I wondered when I would possibly learn people's names or find my way around the building.

We returned to Tom's office and continued my orientation. I was introduced again to Sylvia, the lady at the main desk of our QA department. She was middle-aged with a short hair dyed blond and brown. She wore a conservative dress and her makeup hid some of the age spots on her face. She was neat and tidy and close to retirement. 'This is Sylvia, the secretary for the department,' said Renata. 'Well I'm not actually the secretary, I'm the QA Coordinator,' said Sylvia. 'Oh yes, coordinator,' said Renata. The tension was amusing and I smiled to myself.

As we approached Tom's office, he was gossiping loudly on the phone with someone who may have been an old colleague. 'Hello old buddy, old pal. How're you doin'? I was just playing catch up with my buddy.' Tom was loud. In fact, I was sure anyone at the end of the corridor could have heard him screaming into his phone. He had to say farewell to his buddy when the new gal was deposited in his office. 'Hi Jennylynd, how are you settling?' he asked. 'Well, I have a lot to remember,' I admitted. Tom took me to visit other people in the department and we overheard Sylvia bragging to a friend on the phone. 'Yes this weekend I'm going to my ranch up north. Yes I have a ranch. Ha! Ha! Ha! I try to go up north every weekend. You know… to get away from it all. Hmm Hmmm.' I wondered what her ranch looked like. I was going to have to ask her to tell me about it one day.

I met Bridget who worked in the smaller office next to Tom. She was skinny, with big blue eyes, and shoulder length brown hair with highlights. Her finger nails were immaculate and so was her well-pressed suit. Everything seemed to be in place. Her desk had organized piles of paper and she was busy labelling file jackets to be placed in the correct location. She was well-mannered and spoke confidently. I wondered how I could possibly match her neatness. My desk in the past looked like a mountain of rubble and files. I usually knew where everything was located, but the casual observer's heart would skip a beat at the apparent disarray. I was going to have to improve my organizational skills to match my current environment. We then met with Randolph whose office was next. He was packing to move to another department in a few weeks and was pouring through his documents to clear space for the new Ph.D. recruit. He was a pleasant man with dark brown hair, deep blue eyes and spectacles. Why did everyone wear glasses, except Bridget? Would I end up wearing glasses like the rest of them? Was that a side effect of the job? Another office space was empty at the end of the corridor.

Tom asked which office I preferred. I had two options before the other new Ph.D. started. I could either take Randolph's smaller office with a large window over-looking the grounds, or take the larger office in the middle without windows.

The small office had a desk and wall unit and a window ledge but not much wall space. The bigger office had four walls which in my mind could be decorated with my certificates and framed prints. It had a large wooden desk and a big leather arm chair with wheels. And two arm chairs were perched in front of the desk to entertain guests. One wall was well-outfitted with a wall unit to be used as storage for notebooks and documents. I liked the big storage space since I tended to generate a lot of paper on the job. There was even a side table with a silk plant and two beautiful chairs for more guests. I selected the bigger office. It looked important and classy. I told Tom if I needed to look outside it would be easy to walk around.

The following day was spent setting up my office and putting framed copies of all my academic certificates on the wall behind my desk. This was to remind me and anyone who visited the office that a qualified food scientist was on the job. I brought a vase with dried flowers and also some family photos to decorate the ledge. While getting organized, there was a great deal of commotion near Tom's office. I heard loud laughter from Sylvia as she joked loudly with an old British gentleman. He had almost no hair and whatever was left, was white. He was tall and skinny and sported large round spectacles with curious pale grey eyes, a long pointy nose, and the appropriate shirt and tie for the corporate office.

It was Mark. I heard he was about seventy years old and in no way ready to retire. He was still active, and travelled on company business several times a month. 'What am I supposed to do, retire and play the ukulele?' He spoke loudly with authority in his posh accent. Mark babbled repeatedly and had Sylvia tickled pink. 'I always say, In the Valley of the Blind, the one-eyed man is king!' Mark was describing a situation in which someone feigned knowledge and was clearly leading people in the wrong direction. He used to travel to South America and to conferences in many countries. He prepared reports and travelled again. He worked with a different team to the one I was assigned. I went across to listen to his jokes and say hello. 'Oh Mark,' said Sylvia, 'This is Jennylynd. She is our new QA Manager for tropical fruits,' said Sylvia. 'Allo dear. Welcome to the team.' Mark grinned from ear to ear and I could tell he was waiting to hear me speak so he could guess where I was from.

I said hello and asked him what was so funny. What had made Sylvia laugh so hard? He recounted his silly story and I laughed too. He asked if I was from the Caribbean and I confirmed I was from Trinidad. 'That's splendid! So we can chat about cricket! Nobody around here knows about cricket! They are all uncivilized!' Mark expressed great joy about being able to discuss one of the favourite games of many former British colonies. I did not want to disappoint by stating I never watched cricket and was not in the least bit sporty. In the United States it was not easy to find a TV channel which carried information about cricket matches. I did not look for cricket news except for the usual blurb in an online newspaper from Trinidad.

'Yes Mark. We can yak about cricket. Have you heard about Brian Lara … one of the greatest cricketers from Trinidad?' I asked. 'By George, I must admit he's good,' said Mark. 'Captain of the West Indies cricket team. He scored four centuries in the last test match!' I boasted. 'Of course I've heard of the young fellow. You people must be proud of him,' said Mark. 'Yes, he's amazing! OK, take care,' I said, leaving the discourse at that point to avoid being asked about a cricket test match taking place in Australia or some other part of the world.

Bridget came to my office to see how I was settling in and we had a brief chat. She had worked in the office for a year and knew many people in the building. We had lunch together and I learned about her husband's investment business and their house in the Westlake area. They were disciplined with spending and planning for their future. I listened intently wanting to learn as much as possible from this upwardly mobile couple.

Bridget explained she worked as a waitress in the evenings at a local up-market restaurant and would sometimes see people from the company out to dinner in Westlake. 'Why would you work there?' I asked. 'You already have a job.' 'Well, we have big goals, so it doesn't matter what other people think about me. I get huge tips. I'm working for the tips because they go in my pocket,' she said. I was shocked that someone so smartly dressed in the day in the corporate setting did not mind working as a waitress at night. It was a lesson in discipline and humility that I had not seen before. She would also exercise after work and frequently spoke about going to the gym and forgetting to eat. That was something I would never emulate. How could anyone forget to eat? I was always hungry. As I finished decorating my office on the first day, I listened to the noises from the other rooms. There was Sylvia, boasting about her ranch up north, Tom was bragging with an old buddy and pal, Mark told jokes in his finest British diction to some unknown character on the phone, and Bridget typed furiously at her computer with precision. I was going to get used to the team.

Working at the company included many perks besides having the most luxurious environment. The company hosted lavish Christmas parties for staff and family. I was also to learn about our free invitations to golf tournaments at the Sherwood Country Club in Westlake Village. Every year staff received two tickets for the grounds and we could follow the famous golf stars around the course. I was determined to go to whatever the company offered us. The subsidised lunches at the restaurant and a full gym with televisions sets and equipment were some of the benefits of working in the building. We did not have to leave to get our exercise during the day. Staff included professionals of every nationality. The company provided a rich opportunity for an international experience under one roof. We interacted with associates in conference calls or by sending messages to many parts of the globe. I revelled in the experience.

I had to undergo several orientation programs arranged by HR, in the first six months of probation: leadership in the workplace, technical writing, conflict resolution, Microsoft software skills, and others. The company spared no expense in training its managers to ensure they functioned efficiently.

More Office Stories at the Big Company

As time went by, the new Ph.D., a Chinese food scientist called Jun, came to work with us. He specialized in a different discipline to mine and plunged right into his role. As he organized his little office, Jun ran out of space for all his things and was about to throw out an elaborate ceramic Goddess. 'How can you throw her out?' I asked. 'Well, no space. No space,' he complained. 'Who is she?' I asked. The ceramic figure was that of a Chinese woman in a gold gown, seated with legs crossed and one hand lifted near her face. 'It is QuanYin, the Goddess of mercy and fertility,' he explained. 'I'll take her,' I said. I was thinking I needed a goddess of fertility since I wanted to have another child one day. Anything would help. That evening I went home with my oversized ceramic trinket and then searched for a corner to deposit her.

The following week, a QA lab supervisor, Angeliki was hired to analyze samples coming in with consumer complaints and other manufacturing issues. Angeliki was a flamboyant Greek woman. She was short, compared to the other ladies in the department, with short hair dyed jet black and eye-liner, which accentuated her dark eyes. Her skin was pale and she had a ready open smile. Angeliki was so open, in fact, she told us everything about her life, whether we needed to know it or not! 'I was a house wife for five years! FIVE YEARS! Den ah got tired of it!' explained Angeliki. 'Nobahdee can ah take care of my children. Ah refuse-ah to go out!' she shouted. 'But that doesn't make sense,' I said.

'Don' ah let anyone fool you. Stayin' at home with small children is boring. Ah walkah around dah mall five times. I knew all dah stores. I knew all dah sales and bargains. Don' ah let anyone fool yah. Eeet ees boring!' For me, her story seemed like a radio show called "Confessions of a housewife". 'I believe you,' I said. 'I never wanted to stay at home talking baby talk. Couldn't do it.' The truth was that it was never an option for me. When Tiffany was a toddler my ex-husband and I both worked and Tiffany was placed in childcare. When I got divorced, I still worked and Tiffany was in school and in childcare.

'Ah always say nobahdy can watch ah mah kids! Nobahdy! I don' ah evah go out!' she continued. 'But Angeliki, one day you and your husband will have to go out and socialize,' I teased. The idea of not going out was so foreign to me. 'No!' she challenged. 'The kids go with us wherever we go!' 'OK,' I accepted her argument because there was no winning or convincing her. What would she think of me? I went out dancing almost every weekend and asked a friend's teenage daughter and others to babysit. She would have been upset with me. I made a mental note to never tell Angeliki the details about my outings ... and never about dating men. I would be in her bad books. I could just hear the reproach if I told her about going out ... 'Da poor child... Da poor child! How could you?'

We got lessons in Greek culture and food. 'I am from ah Greece. When we are cooking, the first thing we do is put a cup of olive oil in ah da pot!' she said with relish. 'Oh that's interesting Angeliki,' I said as I took notes on Greek cooking. 'When we were growing up in Athens we had an apartment. Everyone would hang laundry on lines to dry. Even underwear we'd hang outside. Everyone could see your underwear!' she explained. 'Athens must have been an interesting city,' I said while trying to imagine different coloured underwear flapping in the wind on lines overhead, as business carried on in the streets below. She explained, 'When ah visited relatives in da country yah could smell da house before yah gat dere.' 'Why is that?' I asked, looking forward to a logical explanation. 'Well,' she continued, 'Dey would roast a lamb on a spit in the front yard when relatives came to visit. The whole lamb would be roasting. Yah could smell it far away!' I then tried to picture the lamb on the spit, the dry terrain, and white washed Mediterranean buildings. It must have been an interesting country scene.

Our boss, Tom decided to take the small group out to dinner for Christmas. This was in addition to the annual company Christmas party for employees and families. Everyone was coming with a spouse except me. I had to tell my boss I was coming alone. 'You're not married? So you're coming alone.

So it's just you?' he asked again. 'Yes it's just me,' I confirmed. He seemed to have difficulty understanding this. What was his requirement for my being married? I couldn't understand. Sylvia said she was going up to her ranch that night and would be away for the weekend. I asked Bridget what she knew about the ranch and got an amusing story. 'Apparently she has a trailer on a little patch of land. It's not a ranch. I don't know if she even has running water,' said Bridget. 'What?' I was shocked at the gossip. 'So it's more like camping. I thought her ranch was sprawling like the ones seen on television with horses in a corral and extensive land,' I said. 'No Jennylynd, anything is called a ranch in California, and everyone talks about owning a horse. No matter what little old nag you own and pay to house at somebody's stable, people like to talk about owning a horse.' It was a great lesson in Southern California's bragging rituals.

The next week, Sylvia was again on the phone boasting about going to her ranch for the weekend and missing the office Christmas party. 'You know, I have to get ready for the winter up there at the ranch.' She spoke loudly so everyone could hear the conversation. As time went by, I made friends with many staff members in all departments. I eventually became a counsellor for quite a few people who came to my office to complain about their boss and tell some scandalous news. Did I have a face that said "I'm a good listener"? Or maybe it was because of the extra chairs in my office. It looked like a psychotherapist's office and I made friends quickly.

Dating a Giant

Posing as Ms. Red Car Long Legs, I again went online to search for Mr. Right. I wanted to meet someone really tall because I loved to wear high heels and found great comfort in looking up to a man when I was actually wearing heels. In my tall sandals I could readily stand at six feet. One dating requirement was to search for someone well over six feet. I came across a man in his thirties from Ventura. His profile said he was six feet six inches tall. Wow, what a giant. I had to meet him and sent a message. We corresponded a few times then after chatting at length about ourselves, we agreed to meet for dinner.

Luke invited me to his favourite barbecue restaurant in Goleta, just north of Ventura. Without thinking about The Rules which said a woman should meet close to home on the first date, I hastily agreed to meet in his town. I drove out to the restaurant which was described online as offering a "Hoe-down" time. I imagined it had a Country and Western theme and should have been interesting.

At the entrance, I noticed the entire floor was covered with saw dust. Was that the manager's idea of a joke? There was an outhouse built in the middle of the entry way. A bath tub was perched next to the soda fountain and there were random objects on the walls. It felt a bit odd, especially as I was wearing high heeled sandals and the saw dust got in between my toes as I tried to step gingerly across the floor without falling. My giant date met me near the entrance and suggested we sit off to the side so we could have a chance to talk. The music blared and the atmosphere was happy. It was not ideal for quiet banter, however.

I stared at the tall, blonde man before me. He was quite good looking with short cropped hair, baby blue eyes and a wicked smile. Was he good husband material or just looking for a quick roll in the hay, or the saw dust? Only time would tell. My animal instinct said I should keep him, but my logical brain asked me to control my irrational behaviour and dig deep by asking pointed questions. Luke was a divorced dad with three boys. He lived in Ventura close to his mother who would watch his boys for him while he worked or went out.

Hmm, three boys would be a bit too much for me as a stepmother. I sat and wondered what life would be like as Luke talked about all his responsibilities. He was good looking, but he came with a small army. Our date went smoothly and we were both physically attracted to each other. Luke was not the traditional University graduate and professional I craved. He did some office work and odd jobs. However, my irrational side was willing to forgo those minor details because he was tall and cute. I could not think straight. All I could do was force myself to wait and take things slowly. After our date I could not wait to go home to wash the sawdust off my feet!

Our next date was a walk out on the Santa Barbara Pier. I had not been out to the Pier before, so that was going to be a treat for me. I drove up to Santa Barbara and parked on the coast road. We had arranged to meet just in front of the Pier for a walk. On a Sunday afternoon, the atmosphere was ideal. Many other couples were walking on the boardwalk and the Pier. I was in heaven as tall Luke grabbed my hand and said, 'Let's go out.' At the end of the Pier, were a few shops selling souvenirs and snacks. We stopped and gossiped with some people who were fishing along the way. When we got to the shops, Luke asked if I wanted ice-cream.

'Sure,' I said, even though I did not have a sweet tooth and would probably take ages to finish it. 'You have to lick it,' he said laughing as I held the ice-cream for ten minutes talking and barely touching it as the sticky mess ran down my hand. We giggled about nothing and he volunteered to finish my cone for me since he had inhaled his in a few minutes. We continued to hug and giggle. It was a match made in heaven. I was completely mesmerised by his good nature and simplicity. Those big arms felt right when he wrapped me up in them. Luke said he could help me with projects around my house. He was a good handy man.

'Well,' I said, 'I have just the job for you. I'm painting the inside of all my closets. It looks like they were never painted.' Luke volunteered willingly offering to come any evening. Since I did not want Tiffany to see him so soon in our relationship, I asked him to come after 8:30 pm when I knew she would be fast asleep. I saw no point in having my child meet a prospective suitor unless he was serious. We set to work painting my closet and of course in such close proximity to each other, my painter became aroused. He grabbed me and planted a big kiss on my lips. I responded with more breathless kisses but managed to regain my composure enough to pull away. 'Let's focus on the painting. Let's not get carried away,' I said, trying hard to control myself as much as I was trying to control him.

With great difficulty and concentration, we managed to finish my closet interior. Luke suggested we take a rest and tackle the other rooms another day. That was fine with me.

We moved to the living room for a drink and a chat. Again his big arms engulfed me. I kept telling myself nice girls do not hop into bed so soon with strangers. I then had to decide whether Luke was still a stranger or he was accepted as a boyfriend. I had not met any of his friends or families, so that was reason enough to consider him a stranger.

I hopped across to the other sofa to create some distance between us. The tension was unbearable. 'We can talk while I sit over here,' I said. 'So tell me a little more about yourself. Have you dated black women in the past?' 'Yes, I used to go out with a divorced black woman in Ventura. We'd meet a lot at her house, but the relationship didn't get too far,' he said. Hmm, that sounded familiar … meeting at her house … was this just casual meeting to hop into bed? Was he thinking he could set up the same pattern with me? Was I going to be part of his statistics? I started to analyze the situation and decided to err on the side of caution.

'So when am I meeting your family,' I asked, to see his reaction. 'Well, it's a bit too soon. We'll have to wait a while for that,' he said. 'OK,' I said, judging his low level of commitment to our relationship. He hopped over to my sofa and started kissing me again. This time he lifted me with his strong arms and put me to sit on top of him. How was I supposed to resist his charm and his warm muscular body? I began to shiver with delight. My sensible self told me I should get him out before I yielded to his charm without any commitment to a relationship.

'I think you should leave now Luke. I have to wake up early for work and it's getting late,' I urged. 'No Lindy, No. I want you so much,' he said. 'Well, I'm not ready yet,' I lied as I struggled to control my body's natural yearning for him. 'It's time for you to leave,' I said. 'Lindy, you are so conservative,' he said. 'Well, I don't consider myself conservative. I am the one who moved to California not having any family or friends here. You are more conservative than me. Your mother lives around the corner from you.' With that I jumped up and walked to the front door to put him out. The easiest way for me to let him go was to be angry with him. 'Just leave right now please. I'm not conservative,' I screamed.

Luke got up reluctantly from the sofa and headed for the front door. 'I'll call you tomorrow. Chat soon,' he said. 'Bye, bye.' He tried to kiss me but I would not let him. He left in a huff and a puff, leaving his ladder and a few tools behind.

It was important to determine how much I really liked Luke and what were the real benefits of being with him. Would we really have a solid future together or would I just be available for the odd rendezvous. After experiencing previous bad romances, I was in no frame of mind to accept another. I was prepared to put him to the test to evaluate his intentions. If he only wanted casual sex, as tempting as it might have been, I was prepared to let him go. The next morning, Luke called promptly to see how I was doing. 'I'm just fine,' I said. 'How about you?' 'Hopin' to see you again soon,' he said. 'Perhaps one day.' I replied.

After meaningless chatter back and forth for a few days about the meaning of our relationship, I was able to glean that he needed someone to sleep with, but could never commit. 'After all, I have three boys to take care of,' he said one day in conversation. 'No problem,' I said, struggling to control my disappointment. 'Don't forget to come to collect the ladder and tools you left behind,' I said. 'Oh, I'll want more than that when I get there,' he replied with a hint. 'I don't think so mister. Just the ladder ... Will meet you out front.' And so said, so done ... I was able to resist the temptation and met him in front my house when he arrived. The ladder and box of tools were already deposited at my gate. 'Thanks so much for your help. All the best,' I said.

As I was speaking to him, Tiffany ran outside to see who was there. She became terrified when she saw the giant and ran back indoors. 'Bye bye. Take care,' I said. I went in after her and closed the door. 'Who was that mommy,' she asked. 'Oh, just a tall man,' I said.

Double Booking

Wonderful friends in PWP had tried to match me with single men they knew to see if anything would materialize. Mona said she knew a good natured real estate agent who was perfect for me. She planned to invite him to one of our group evenings out and we would let nature take its course. She gave me the eye when Derek appeared at the bar and she then rushed to introduce us. 'Hi Derek, how are you?' I asked.

Derek was middle aged with short cut salt and pepper hair, strong black eyebrows, a circular face with a short moustache and beard. He barely had any chin and his face seemed to morph right into his neck. Derek was of medium build and height and he was a smoker. He would smoke outside then come back into the bar. I wondered if I could put up with the smoking, but realized I had dated smokers in the past if they didn't smoke around me. He worked for a real estate office and mortgage brokerage firm. Well, perhaps he would make a good friend and contact when I wanted to borrow money or buy and sell my house, I thought.

'Hello,' he said shyly. 'Mona's told me about you. I wondered what he had heard. Yikes. Hopefully it was just that I was single. I hope I did not appear desperate with friends trying to hook me up with any available man. Derek sat quietly and drank his beer. He laughed at most of the jokes given by the PWP friends but did not join in. I barely got a few words from him, but he did ask me to dance once. When it was time to leave, Derek asked for my phone number and I was delighted to give him. 'Chat soon,' he said. The man was so quiet. How was I going to manage with a quiet man?

Around the same time, one of my male friends from PWP would visit with his two children. Gary had been married twice and had a child from each wife. It was funny how the children resembled him exactly. His genes were strong. Brenty and Cindy would come over to swim with Tiffany in the pool near our house. Gary and I would dip in the hot tub next to the pool, keeping an eye on the children. We spoke about every topic under the sun and sometimes told jokes about other PWP members. Gary was tall and good looking with a full head of prematurely grey hair. He had a ready smile and almond shaped blue eyes.

He boasted about his Irish heritage and would sometime invite Tiffany and me to his house in Ventura where he kept a book about Ireland on the mantelpiece. 'Have you been to

Ireland, Gary?' I asked. 'No, not yet. But I know my great grandfather was from Tipperary. That's all I know,' he would say. Gary was notorious for making passes at the ladies in PWP and the Ski Club. The more seasoned members knew about his antics while new members didn't. He was so likeable, it was easy to get taken by his charm.

For me, he was a good buddy and friend. He was reliable and helped me with handy work around the house. We were also happy for our children to play together. Gary would sometimes tell me about his girlfriends and exploits as if I were another man or a buddy. I listened with a neutral face and tried not to make any judgemental statements. That's what a buddy was supposed to do. If I reacted like the average woman, I would be taken off the buddy list for sure. He would notice I was indeed a woman.

Well, one day, his animal instinct kicked in as he realised he was swimming in the hot tub with a voluptuous woman in a bikini – unfortunately, it was me. He cornered me when the children were not looking and planted a big kiss on my lips. 'No Gary, No. We're just friends. Remember?' I urged. I protested quietly knowing he was attractive and I had resisted any emotion towards him for ages. 'But Lindy you're a gorgeous woman and I know you're not seeing anyone,' he said. 'Well Gary, you're a gorgeous man, and I know you're seeing one girl full time and two or more others on the side. No. I know too much about you. Let's just be friends.'

'Aw man,' he said with a defeated tone. 'You're such a good girl,' he continued. 'Yes I am and I've told you so,' I said. Gary did not hesitate to try again that night, just in case I was not serious. He cornered me in the powder room for a kiss before he changed out of his wet swim suit. 'Come on Lindy. What's a little hanky panky between friends?' I turned my head so he could only reach my cheek. He tried again to kiss my lips. He was completely aroused. 'Well, then we won't be friends. The answer is still No,' I said emphatically. 'Aw man ... that's too bad,' he said dejected. 'No means no,' I said, confirming my position as I released myself gently from his hug. 'OK, my friend ... OK.' He surrendered with his head held down. He backed away to calm down, while I quickly went upstairs to my room to change.

I invited Gary and his kids to my choir's concert at the Buenaventura Mission. Since it was close to his home, we thought it would be a good idea for all the family to come to the show. He promised to bring the kids, even if they slept through it. They had no interest in classical music, but the experience would be good. Gary was just trying to please me and I appreciated it.

In the meantime, while conversing with Derek during the week, he asked about my hobbies. I told him I sang with a big choir and we had a concert coming up that weekend. I then invited him to the show. 'Sure I'll come,' he said. I looked forward to singing to Derek in the audience and impressing him. He may or may not have liked classical music, but it did not matter. The days passed swiftly and when concert time came the choir stepped into the church to sing to the crowd. I had butterflies in my stomach, but for the wrong reason. I was looking out for my new boyfriend, Derek in the crowd, but did not see his round face. Even though it was a bit dark in the audience, I was still able to see when he slipped into the back row during the second song. As he sat down, I looked at the faces along the row in front of him and sure enough I spotted Gary and his brood. I did not think he would seriously come and bring the kids too.

Yikes! Maybe he was serious about me after all. How was I going to explain Gary to Derek? Or Derek to Gary? Would he understand Gary was just a friend? I knew at the end of the show Gary would give me a massive hug, and perhaps try for a kiss? How was I going to explain Derek to Gary since I had not told him about this potential new boyfriend? How was I going to be able to play the nice potential girlfriend with Derek when I had double booked? Derek would be upset to see me fraternizing with another man when he had made the trip from Thousand Oaks out to Ventura to sit through my concert?

I had to think quickly while singing my music and acting my part on stage. My solution was to signal to Derek to meet me out back, after the show. That way I could greet Gary and the kids quickly, say farewell, then slip around back stage and spend time with Derek. Then he could invite me for an after-show drink. I worried my way through the first half of the show. During the break I did not dare go out to say hello. I hid in the sanctuary with the other choir members, resting our feet and drinking water. I decided to send Derek a text message and hoped he would check his phone.

Learning to use my new cell phone and the many features it offered was a big feat. In sending text messages, each button had one number and several letters. One had to press a button a few times to get to the right letter and spell out a word correctly. Then pressing the space button at the bottom I entered the next word. "Meet me back stage behind the church after show." I hoped he would get the message so things could work smoothly for all concerned. By the time I figured out how to send this long message, it was time to line up and go back out to perform. The mission was accomplished. As we lined up on stage, Derek smiled at me and gave a thumbs-up signal. I smiled back and sang merrily through the second half.

As soon as we filed off the stage and people went in all directions, I rushed through the main church, and down the aisle. 'Hello Gary. Great to see you and the kids. Thanks so much for your support and coming to my concert,' I said. 'Great show Lindy. They couldn't keep up, but I did,' said Gary. 'Thanks Hun,' I said. Gary gave me a big hug as usual. 'Are you coming over to the house?' he asked. 'Oh, I'm so tired.' I stretched and yawned. 'Think I'll call it a night,' I said. 'OK. Yeh. Takes a lot of energy to sing for an hour and a half,' he said. 'Yes it does. Will call you tomorrow. Bye,' I said.

With that, I was off to the back of the church to meet Derek who I was sure by then was waiting at the back door as the choir members filed out, one after the other. I rushed to the side room, grabbed my bags and headed for the door. 'Hi Derek. So good to see you,' I said out of breath, with great excitement. I gave him a hug and he smiled. 'Nice show Lindy,' he said. 'Well glad you enjoyed it,' I said. Derek, as usual was quiet. I never knew exactly what he was thinking and there was a short pause. Then he asked awkwardly, 'Would you like to go for a drink or something?' I responded with zeal, 'Sure! Lots of places on Ventura Boulevard. Let's do that.'

And so that night I went with quiet Derek to hang out briefly after the concert. It became evident that Derek was way too quiet for me. He never made the first move and I wondered if he did not really like me. I decided we would just be platonic friends and forget about a romantic interest. It would just ruin our friendship anyway.

Family Visits

As Tiffany and I settled in our new home in Westlake Village, various family members came to visit. My sister came with her sons in the summer and also for Christmas holidays, and we braced for the noisy crew. Another time my mother returned for a visit. My father who had been suffering from heart disease, as well as complications of prostate cancer, came to visit and help with babysitting Tiffany, even though he was not feeling well at the time. And in the fall, my brother and his wife came for a visit with their first son, Marcus, a toddler in arms. My retired aunt, Audrey was enlisted one summer to help me with Tiffany, since I had to travel to various conferences in close succession and needed an extended period of childcare. We were fortunate to get this help when we needed it.

I became quite skilled at showing the sights and sounds of Los Angeles to family and friends. I should have been hired as the city's executive tour guide. All visitors were taken for the drive on Highway 101 from Westlake to Los Angeles. We would exit on Santa Monica Boulevard or Sunset Boulevard and drive along taking in the views of famous and not so famous restaurants, clubs and cafes. I would point out major places along the way like UCLA and the big houses. A major detour would be to drive through Bel Air gawking at the dwellings of the wealthy.

'Oh look at that house. Oh my God, the gates are so fabulous ... And who did the landscaping there?!' I would get lost and have to double back to try to get out of the "Private" neighbourhood. We sometimes got out of the car if there was no traffic behind, taking a photo next to the sign that read "Bel Air", just to prove we were there. Drivers in LA would let you know they were upset. They blew their horns often and loudly. The next stop would be the Will Rogers Memorial Park in Beverley Hills. We would park quickly, get a photo next to one of the fountains, and try to get a shot with the pink Beverley Hotel in the background, and then head on. Rodeo Drive, the street with the most expensive designer shops, was the next stop. Parking was essential if we had to walk around trying on clothes and posing with fancy accessories. It took little effort to feign interest in buying some expensive item. Some stores would be closed to the public on occasion if a special celebrity was shopping there. Security would keep the plebes at bay. In general, sales people in stores were gracious. They never knew who had money and who didn't. Boutiques would be teeming with tourist from many countries. It was an open air version of Harrods of Knightsbridge in London, United Kingdom, but with American big and brash opulence.

After Rodeo Drive, we would be hungry and have to eat in the area at one of the many restaurants on the side streets, or drive to Hollywood to get junk food. One of my favourites at the time was the Hard Rock Café at the Beverley Centre. Parking was tricky around Hollywood. With every block away from the main drag, the price of parking decreased. However, taking elderly parents or small children, I generally parked nearby. We would "worship" the stars on the sidewalk on the Hollywood Walk of Fame, looking for our favourite movie stars and performing artists. Of course, we had to stop for a photo next to Michael Jackson's Star. The Mann Chinese Theatre with handprints and footprints at the front always attracted large crowds of tourists, as well as pick pockets. As the tourists gawked, a skilled thief could enjoy care-free rounds. It was worrying how many shady characters roamed around Hollywood Boulevard in those days.

Another well traveled point was finding Griffith Park and driving to the summit to look out at the city of Los Angeles from many angles. Parking was tricky in the summer as the whole city of Los Angeles and every summer camp seemed to be at the summit touring around the Griffith Observatory. The Observatory was free to explore with museums about the planets, rocks, and astronomy. A lengthy stay would be needed to explore the museum thoroughly but my tours tended to be sound bites of the city.

When my sister, Colette and her boys came to visit we arrived at LAX to collect them in my red Mitsubishi Eclipse with the sun roof. It occurred to everyone that three children, two adults and several large suitcases could never fit in a sporty car. 'Lindy, what were you thinking? We can't all fit in that capsule!' Colette yelled. 'I'll have to rent a car.' Well, I imagined it would be best for her to rent a car anyway because I was going to be at work every day and they would have to find things to do. We waited in the long line at an airport car rental company and finally were able to secure a car for the two weeks. I had to use my credit card for the transaction which was not a wise decision. I knew I would be stuck with some of that bill. When family members visited, one has to grin and bear it.

'Khadir come back here! Amiri stop lagging behind!' Colette had to repeatedly call after her boys who never listened to her. Khadir was about three years of age and quite mischievous. He never stayed still for one minute. He had almond shaped, bright eyes and the broadest smile. He enjoyed the attention strangers gave him when he would approach them with baby talk and his smile. He was quite spoiled. Amiri was a tall, skinny 13 year old. He too liked attention and would sometimes wander off to talk to strangers. 'We're visiting from Atlanta. Yes, we came to California when I was younger. I'm not sure how long we're staying.' Amiri told random strangers his life history. When we finally got to the house, I gave the visitors my room since it was a little bigger and decided to share Tiffany's room with her. As I moved some clothing across to Tiffany's room I heard a loud shout. 'Charge!' That's all we heard as the lanky teen, Amiri dove head first down the carpeted staircase for fun! I knew it was going to be a long few weeks with them and my nerves would be frazzled.

We used the rental car when going out as a group. I was still singing in the choir at the church in Camarillo, so decided the whole family would go to church on their first Sunday in town. We had to leave early so I would be in time for the voice warm up. During the service, Khadir could be seen crawling under the pews for "fun". He popped up at various places to greet the stunned parishioners. "Hello!" He then continued his exploration under the pews as he wiped the floors with his lovely suit; "his Sunday best". Amiri sat sulking in the pew, waiting for the long service to be over so he could walk around. Colette sat shaking her head and giving Khadir "the eye" every time he popped up. 'Come here,' Colette whispered with venom. He ignored her and continued on his adventure smiling happily. 'You'll see when I get my hands on you,' said Colette. 'Oh leave the child. Let him have some fun,' said one or two older ladies. Tiffany giggled continuously at the scene. It was her most funny day in church to date.

On the way home after the service, Khadir received a stinging pinch and a severe scolding from Colette. He responded to this with two minutes of loud bawling. Afterwards, he was back to normal and ready for more mischief. Colette decided to take Amiri and Tiffany to see the new Harry Potter movie. It was a big craze at the time and Amiri had read all the books. Small children were not allowed at the movie. An age restriction was in effect. This meant Khadir had to stay at home with me. Colette left home doubting I would be able to manage him since she never could get him to sit still.

Khadir bounced around the house in disappointment. 'Haddy Podder mommy! Haddy Podder!' he screamed. 'You can't go. You're too small to go!' I explained. 'Haddy Podder mommy! Haddy Podder!' He screamed even louder. I was sure he had no idea what he was screaming about. He knew they were going somewhere without him and he didn't like being left out. I re-assured Colette everything would be fine, and they left for the movie. Khadir screamed and bawled for a solid three minutes. 'Haddy Podder mommy! Haddy Podder! Mommy!' When he saw I was not taking notice, he stopped crying abruptly and looked at me. We were in the bedroom. I looked at him and quite sternly said, 'Your mommy is out. Now stop crying and go to sleep right away.'

He saw that Aunty would stand for no nonsense. He stared at me for a few seconds with his eyes wide open and a strange look of terror in his face. He then closed his eyes and put his head on the pillow. Within a few minutes, he fell fast asleep. He never woke up until the noisy clan returned from the movie. 'You see I told you everything would be fine!' I boasted to Colette.

While they were visiting, repairs were being done on my kitchen. Mould was discovered in the insulation behind the kitchen sink. The Home Owner's Association (HOA) was using insurance funds to cover the cost of gutting the kitchen, replacing the mouldy insulation and replacing all the cupboards and shelves in that area. It was a project that was taking weeks to complete. In fact for a full week Tiffany and I had no access to the kitchen. We bought meals and also stocked up on frozen dinners. When the visitors came we had access to the kitchen but the cupboards, shelves and sinks on that side of the room had not yet been replaced. Khadir knew his way around the dinner table and kitchen after months of coaching from his mom. He knew after a meal, he was to scrape the remnants of his dish into the bin, and then place his dish in the sink. The pint size boy dutifully scraped his dish then looked around thoughtfully to follow procedure. He looked and looked. He walked back and forth. Then he looked at all of us confused. 'Where's dah sink?' he asked.

We all started laughing. He was cuter than words. Khadir's

question became a classic joke for their visit. 'Don't worry baby. I'll take that,' I said. I had been improvising using a stand pipe in the patio coming off the kitchen. A large bucket was serving as the sink. The extra tables served as counter tops and I managed to cook a four course meal in the mêlée that day. Everyone was baffled at the elaborate meal.

Living in a complex with many swimming pools had its joys, since my visitors could hang out at the pool when I was away at work. One afternoon, everyone got dressed in swim suits and we walked a little way up Via Colinas to the closest pool located in the middle of a group of townhouses. I showed the kids where they could swim while I was at work. I also gave them the key for the pool gate. The area was to be kept locked at all times. 'Geronimo!!!!!' screamed Amiri as he jumped into the pool with a big belly flop. 'Yippee!!!!' shouted Khadir. I hoped Colette would keep a close eye on them since they splashed in different directions while Tiffany swam quietly.

As the noise level grew louder, I noticed a few drapes open and close at the houses around the pool. The neighbours no doubt heard the uproar and wondered what tornado had landed. I calmly called everyone together and suggested we move to the pool on the edge of the complex. It was near the main road and away from houses. They could make as much noise as they wanted at that pool. 'Khadir don't run so fast. You could fall! Amiri keep an eye on him! Wait!' screamed Colette after the boys. Tiffany walked with Colette and me quietly. I was appreciating having a little girl as opposed to two energetic boys. I was thankful we had some options in pools otherwise the HOA may have put me out for causing a disturbance in the neighbourhood.

I planned to take the visitors up to San Francisco since it was one of the main attractions in California. They had to see it at least once in life. This was a lengthy six and a half hour drive from Westlake Village. We were to leave early in the morning and I booked a cheap hotel online to stay overnight. We were going to drive back down the next day. As we drove along the way I pointed out some of the beaches and towns: Ventura, Santa Barbara, San Luis Obispo, and more, until we came to desert highway with just rough terrain for miles. 'All the beaches look the same,' griped Colette. She was not one for sightseeing.

When we arrived in San Francisco, the rain poured. We had hoped to take the ferry around San Francisco Bay. That day, opportunists sold light plastic rain coverings to unsuspecting tourists as we stood in the rain trying to eat seafood chowder at Fisherman's Wharf. A tourist tradition was to stand on the sidewalk next to the vendors and buy the thick white soup that was served in a sour dough bread bowl. Another was to wander around the Ferry Terminal and visit the Piers, especially Pier 39 with its fancy shops and fast food restaurants. Colette wondered out loud to me, 'Why are we walking in the rain?' I responded, 'Because we're in San Francisco and it can rain and get foggy at anytime.' We wore our make shift rain coats and continued the walking tour.

We passed a man at the street corner drenched to bone with a sign that said, "NEED MONEY TO BUY WEED". He was creative and honest and he actually collected a few coins from pedestrians and passing vehicles. 'Girl, where are we?

Too many crazy people around here,' said Colette. 'We're in Frisco. No problem. Go with the flow,' I said. 'You have to at least go on a boat around the Bay to see Alcatraz. That's where they kept hardened criminals!' A man approached me with a wad of soaked brochures. He was wearing a sturdy rain coat. 'Half price, half price! Lady yah wan' ah half price boat ride?' All trips were reduced since tourists were turned off by the weather. We drove six and a half hours to be there, so by hook or by crook, we had to see something!

I told him we would take the half price tickets for the boat ride. By then Tiffany, Khadir, and Amiri were soaked to the bone. The boys probably wondered why Aunty Lindy was still continuing with her tour of San Francisco. The boat ride took us around the Bay and the recording was the same as if it were a sunny day. We circled Alcatraz and heard stories about attempted escapes. As the water became choppier, the boat headed back to the ferry terminal, but not before we said hello to some seals that were resting comfortably on buoys and random logs nearby. 'You can't come to San Francisco without riding on the trolley car,' I said. So we paid and hopped on. The trolley went up a big hill and down another. It was the 'Frisco experience not to be missed, especially when drenched by the rain and wearing useless yellow plastic rain coverings.

Our overnight hotel, booked online turned out to be a seedy dive that may have been used by "people of the night". It wasn't clean and thankfully we were there only one night. People seemed to come and go all through the night in the rooms around us. Miraculously the rain stopped on our journey back to Westlake Village. I decided to make a detour through the Carmel 17 mile drive to show Colette and the boys the famous Pebble Beach golf course and cedar trees advertised on all tourist brochures about Central California. I didn't mind paying for the drive. It was a rare opportunity for the family. As I drove around pointing out the beautiful scenery I turned to see Colette dozing and snoring. 'Hey I paid for this drive so take a look!' I said. 'I don't know why you wasted your money,' she said. 'I don't like scenery. Show me the malls!' It was a silent trip back to Westlake that day. Everyone was upset.

The following weekend, I decided to take another long drive with the visitors to Las Vegas. It was a drive I had done on a few occasions. We had to visit the city that never slept. I remembered all the kid-friendly and free entertainment: the Caesar's Palace fountain show, the Treasure Island Battle, the Bellagio water fountain show, the MGM grand show with the tigers, walking around the streets of Paris, watching magic shows at Circus Circus and many other gems. We were on a tight budget so free activities were part of our agenda. We journeyed through the Mojave Desert and arrived at midday ready to explore. Staying at an inexpensive motel obliquely opposite Treasure Island, we were on the strip and at the heart of a lot of action. We just needed this place for one night and planned to drive back the following night.

Our first stop was Circus Circus, marketed as the most kid friendly joint. I had to keep a close eye on Khadir and Tiffany since they were fascinated by the lights of the slot machines and kept rushing towards them. 'Ma'am, kids are not allowed near the slot machines.' The security guards were ever-vigilant. Amiri was older but would also wander off and have to be reined back in. 'Keep an eye on your brother,' Colette would yell. 'But I wanted to see the Magic show!' he protested. We gave him one hour to himself and arranged to meet back at a certain spot. Colette and I had to take turns in physically holding Khadir and Tiffany, so they would not get lost in the throngs of parents and children at Circus Circus.

She took her ten minutes at the slot machines, while I held the children. Then I spent my five dollar budget at the slot machines while she held the children. That was all the gambling we needed. As soon as Amiri returned, we walked from one hotel to the next, taking in the attractions and sometimes eating junk food. 'There goes one bride. Hey there's a bride and groom!' Amiri counted the married couples or those about to say "I do", as they roamed around hotels in full wedding regalia. This was also one of the attractions in Vegas. It was an exciting but hectic two days in Sin City.

As these visitors left, more family came. While my father was visiting relatives in New York, I suggested he come out to California to see us. He agreed to help with babysitting Tiffany when I left a few days on a business trip. It was a scare when I had to take him to a local health clinic the day before travelling to get medication for his dizzy spell. He had been taking medication for his many different ailments and was not the strongest physically. I took him on my LA highlights tour and we also visited Monterey, San Francisco, Carmel, Big Sur, and the famous Hearst Castle, former residence of publishing tycoon, William Randolph Hearst. Daddy was particularly tickled when we visited the wilds of Venice Beach where we saw an elderly couple dressed in beach gear. The man wore swim trunks and the old woman, a bikini with tall boots, possibly imitating Wonder Woman. 'Lindy, what kind of place is this?' My father was surprised at the madness before us. 'Don't worry. It's Venice Beach. Everybody crazy comes out, even in the daytime,' I confirmed.

I shed a quiet tear as Daddy returned to our cousins on the East Coast before going on to Trinidad. I was to cry again when my mother was leaving us after her second visit to California. Three years after her first visit, Gloria had not been in the best of health. Arthritis was affecting her knees and she could not walk quickly anymore. Walking was painful. I advised her to get wheelchair assistance while travelling. She did not like the idea of sitting in a wheelchair.

'I'm not an invalid. Why would I need a wheel chair?' she challenged. To this I replied, 'Well then use a walking stick!' She was shocked at my suggestion. 'Are you kidding? Walking sticks are for old people. Do you really expect me to use a walking stick?' Her pride was bigger than the practicality of getting assistance. I could not believe her swift decline in a matter of just three years. It was winter time and good weather to visit Las Vegas. We drove through the Mojave Desert one more time to do our highlights of Las Vegas tour. More interesting hotels had opened so there was more to see that year. My mother enjoyed visiting my fancy office at the big company and meeting my new work colleagues. She was proud that her daughter had stepped up to a higher paying job and an impressive office. I would never forget her face as she looked around my office with pride. After a short stay, the vacation came to an end. We had to order a wheel chair when she checked into her flight to return home. I cried all the way as she was wheeled off into the distance.

As California's official tour guide, it was always good to see family.

8

GALLO PINTO AND THE COSTA RICAN ADVENTURE

The Cloud Forest

I had gone to San Jose, Costa Rica with my manager for a regional meeting of all the company's leaders in Latin America. This annual event saw managers from operations in Columbia, Ecuador, Chile, Honduras, and Costa Rica gather to discuss issues in production and other matters affecting trade to Europe and North America. My role was to discuss food safety at farms and packhouses. I was also encouraged to give my presentation in Spanish since everyone at the meeting spoke Spanish. This was a daunting prospect but one had to be ready for the challenge. The company had provided me with a Spanish tutor who came once a week to help me with my spoken Spanish. This was a huge benefit and I felt obligated to return the favour of the free lessons.

We rose early in the morning, having flown to San Jose from California the night before. The four star hotel consisted of sprawling Mediterranean style buildings, cream with red-tiled roofs. Opulent gardens surrounded us and a hot tub was located in the garden, according to the brochure in my room. I was determined to visit it one evening if it could be squeezed into the hectic schedule. In fact, I was determined to squeeze many activities around the pre-planned program, but had to keep my plans quiet.

The typical big American breakfast buffet was augmented by a host of fresh fruit and pico de gallo, the favourite black bean and rice dish served with every Costa Rican meal. I helped myself to a bit of everything, always conscious of the fact that I did not know when the next meal would be. After gorging myself, I did not feel well. The driver came to meet us at 8:00 am and we were also joined by Hans, the QA Vice President of European operations. He had lived in Costa Rica in the past and was familiar with the country and the company's production staff.

'Hello Hans, old buddy. How are you?' My boss was delighted to see him and they exchanged generous handshakes. 'This is Jennylynd, a rookie with the company … QA Manager.' I shook hands with Hans. 'Hello. How are you?' I said. He was tall with salt and pepper hair cut conservatively, and large glasses. His salt and pepper moustache partially hid his broad smile. 'Welcome to the company. I'm sure you'll enjoy working with us!' he said. 'Thanks,' I said. I already enjoyed working with the group, even though I had to travel far from home. When we got to the office, I was introduced to Norma, the corporate secretary for the Latin American division. She was an attractive, black, middle-aged woman with copper brown skin, bright eyes and neat business attire. 'Hello Jennylynd. Welcome to San Jose,' she said. 'Thanks so much. Pleased to meet you,' I chimed.

As people assembled in the large conference room, I noted the difference between this office building and the one in North America. The head office in North America was all enclosed with concrete and glass. We had no windows that could open. Air conditioning or heat ran all day through a central air circulation system. In the Latin American office, the building was no more than two stories high. Parts of the building were interrupted by gardens with beautiful tropical shrubs and flowers. All offices had louvers that could be opened at will to let in fresh air. The conference room had air conditioning units that could be turned on or off as needed. I imagined when North Americans like us arrived, we had to be pampered and the cold air was turned on. The large ceiling fans and open louvres would have been enough to keep fresh air moving through the room.

In looking around the room at all the faces, I realized I was the only woman in the meeting. Reviewing the names on the program, twice, sure enough, I saw my name was the only female one. Apart from Norma, who ran back and forth supplying copies of documents for the meeting and the lunch lady who set up coffee and snacks, I was surrounded. Yikes! I had to mentally convince myself it was a unique opportunity to embrace with joy. However, intimidation and uncertainty were flooding my mind with my half hour presentation looming the following morning–in Spanish!

All the managers knew each other from previous meetings and they exchanged greetings with great gusto. They were friendly and it was good to put names to faces as I was introduced to everyone. We had corresponded by email over a few weeks about food safety programs at the farms and their names were familiar. A hectic program was planned for a few days. Every night, dinners were planned for the group. How was I going to squeeze in a little fun for myself if every waking moment was scheduled? During the first day, a manager from each division gave a report of production issues and exports. 'Blah, blah, blah.' I tried to take notes to stay awake and welcomed the tea break and lunch break so I could talk with people.

The presentations seemed to go on and on. I could not participate in discussions, because I was not familiar with the business. I just had to sit there and learn. According to the printed schedule for the following day, we had presentations in the morning and an afternoon off. Following this, we had a planned group dinner and evening entertainment. My reward, following the knee bucking exercise of presenting in Spanish in front of a learned audience, was to plan a trip during the free afternoon. I asked John, the regional operations manager, if he could recommend a cable ride or other forest adventure. He told me to ask Norma to arrange everything. Before heading out that afternoon, I spoke to Norma about a cloud forest adventure I had seen on the internet. 'Is that what you want to do?' she asked to confirm. 'Yes of course. It looks wild. People jump from tree to tree on cables,' I said. 'OK Jennylynd, if that is what you want, I'll ask Felix, the company driver to take you over there in the afternoon. He will wait for you and then bring you back to town. It is about an hour's drive from here. You can pay Felix directly,' she said.

Norma was a gem. She called the tour company and made a reservation for me. All we had to do was show up and I would get my ticket on arrival. I had perused the cloud forest adventure website before leaving California. The photos showed exotic parrots and toucans and promised tourists the chatter of monkeys and an opportunity to mix with wild life. I looked forward to the break from the formal meetings. That night, I could barely sleep. I agonized over my presentation in Spanish and practiced ten times. Norma had already printed out the PowerPoint notes to give attendees. Everything was in place for the following morning. At 10:00 pm, I decided since the swim suit was in my suitcase, there was no harm in going for a dip in the hot tub to soak and relax. I was wide awake and perhaps the hot water would help me sleep.

The hot tub was partially hidden in the garden by a bed of shrubs and flowers. It was a beautiful, well maintained garden. As I turned on the jets and walked into the hot water, I imagined myself in absolute paradise. This was the calming effect I needed. 'Relax. Relax,' I told myself. My tranquility was interrupted when I saw Hans walking around the garden late at night smoking his cigar. 'Jennylynd! What are you doing out here late at night?!' asked Hans. In my mind I was thinking, 'Trying to get away from the meeting delegates like you so I can relax a little.' Of course I could not get away from them. Some of the managers from other divisions were also staying at the hotel. I calmly jumped out of the hot tub, put on my robe and went briskly to my room. 'Goodnight Hans. See you at the meeting in the morning,' I said. 'Goodnight Jennylynd,' he responded. I did not like the idea of a senior manager ogling at me in my tiny bathing suit late at night. It was not a comfortable feeling.

Sleep finally came late that night and it appeared like only a short time passed before the phone rang with my wake up call for the day's events. I packed a small bag with adventure clothes for the afternoon. The driver was to take me directly from the office to my tour and then back to the hotel in time for the group dinner. I could barely eat from the splendid breakfast buffet that morning. 'Just let me get through this with flying colours,' I kept telling myself. As we got to the main office, I went around the room giving the delegates my pre-printed hand outs and set up the computer with my Power Point presentation. 'Come on, come on everyone,' I said silently. 'Get into the room quickly and stop gossiping with friends'. We started at five minutes after nine and it was a long five minutes for me to wait.

'Seguridad de alimentos en las fincas es muy importante. Es necesario que los empleados lavan los manos despues de usar la toaleta y despues de fumar,' I started in my best Spanish. I wondered what the managers thought about my rudimentary Spanish presentation. It was what I thought to be common sense hygiene practices in operations. Would they ask me questions? Would there be an awkward silence when I was done? Any discussion? As I approached the end of my well rehearsed monologue, all fear had disappeared. I felt like I was talking to my peers. Forgetting about being the only woman in the room, I was less self conscious about what may have been considered a macho environment. Everything was fine until one of the managers asked me a question. 'Otra vez por favour,' I asked him to repeat the question.

I had no clue what he asked. My boss who was fluent in Spanish jumped to the rescue and answered the question for me. I was able to answer two additional questions and mercifully the time was up. I felt free and stopped sweating. A relaxing air descended on proceedings. The cloud forest was waiting for me. It was just a matter of sitting through the remaining presentations of the morning, then off to freedom.

I ate many pastries during the break to make up for the sparse breakfast. I also swallowed a few sandwiches provided for lunch and told everyone, 'Farewell and see you later for dinner.' We all went in different directions. The group dinner and outing was planned in the mountains where we would dine on fine Costa Rican cuisine and be entertained by folk dancers and singers. It was something everyone looked forward to. 'Jennylynd I hope you have a large jacket or pauncho for the evening. It's really cold in the mountains,' said one of the good natured managers from Peru. 'A jacket? I didn't bring anything,' I replied. I assumed Costa Rica was tropical and never thought of packing warm clothes. I would just have to wear my work suit which was made of light fabric. The sleeves were long but the skirt was short. The only other clothes were casual Bermuda shorts and a T-shirt for the forest trip.

'Enjoy your trip,' said John, the regional manager. He knew I was planning something but did not know where I was going. 'I will. I will,' I chimed with glee, not telling him much. He appeared conservative and had probably never gone. I had changed into my Bermuda shorts, t-shirt and Costa Rica cap; Jennylynd of the Jungle! Felix, the good natured driver came to collect me. Trying to make small talk with Felix was no easy feat. He spoke absolutely no English and my Spanish vocabulary consisted of basic food safety facts. An ordinary conversation about the weather in Spanish would take me ages to construct. Luckily, we had a car radio with music to fill the gaps.

After an hour's drive out of the city, we came up to a building with a large sign out in front that read 'Cloud Forest Adventure'. It was a small wooden building and I did not see any tourists; it was a Wednesday afternoon in the middle of the school term. However, tourists should have been on tours too. The ground in that area was flat and sparse. Apart from a few bushes, I could not see any trees around the little building. I did not hear any chattering monkeys or see toucans. Where was the forest? Was this some elaborate hoax? As we stopped in front of the building, a neatly dressed gentleman came out on the porch.

'Buenos Dias. Como estas?' said the tour operator. Felix explained quickly that I was there for the cloud forest tour and we had to drive back to San Jose afterwards for a meeting. 'No problem,' the man continued in Spanish. 'We will have her out of here in no time.' He called two young men who were hanging around and said they would be my tour guides. The place was so empty that afternoon, I had two tour guides. Was I lucky or what? 'English or Spanish?' one of the men asked me. 'Español por supuesto,' I replied. I was on a role practising my Spanish conversation with Felix and wanted to continue the chatter. He explained we had to hike a little way into the bushes before we came to the forest with tall trees and platforms.

'How far do we have to go?' I asked, a little worried poor Felix would be stranded for hours with nothing but his cigarettes. 'It's not far,' they said. I know the words "Not Far" were usually relative to what the person was used to walking. "Not far" had no real meaning. For me, "Not Far" in the bush was far enough. I was a city girl or perhaps a suburbs girl. We walked and walked, and then walked some more. A mosquito attacked my leg. I asked the men, 'Where are the chattering monkeys or the toucans?' I couldn't see a tropical bird for miles around. Nothing looked like the posters online. They explained it was the dry season and a lot of the wild life went deeper into the forest. I imagined the tourist traffic would have scared off all wild life during busy times.

After jumping over a few tree stumps and walking along a trail, we finally came upon an area with tall trees. The forest was not dense but the trees seemed to go for miles into the air. They gave me a pair of gloves with good grip and a helmet. They put on helmets too. One guy explained how I would jump from one tree platform to the next. 'Don't look down,' he said. 'Just look ahead.' Following instructions was not one of my skills. I would have to see what transpired. We put on harnesses which were to be attached to a pulley on the steel cable, strung from one tree to the next. Slowing down the pace was done by pressing down on the cable while in motion. Most of the information went in one ear and out the other. How did they expect me to understand and remember all that information when I was terribly afraid? I wondered if it would make sense to turn back and ask Felix to just drive me back into town. He would probably laugh at me. I was supposed to be the brave manager from "America". He had never done the cloud forest adventure. This activity must have been reserved for crazy foreigners.

As I stood on the wooden platform built around the large tree trunk, I stared at the harness around my body. Touching the tiny helmet and looking down at the forest floor, I felt so sick. Why did I eat that extra sandwich at lunchtime? It seemed like a good idea at the time. However, it felt as if the sandwiches wanted to come back up. 'Don't look down. Look straight ahead,' yelled one of the men. 'I will jump first to the other platform and wait there for you. He will come after. Just stretch your feet out and step off the platform.'

'Wha' wha'…' Before I had time to respond, he was gone. He jumped off the platform and went flying. Within a few seconds he was at the next platform built around a massive tree. It was then my turn. My back up tour guide said I had to do about thirteen jumps and the last one was the longest. Yikes. I was so nervous, I didn't know whether to pee my pants or save face and act like a lady. It was too much pressure in one day. 'Jump! Jump now!' screamed the tour guide. The guide behind tried to get me to leap from the platform. I was momentarily paralyzed and looked down at the forest floor which appeared miles and miles below us. How could a mere helmet protect me from a fall to the forest floor?

I was holding onto the handle of the pulley for dear life. After the first jump there was no turning back. One had to finish the course or get stuck in the forest. It was a long way down. There wasn't even a visible hiking trail. 'Jump now!' He looked like he was getting impatient. 'OK! OK, I'm ready!' I said, but was I? Saying a quick prayer, I closed my eyes and jumped. In a split second, I remembered the instructions to keep my eyes wide open to alight onto the next platform.

'Aaaahhhhhh!'

Every bird, every monkey, and every tourist for miles around must have heard me. I had never been so terrified in my life. A million thoughts went through my head at the time. This is what they call fun? Why would anyone pay to do this? It is insane. Where were all the lovely birds they promised we would see along the way? Had I frightened them away? The first tour guide was at the next platform to help me gain my footing. Another second and I could have flown right into the big tree trunk.

'How was it?' He asked. 'Well, ah, well …' I could not speak. My heart was racing. The other guide jumped onto the platform and without another word, the first guide took off for the next tree. I noticed by the third jump I was actually gaining confidence. By jump number eight, I felt like I did not need the guidance and coaching as in the beginning. By jump number eleven, I was howling like Tarzan while flying through the trees. Don't look down. Focus on the approaching platform. I followed the advice and did not need any more help to land. The last jump had the longest cable ride; however, I knew how to speed up or decrease the speed. It was a thrilling ride.

The course was finally over and we climbed down a big ladder to the floor. We were safely on the ground once more. It was the thrill of my lifetime and a ride I will never forget. After a short hike through the bushes, I returned to Felix chattering in English about my amazing adventure. 'It was the greatest achievement of my life! If I can jump from one platform to the other, I can do anything! I'm ready to take on the world!' I screamed.

All poor Felix could do was smile. He spoke no English.

That evening I met the other managers at the front of the hotel and a minibus took the whole gang up to the mountains for dinner. It was many hours since lunch and I was ravenous. We had to wait for everyone to assemble before ordering and being served. The beautiful restaurant was up in the mountains overlooking San Jose. It was already chilly and I had nothing warm to wear. The menu was superb and the dancers and musicians performed with great skill. We got a true flavour of Costa Rican hospitality and culture that night.

In conversation with John after dinner, I mentioned I had a wonderful time in the afternoon. 'Oh yes the cable car ride is usually interesting,' he said. 'But I did not go on the cable car. I went on the Cloud Forest adventure,' I said. 'You went where?' he asked. 'You know; the one where you are in a harness and jump from one tree platform to the next by a thin cable?' I continued. The man's eyes bulged. 'What? What did you do?' he asked again. 'I was flying from tree to tree like Tarzan!' I boasted to him with a big smile on my face. 'How could you do that Jennylynd? It is dangerous! Something could have happened. How could you do that? Are you OK? Oh my God! Jennylynd!'

It was amusing for me to see his shock. This was no laughing matter however. If one of the visiting managers from "America" were to get injured on a visit, he would have been responsible. 'Yes but nothing happened. I had a great time. Don't worry about it John,' I said. The poor man was stressing from the fear of what could have happened. I smiled happily knowing I had experienced the adventure of a lifetime in the cloud forest. I was ready to take on any challenge the world threw at me.

Private Jet into the Green

I had come to Costa Rica to learn about the food safety programs in Operations and also find ways to improve them to match what was happening in our industry in United

States. It was thus important for me to visit farms for a first hand view. Arrangements had been made to see plantations in the East of the country. One manager, Rudolpho, was to travel with me on this assignment. Rudolpho said we would meet at 7:00 am next morning and fly to the area in the company jet. Flying on one of the company's planes? How exciting. I immediately felt like a celebrity making cameo appearances in cities around the globe. The red carpet would be rolled out as I landed in my private jet. Photographers would try to get the perfect shot as we left the tarmac. This of course was idle fantasy. We were visiting farms and this was a three or four-seater propeller jet.

Waking early next morning with butterflies in my stomach, it was hard to swallow my breakfast. I was going to fly on a small plane and had no experience with this. As I got to the hotel entrance, Felix and Rudolpho were waiting and within ten minutes we were at the light aircraft section of the international airport. Without fanfare, we entered the small building then onto the tarmac.

El Capitan, the pilot, was waiting for us. 'Buenos dias!' He was a short, skinny gentleman with dark glasses and a pilot's white shirt, black pants and pilot's hat. We had to bend over to enter the little plane since we were taller than the interior. I was so excited. I could barely breathe. Rudolpho and El Capitan were used to the exercise of flying around the country in the little jet. They probably assumed I was a regular too, until I acted like a child in a candy store. 'What's this for? Oh what's that? Oh my God, I'm in a small jet. Woohoo! Everybody look at me!' I shouted to the imaginary friends on the tarmac, and my travelling companions just smiled. Wishing my friends back in

California could have seen me, I felt so elated. I also wished Tiffany could have been with me to share in the experience.

As soon as we fastened our seat belts, we took off. As we climbed into the sky, the constant din of the propellers was apparent. It would not be a silent ride like a big aircraft. However, we would only be airborne for twenty minutes. I noticed that we flew closer to the ground than the typical big plane. I could see all the cars and roadways. We then hovered over a more rural area outside the city. The most spectacular sight was the many tall mountains and dormant volcanoes that dotted the landscape. Rudolpho pointed out some of the major sights on the way and I reacted with loud cheers.

Within fifteen minutes, we started our descent. Down and down we went at what appeared to be break neck speed. As I looked below us, all I could see was a wide expanse of green. Where was El Capitan taking us? I didn't see any place to land. Were we going to land on the tree tops? This must have been in the middle of a plantation. I started to panic and tried to take deep breaths. The man must have known what he was doing. Why was I panicking? Feeling a little sick because the descent was rapid, I tried hard to see a landing strip. We were coming close to the trees then, and all I saw was more and more green space. I decided to cover my eyes to spare myself the agony. 'Jennylynd, why are you covering your eyes,' asked Rudolpho. I shouted, 'I can't look! He's gonna get us killed! I can't see where we're landing.'

Before I could say another word, we hit the ground, moving forward on a dirt landing strip. I knew we were still alive and only then could I exhale and unblock my face. Rudolpho was looking at me, the mad woman, and I was defending my actions. 'Well, it's my first time in a small jet. What do you expect?' I wiped the sweat from my brow and looked around. We had landed on a small dirt track cleared in the middle of a massive plantation. We were surrounded by thousands of trees and it was intimidating. I thanked El Capitan profusely for bringing us to safety and asked him to pose with me for a photo next to the jet. I was determined to show that photo to everyone I knew.

We visited countless farms that day, speaking with supervisors as I learned about production and took notes. The company owned what could be described as small villages with housing for managers, supervisors and junior staff. Some of these small villages even had a dry goods store, a health centre, a school, and a post office. Never in my life had I seen such a large operation where thousands of lives revolved around one company; it was difficult to fathom. I could not decide on my feelings for this type of organization. On the one hand, it was good to create so many jobs for people. Most of the food was bound for North America or Europe and would feed millions. On the other hand, was I witnessing a form of slavery? These people were giving their whole lives to the company. With amenities right on site, they lived to work. Yes, they got a wage. Yes, they could leave if they wanted, but where would they go? The money must have been just enough to keep them working on site. Their children would be trained just enough to work for the company when they became adults. It was a moral issue I could not cope with. I tried to blank it out and focus on the tasks at hand: Learn about the operations, do inspections, make recommendations. I proceeded with robotic precision. I would become one of the working masses; working for the big company.

We had lunch in a small restaurant in the seaside town of Limón on the coast road and I spotted many black people. 'Who are these people? They look like typical Caribbean folks,' I said. I was puzzled since I did not expect to see such a large concentration of people who looked like me. I thought Costa Rica was populated only by people of Spanish descent. Rudolpho explained, 'Many people had come over from Jamaica to work on the plantations in the past. Remember we are now on the Caribbean coast of Costa Rica.' I stared at them in awe as we walked through a shop in Limón looking at the snacks. The trip was a time for wonder and discovery; an educational experience from a social standpoint. I was certainly learning a lot about Central America.

9

A MOM'S LIFE

Marry Well

I was under the impression that the people of California were modern thinking and well ahead of the rest of the country in all social beliefs. It was true many new religions, new food trends, and new businesses started in California. The State had a wonderful atmosphere for nurturing entrepreneurs. Some of the highest divorce rates were also noted in California. I wondered what this meant for a single mother like me to settle and work there. In my mind the average person in the population should have been used to single parents and independent women. However, I discovered pockets of traditional societies where we lived. Some pockets in society were fixed on the traditional family structure and frowned upon anything out of the ordinary.

'You have to marry well!' I heard one woman say at the office as she trudged through her boring 9:00 to 5:00 responsibilities of shuffling papers and taking calls from complaining customers. 'What do you mean? What's *Marry Well*?' I asked a bit bewildered by the statement. 'Look at me. I would not be here if I'd married well. Find a man with money. I'm telling my daughters to marry well so they don't have to work,' she confirmed.

I was taught to study hard, go to university and find a good career. That's how I was raised, growing up in the Caribbean. You were to go to the best high school, go to the best university, and become the best career woman. However, I was living in the United States in the 21st century, listening to a woman talk about marrying well and staying home. I could hardly believe my ears. It was evident she did not want to work. Was there something bad or unsavoury about working? Was she being lazy? I tried not to judge, but found her job easy, even if it was boring. What important things would she be doing if she was not working? Would she have a daily purpose in life if she did not have to get dressed every day and come to the office? How would she save the world when she was not working? 'You have to marry well,' she said again as her head hung low and she continued her drudgery. It never occurred to her that if she went back to school and got more education she could earn more money without marrying well.

School Moms

I decided to observe the mothers who were active in picking up and dropping children off to school and those taking children to activities, day after day. Those who married well seemed pre-occupied with their children's activities. They had given up their own goals and aspirations and lived their lives through their children.

At the elementary school in Westlake, the moms made a vicious attempt every morning to drop off their children ten minutes before starting time so they would not have to wait around too long. As a result there was great road rage and tempers flaring as everyone arrived in large family cars to the limited curb space. Brands like Mercedes, Lexus, and BMW were the order of the day. And instead of a simple car, the vehicle had to be larger than life, even if the mother had one child. I couldn't understand the logic since it must have been expensive to maintain the large monsters. However, at curb side the big cars commanded a great deal of attention and power. My tiny Mitsubishi Eclipse was in peril of being run over on many occasions as people jostled for a spot.

Those moms who had other responsibilities left swiftly. However, there were some who parked away from the school and walked in to "help" the teacher in the classroom. Teachers, they assumed, needed help in grading homework, collecting papers, and managing students at lunch. This too was a fight and a jostle to see who could be assigned to help the teacher. If these mothers had married well and had so much time, why did they need to be in the classroom all day long? Teachers had to draw lots for those interested in helping in the classroom. At one parent teacher meeting, the teacher asked for names of those who were interested in helping and then she drew the names on a lottery basis to select different women for different days. I was amused by the process since I never submitted my name. I was always working at the office or travelling to a country far away.

I wondered what could be the benefit of helping in the classroom, apart from escaping boredom at home. Then one day Tiffany came home crying and saying she did not get a good part in the school play. 'Alexa got to be the main girl in the play! Her mother is always there and teacher gave her the part.' Poor Tiffany was inconsolable. I guessed the teacher felt obligated to the extra-helpful mother. Her child was elevated to the main part or she would face maternal rage from a daily helper. Other mothers boasted out load about going to Pilates class in the morning, then going to the café for lunch. I had no idea what the word Pilates meant so had to go online to look it up. I was relatively skinny but kept fit by waking up early in the morning and doing my own aerobics routine to calypso music. Sometimes Tiffany would hear to music and come downstairs to join me in exercise. On a limited budget, I was not about to add additional gym fees to my bills.

Ballet Moms

'I left my job to stay at home with my children one woman boasted to the other.' The listener agreed, 'Yes, I would never want any strangers raising my children. That would be terrible!' the other said. I listened attentively as I waited for Tiffany during her ballet class. I did not dare join in the conversation, since I never stayed home to take care of my child and was out to work as soon as I could get going. I did not want to be judged as a bad mother by the majority, so I kept quiet. One mother asked, 'Where are you from?' She looked at me with the innocent eyes of someone who had never travelled and was quite contented in her little world. She had heard my accent as I chimed in with a statement to another mom. 'I'm originally from Trinidad,' I said. Her vacant stare told me more than words could say; she had no idea where this country was located. I became annoyed was trying hard to control my emotions. 'So how did you get here?' she asked, looking down her nose at me. At that point I was boiling. Instead of giving a long convoluted answer of having studied at university in Canada, then working in Florida, then applying and getting a job in California, I pounced like a wild cat. 'I came on a plane,' was my short answer. I had been tempted to say I rowed on a boat all the way, but that would have been too much. She saw my annoyance and stopped at that question. She would have to go home and look on a map to find out where Trinidad was located.

Stay at home moms tended to channel their lost aspirations of greatness through their children. Some children at the dance school were fully booked for classes on week days and weekends. I had signed Tiffany up for ballet and tap dance at the California Dance Theatre when we moved to Westlake. It was not easy running away from work mid afternoon to do the pickup and drop off. Sometimes I negotiated with a fulltime mom to watch her for me until I finished work. Some children would be in ballet, tap, hip hop, jazz, and musical theatre, never having a day off. They arrived directly from school to the dance theatre. At the end of the year when concert time came, the moms were more nervous and anxious than the children to ensure their children got good parts in productions.

I experienced a small crisis when Tiffany and her friend Garyanna auditioned for the part of a small child dancing with a doll during the opening party scene of the Nutcracker Ballet. In the audition, the dancer had to hold the doll, then turn to the left lifting the doll, and then turn to the right lifting the doll. After that, she would wander around the stage with other children in the party scene in the background. It seemed simple enough and both Tiffany and Garyanna were understudies for each other. We had to sign contracts to say we would be present on the performance day. One child was assigned the Saturday performance and the other the Sunday performance.

'My Garyanna is a natural actress,' said her mother. 'She's been on stage since she was a toddler.' While she boasted, Garyanna would be off doing some mischief in a corner. 'Garyanna come here this minute! Garyanna I'm going to count to three ... one, two, three ...' It was amusing the way

Garyanna ran in different directions like a spoiled brat completely ignoring her mother. She was blonde with blue eyes, pale skin, and the cutest face of disobedience. 'You should have seen my Garyanna act as a little kitty cat in the local play last month. It's as if she was possessed by the role,' the mother continued. 'She purred and meowed on the stage like a pro. She's going to be big in Hollywood one day,' she boasted. I listened and smiled imagining the mom wanted to be on the stage in Hollywood one day too.

When we were backstage during the dress rehearsals, the costume coordinator told us we did not have to worry about dresses for the girls. They had a stock of Victorian dresses they would lend us. I was thankful, even though I knew Tiffany had many pretty dresses she could wear for the occasion. Garyanna's mom said she would do me a favour and lend Tiffany a lovely lace bow clip for the occasion. 'That's quite thoughtful of you,' I said. 'Well you know, we have so many bow clips, it's the least I can do,' she said. I thanked her wondering if she thought we did not have a stack of bow clips at home too. With only one daughter I had gone overboard purchasing frilly dresses with hair decorations to match each dress. I had curled Tiffany's hair for the dress rehearsal and put in the bow clip. We waited backstage for the assigned dress and Tiffany wore tights and a tunic. The costume coordinator approached giving me a green velvet dress with excess pleats and white lace at the bottom. She then gave Garyanna's mother a cream lace dress for Garyanna. The mom looked absolutely distressed. A cream dress would never show on stage on a pale Garyanna. She looked at the beautiful green velvet dress that Tiffany was carefully stepping into. I then saw her mutter as she approached Tiffany and yanked the bow clip out of her hair.

She said she had decided that Garyanna needed the bow clip. 'Suit yourself,' I said. Tiffany frowned and came to me to complain. I told her she shouldn't worry. We would get a nice bow clip at home. I could not believe the competitive nature of the back stage mom, fighting over a simple dress. The girls had maybe three seconds of fame in a two hour performance. But, such was the psyche of the dance mom.

I joined a mom's ballet class that was advertised by the dance school as a way to keep fit. I think some of the mothers, like me, secretly wanted to be that ballerina on stage and never had the opportunity. I remember as a child, begging my mother to send me for ballet lessons. Her constant answer was that she had no time. She was a music teacher at a high school and on evenings after that job, she gave private piano lessons at home to all the kids in the neighbourhood. I was fortunate she gave me piano lessons but could not see it at the time. When I got older, I managed to get a Saturday morning part-time job playing piano at a ballet school in town. It was great pocket money for me, and I was able to come close to ballet dancers as they pranced around the room doing their routines. They all looked so graceful and proud. I secretly envied them because they appeared so confident.

When I saw the Mom's Ballet class advertised, I signed up right away. It was at 7:00 pm on a Wednesday evening. This worked out perfectly for me. I had enough time to come home from work, feed Tiffany and do homework with her. Then we left for my class. I would take Tiffany and she sat quietly in a corner observing the mothers. The first evening back home, Tiffany scolded me. 'Mommy you don't know how to point. That's not the way. You have to bend your foot like so ...' She showed me how I should bend my toes. My poor feet ached from the exercise and I wondered why we pointed and pointed. As the weeks wore on, I learned how to point and how to focus on a corner as we did turns to go in that direction.

I spoke to other mothers in the class to find out why they were taking ballet. Some had danced before, however others, like me had children in the dance school and decided to do ballet to keep fit. One mother who had married well and was home all day wanted to get out on evenings. Her husband watched the children while she did her own thing. At the time I was travelling a great deal to Latin America for work: a few days in Costa Rica one week, then Honduras the next. This mother asked me what I did and I told her I was a food scientist who travelled. She was intrigued by the idea of a single mother having a career and could not wait every week to grill me with questions about where I had travelled and what I had seen. Her interest was admirable, even though it was distracting during the one hour of instruction.

Church Moms

I did not get the same reception, however, when I joined the mom's club at my church. When we moved to the new neighbourhood, I decided to go to an Episcopal Church in Agoura Hills which was closer to my neighbourhood. After attending a few Sunday masses, I wondered how I could make new friends in the area. People left promptly after mass saying a quick hello to the priest who shook all hands at the front door as we left. One Sunday I stopped and told him I was new in the neighbourhood and wanted to make friends. Being a thoughtful man, he paused for a moment, looked at Tiffany and me, and then suggested I meet with the Mom's club. Apparently, they met once a fortnight at various homes in the neighbourhood. He felt it would be a good opportunity to bond with other mothers. I jumped at this idea and he gave me the name and number for the coordinator of the event. No children were allowed because the mothers were supposed to have a night off.

I called the organizer and took directions for the meeting the following week at Sally's house. We just had to bring a snack and get ready for lots of conversation. I had to travel early in the week, but I was free on the Friday evening they were meeting. A friend agreed to watch Tiffany for me when I went for the short social. As I approached the large house in Westlake, the wealth seemed to ooze from the lawn and front porch. I had feelings of inadequacies as I remembered my own modest little townhouse on the other side of town. What if these moms did not speak to me? What if few people came, then I would be forced to talk. What if it was overcrowded, then I may have been alone in the crowd with the familiar folks speaking only to people they knew.

As I rang the doorbell nervously, I wondered if I had made the right decision to go there. I could hear a tiny dog barking and running around near the front door. 'That's OK, that's OK,' I heard a woman's voice say as she approached the door. 'Hello, I'm Marge,' she said, as she opened the door and looked at me from head to toe. I had a lump in my throat but got the courage to speak up. 'Hi, I'm Lindy. I'm here for the Mom's club.' I feigned a smile of courage and held out my hand for a hand shake. I had been so used to greeting people in the formal business setting with a handshake that I could not get away from this. 'Come on in,' she said with a friendly smile. 'Come right this way. A few of the girls are here already.'

We entered a spacious hallway with plants and Marge led me to a sitting room which was off to one side of the main hall. Five other ladies were gathered there yapping away. Marge introduced me and in a whirlwind I heard everyone say their various names. 'Don't worry, we're going to do this again once everyone gets here,' said Marge. After chatting with the ladies, it appeared most had young or elementary school children, so we had some of the same experiences in child rearing. When everyone arrived, at least fifteen women were at the gathering. One of the organizers said we had to get together one day at the park. 'I usually take Johnny to the park to play at 11:00 on mornings,' she announced.

'Well, I'll join you over there,' another one chimed in and then another. I knew I would be in the office at that time, so I kept quiet. Most of the mothers did not work and were available at a moment's notice to go to parks and other places during the day. 'Let's do something for ourselves without the children!' one woman volunteered. 'Yes, that's right,' said another. 'Let's go scrapbooking.' I wondered what scrapbooking was and listened attentively. 'There's a new place on Lindero Canyon Road offering scrapbooking. They have all the materials. You just have to pay and go in with your stuff to assemble,' said one mom. 'OK,' chimed in one tall woman. 'Oh ... and if you have any talent at all, don't come!' she said, laughing hysterically while the others chimed in with laughter.

I didn't find anything funny about her statement. It confirmed to me the fact that some women felt worthless even to the point of putting together creative scrapbooks. I used to make scrapbooks to preserve memories of trips abroad or business trips. What was this woman speaking about when she said people with talent should not come? I was too talented and uptight to hang out with them. I was pulled out of my day dream when one woman asked what I did all day. I told her I worked for a large food company and frequently traveled to Latin America on business. She looked at me with pity and said, 'I feel so sorry for women like you who have to work.' 'What?' I asked, completely baffled by her pity. 'You feel sorry for me?' She confirmed, 'Yes, I used to work at a bank. I could not imagine having to get up everyday for work now I have a kid to take care of. My husband pays for everything, so I don't have to bother.'

Well, I felt insulted by her pity. I really enjoyed my job. I looked forward to the adventure of international travel and saw no benefit in looking at a small child all day long or wandering around the shopping centre while a child was in school. I could not wait to leave the mom's club event. I felt like I was stifling in their acceptance of a small life. I also made a decision never to go back to their meetings.

Ice Skating Moms

As Tiffany also participated in ice skating, it was another activity which saw the rage and desires of mothers manifested an all types of behaviour. I wondered who could be more competitive, dance moms or ice-skating moms. I jumped onto the bandwagon of over-anxious mothers as Tiffany progressed through the ranks of the ice skating classes. The toddlers went on through different levels after a ten-week session. They were supposed to come to the ice skating rink during free skating times to practice what they had learned. I took Tiffany dutifully to practice her moves and hoped she would advance quickly through the levels. One teacher said Tiffany was not yet ready to move on to the third level when she was six years old. I protested not knowing quite what was required. 'She needs to build her strength on the forward and backward moves,' said the instructor. 'Oh really,' I protested. 'Well, I think she's strong enough!'

I became as wild as many of the other ice-skating moms whom I criticised. I was envisioning my child skating at the Olympics at six years of age and felt the instructor was holding her back. I complained to another mom who would listen to me. 'I might have to take her out of ice skating. I can't believe she has not advanced,' said one mother complaining about her child. 'I don't think this activity is for her,' The mom continued out of breath. 'We may have to try music lessons or something. She's better at music.' I could not imagine her seven year old child being labeled a failure when her whole life was ahead of her with many years of classes. What did we mothers expect? I had to curb my own behaviour and let things move forward at the child's ability and talent.

One mother had her teenage daughter on the ice for at least two hours during the free skating time practicing her moves. The mother would come with a large blanket, popcorn, candy, and soda pop. She sat fixedly watching the child go through her paces. One day I decided to enquire what was going on. 'I pay for extra lessons for her every week,' the mom told me. 'She's going to make me a lot of money one day. You know how much money I spend on her classes?' I was afraid to ask. I knew group lessons were expensive enough, but private lessons must have cost a fortune. In addition, the dance outfits and time involved would have been exorbitant too. 'She had to come mornings to practice before school. They do ballet too for flexibility,' said the mom. I responded saying, 'That's really interesting.'

I felt sorry for the poor girl and was not sure if she would make it as a famous figure skater. She was a little on the chubby side and most figure skaters I'd seen in the past were slim and trim. The mother sat in a daze watching the child, eating popcorn and drinking soda. It was like a scene from a really bad movie. So, the main lesson I learned from some of the mothers in the area was to marry rich so I would not have to work. Don't think too hard or develop any talents because you don't need to be smart to be married. Above all, volunteer in the teacher's classroom so your child could get good grades and a key role in the school play when the teacher sees you're involved.

10

YOU MAY KISS THE BRIDE

Will He Ever Kiss Me?

A few weeks after we moved up to Via Colinas in Westlake Village, I discovered my choir buddy Sam also lived on Via Colinas. Was this fate or just a coincidence? I called him and he popped over for a visit one evening. He worked from home on his computer and sometimes went into a central office. He had a technology business with several other investors.

One day, Sam invited Tiffany and me to go with him to Shakespeare in the Park which was being held at the California Lutheran University. He said he went every year and everyone would be out with their blankets, food, wine and other goodies. It seemed like a wonderful way to spend the evening with him and I welcomed the opportunity to cuddle under a blanket in the cold night air. He came to pick us up an hour before show time so we could stake out a good spot on the grounds. 'The place fills up fast. We really must get there early if we want to be close to the stage,' he said. 'We're ready. We're ready. I've packed rolls, cheese, grapes, soft drinks, chocolates,' I said. 'Lindy we'll only be there three hours. You've packed food for a nation,' he said. 'Well, we might get hungry,' I said. Being perpetually hungry, if nobody else ate, I knew I would.

The campus grounds were beautiful, with large oak trees and lawns interspersed with modern concrete buildings. This was a private university and their funds were well spent providing beautiful surroundings for the students. We watched the outdoor play and huddled under the blankets to stay warm just like one big happy family. The next day Tiffany said, 'Mommy, I like Sam'. I said, 'I like him too. He's a good friend.' He was such a good friend that he never tried to touch me. He volunteered to come to the Los Angeles Caribbean Carnival with us, then to the Caribbean Treehouse restaurant in Inglewood for Trinidadian food. He had no problem spending hours with Tiffany and me going here and there. However, he never made any romantic advances.

One day I decided to make one last attempt to see if he was interested and then break ties to save myself the mental anguish. My sizeable tax return allowed me to buy a brand new Harmon Kardon stereo; the big rage at that time. Since Sam lived nearby my reasoning was that Sam could come to help me install the gadget. The sales people in the store had shown me everything, but I was going to try the "damsel in distress" approach to see if that would work. 'Hi Sam, how are you?' I asked. 'Just great. What's up?' he said. 'I just bought a new stereo and can't figure out what to do with it. There are tweeters, a subwoofer, turn table, amplifier, cassette player, and a million wires. Would you be able to help me install it in the wall unit?' 'Sure, would love to. Will pop over later,' he replied.

I dressed in really cute shorts and a T-shirt for Sam's visit. This was one of my vain attempts to get him into my home and get his attention. He worked away at the stereo for a while fiddling with all the wires and could not really put everything together. After a while he gave up and said he was going out with friends and would try it another day. The installation was not hard. I just wanted the new speakers and wiring to fit snugly into my wall unit. The amplifier, turn table and cassette player stacked one on top of the other in the middle of the wall unit. 'That's fine,' I said.

After he left, I put together the stereo by myself, passing the wires behind portions of the wall unit so they could be hidden. It did not take long. Finally we had a big stereo sound in the house. I realized Sam and I were just buddies and nothing more. Why didn't he make a move or try to kiss me? My attraction for him was obviously greater or different than his attraction for me. He just wanted to hang out. I decided to nip this in the bud since it was becoming more difficult to control myself around him.

The following week I got a call. 'Hey Jennylynd, do you wanna go check out the new movie theatre nearby this weekend?' he asked. 'So sorry, I already have plans for the weekend. Chat soon,' I said. That summer, Sam moved away to another neighbourhood in Moorpark. He called to tell me he had bought a house and moved. 'That's great for you. Stay in touch,' I said. I knew I would see him at choir practice but the feeling would not be the same. The best medicine for the upset soul was for me to go back online and find new people to date.

Next!

Party Time in Southern California

'Those are real! Those are fake! I spotted some falsies!' yelled Joanie at the top of her lungs as we danced on the outdoor patio at the bar on Lindero Canyon Road. 'What are you talking about,' I asked as the beat went on and on. 'That woman over there has fake boobs!' she explained. 'Can't you see? They're round. Do you have round boobs like that?' I had to admit my breasts were never round, even as a teenager. They just never grew that way. They pointed downwards in general and would never match the 'acceptable' round movie star creations with upturned nipples. 'Can't you tell the difference?' Joanie asked.

After Joanie pointed out the falsies to me, I became aware of the distance women would go to enhance themselves to appear favourable to men. I began to watch people even more at the clubs. Round breasts, fake tanned skin, false nails, false eyelashes, bleach blonde hair, botox to slow wrinkling, chemical facial peels, and of course skinny legs in a mini skirt with tall heels; these were the traits considered beautiful. Everybody was blonde; white, black, Hispanic, oriental; they were all bleach blonde. Some of my friends and I would never make the grade. However, we wore miniskirts with high heels. I had a wardrobe of miniskirts. I owned miniskirt suits for the corporate office. I even put a few high-lights in my hair but could not bring myself to go blonde. Not with my dark brown skin. It just would not look or feel right to me. My long skinny legs and red sports car were a step in the right direction for being considered beautiful in California.

We were always on a diet. I wondered if it was worth the effort. Despite starving and cutting out pasta, rice, potato, bread and other carbohydrates for a year, I still had curvy legs. I still had not been able to attract Mr. Right or be asked to be the MRS; the dream of every single woman I met. We went out frequently and we looked great, I thought. What was I really missing? In contrast, however, many men did not have a six pack stomach. The grey, bald, or corpulent general felt entitled to sport a skinny model on his arm, with little effort on his part to look good. Why were men allowed to have life so easy, while women agonized and spent a fortune on their looks?

A popular night spot was Wood Ranch restaurant. They played 70's Funk music one night a week. The gang decided we would go there every week and see if we could find some eligible bachelors. We would go after dinner time, just for the DJ and dancing. That way, we would not be stuck with a huge dinner bill. Jenna, Joanie, Mona and I met at 10:00 pm and managed to squeeze in a few hours of dancing.

'… Brick … house …' went the music… We screamed and jumped for joy. It was one of our favourite songs. All through the night we looked over our shoulders in case Mr. Right walked by. One or two hopefuls would pass through. If we were lucky, somebody would even speak and ask one of us for a dance. Most of the time, however, this did not happen. We still enjoyed the music though. Another hot spot was Bogies night club at Westlake Inn. This was supposed to be posh and pretty with the possibility of running into a movie star if we were lucky. Several PWP friends met there for Saturday night dancing and we combed the crowd for eligible bachelors and a star or two. The music was always loud and amazing; and we were guaranteed a night packed with dancing.

One night we spied one of the famous Baldwin brothers at the bar. Joanie yelled over the music, 'Don't look now … There's a Baldwin brother.' 'Which one is he?' I asked. 'Who cares? Let walk over there!' she said. We walked by and saw a few women desperately trying to make conversation. We then passed back again a few minutes later, pretending to be looking for drinks at the bar. We passed a third time and he was of course occupied with other hopefuls trying to strike up a conversation. 'Let's leave the poor man alone. I'm sure he's fed up with silly women chasing after him,' I said. We gave up the chase and continued dancing on another side of the room where other eligible men walk around aimlessly. We smiled at a few and managed to get a short dance. The California man was allergic to asking a girl to dance. He would rather stand on the side of the club looking cool and watching the women. What was this?

Joanie was not shy and would strike up a conversation with anyone. I confused myself with accomplishing The Rules, acting coy and waiting to be approached. It sometimes appeared like an exercise in futility. Our friend Mona who lived in Agoura Hills told us about a hot spot called Padri's Martini Bar. They offered a full menu and late night dancing. This was supposed to be even more special than the places we had frequented in Westlake Hills. Anything more special was worth investigating. Joanie and I pulled up in our miniskirts. Because parking was difficult, I suggested arriving in my car and I would take her home afterwards. Within a few hours, Joanie was dancing crazily with a new guy. She took a swig of martini and yelled, 'Woo hoo! I'm doing the nasty.'

She called grinding backwards on a guy, 'Doing the nasty.' It was an education in California lingo. After midnight, I was getting tired of the overpacked room and wondered when we would be heading home. Joanie seemed rather happy with her new find so I could not disturb her. I danced too but did not meet anyone interesting. By 1:00 am, people started clearing the room and heading home. Joanie said, 'You go on home. Rick will give me a ride!' 'What? Are you sure?' I asked, not trusting this new "Rick" and partially drunk Joanie to make it home at all. 'Don't worry. I'll call you tomorrow.' Reluctantly I left her and walked to my car driving home quickly. I had to give Anna the babysitter a ride home, so we put sleeping Tiffany in the car, drove over to Thousand Oaks, and then drove back. I was tired and fell asleep swiftly.

The next day I called Ms. Doing the Nasty to find out how she faired the night before. 'Oh, I have a headache. I must have had too much to drink,' said Joanie. 'Of course you did,' I agreed. 'You should have seen his big house. Oh my God!' she went on. 'You went to his house? Are you nuts? What happened?' I asked. 'Nothing happened. He lived nearby and wanted to show off his place,' she said. 'Of course he did and a lot more,' I chimed in. She continued, 'After I walked around to see the place, I told him I couldn't stay. Imagine, he wanted me to stay over!' This was an obvious follow up. 'Of course he did,' I confirmed, not quite understanding her naive revelation. 'Well I told him I'm not that kind of girl. He had to bring me home right away,' she said. 'Well you're lucky he brought you home,' I said relieved. 'Oh he's a great guy. I can tell if someone is good or not,' said Joanie. I was worried about Joanie when she had too much to drink. Fortunately, everything worked out fine.

Fran, a friend from the McGill Alumni Association sang in a small pop band and invited me to come to Dr. Dan's party at a big house in the Valley. 'It's an *Industry party*,' she said. I wondered what was an *Industry Party*? I asked a PWP friend

Jenna and she suggested it was a movie industry party. Since I was not going to anything like that alone, Jenna suggested she go with me and we would dress like "Industry Types". I dressed in leopard patterned leggings and wore a black and gold halter top. My hair was worn long with a few curls and I put on stage make up. It was a bit excessive, but one never knew who one would bump into at the *Industry Party*. Jenna who was always ready for a laugh decided to dress like a 1970's hippie. She was quite pale with short blonde curly hair with light blue eyes. She was tall and skinny and could readily pass for a movie star. Jenna wore a dashiki and a head band with a *Peace and Love* sign prominently displayed at the front. The outfit was a bordering on crazy. We did not know anyone so it did not matter. 'Let the *Industry people* try to figure out who we are,' she said.

We drove in my red Mitsubishi Eclipse to the Valley. It was all about creating impressions and illusions. When we located the address, we drove past the house twice to scope out the place and also to be noticed in a red sporty car. It was a large house from what we could see. The white Mediterranean style house had a red tiled roof and beautiful sub-tropical landscaping. All the houses on the street were large and imposing. The wall was not too tall so it was possible to observe from afar. People were stationed at the imposing gates sitting at table going through names on a list of paper as people approached. Hopefully my name would be on the list as my friend Fran promised.

Jenna and I walked up. 'Hello ladies. Are you here for Dr. Dan's party?' asked one of the young men. 'Yes,' I chirped. 'Jennylynd James and one guest.' He searched the list. 'James … James … Yes I see it. Welcome to the party. Please add your name to the email list. Drinks are at the bar in the back yard and food is in the kitchen.' I wrote my email on a long list and was informed I would get a notice for the next party. 'OK. Thanks a lot,' I said. We were thinking drinks and food, just like that? Who was this Dr. Dan who would invite random people to his house? Would we even see him? We walked around the back yard and got some soda. Neither of us drank alcohol. We then walked round and round the house observing the guests and trying to look important. When we went inside we saw various dips and finger food on tables and kitchen counters. The food looked well picked over, so we did not touch it. Eating before leaving the house had been a good idea.

It was a funny game. Most people were dressed in casual party clothes. I could not distinguish anyone famous, but then I seldom recognised stars. I was just not that interested. We followed the sound of music as a live band started up. It was Fran and her friends singing Rock and Roll songs in the living room. Many were dancing and jumping around so we did a little dance as well. 'Hi Fran,' I said as we got close to the front. 'Great party.' She was concentrating on her words and did not say anything to me. How could she say hello mid song? 'Yah yah yah. Blah Blah Blah.' The band was OK for a house party, but couldn't make it on the big stage though.

We continued walking around from room to room looking at people who were obviously familiar with each other. They gossiped about nothing and we tried a few times to join in. It was amusing when some party goers spotted me and tried to guess who I was. 'Oh yes, isn't that what's her name? From the film? You know …' said one observer. 'Yes, I think it's her,' said the other. I just smiled, put my nose in the air and continued walking ahead to nowhere. Jenna and I had a good laugh. The place was filled with industry hopefuls, hoping to meet someone important. We acted our parts well until we got tired of them and decided to head home. It was however, a happy and interesting experience. I was on Dr. Dan's email list for life and continued to get invitations to frequent parties. We never went back and I'm still wondering who was Dr. Dan.

Cosmetology to the Rescue

I made friends with Borzena, a Polish cosmetologist whose daughter was in class with Tiffany. We bonded instantly one day, as we dropped our daughters off to school. She was a single mother and lived in our neighbourhood just up the hill at Via Colinas. My ex-husband was Polish, and I had learned to recognize the accent. When I heard her speak one day, I decided to impress her by saying a few greetings in the Polish language. 'Oh, where did you learn to speak like that? That's amazing,' she said. And our friendship began. Borzena was tall and chemically blonde with a short haircut. She was stylish and beautiful. Every casual outfit was accentuated with a matching scarf around the neck. She worked as a cosmetologist at a nearby clinic and also attended to clients in her home. We enjoyed chatting regularly and I asked her to explain what she did.

She would see clients at the clinic who wanted facial peels and Botox injections. 'De ladies, dey have ah lat ah money and dey wantah to look yang,' she explained. 'We are helping dem.' This was a world I knew nothing about. 'What's the Botox injection,' I asked naively to get more information. 'It stops the skin from wrinkling. But dis is temporary my dear. You have to come back to do it again and again. Look I used it on my forehead,' she explained. I couldn't see anything. I guessed the clients at the clinic had enough money to keep coming back. 'I want to have my own business and leave that clinic,' she explained. She already had clients coming to do facials and hair removal.

'I wax everywhere,' Borzena explained. 'I wax eyebrows, under-arms, legs, pussy, everywhere.' I shuddered. 'What? Waxing is too scary. I just use a razor.' 'No darling, waxing is better. You come one day and I will do your eyebrows.' The thought of using warm wax to remove hair was frightening for me, even as an adult. I was unwilling to go through that pain to be beautiful. As single mothers, we enjoyed trading stories of being divorced and survival. We also traded dating stories. We started planning activities with our daughters on weekends and did not mind visiting Ventura town for dinner on a Sunday, or the art show at the waterfront in Santa Barbara on the weekend. I liked exploring and learning about new places and Borzena was a willing adventurer. She taught me about the fancy shops at Melrose Place in Los Angeles. 'Come on darling. We are window shopping.' I enjoyed watching her play with store clerks trying on clothing and shoes, knowing she could not afford to buy them.

'I weel let ah you know,' she would say with her heavy European accent. They seemed impressed by the accent and she had fun playing with them. I wanted to learn how to create the same elusion. I was usually too shy to try on something I could not afford. I looked at Borzena and took lessons. We visited Chinatown in Los Angeles one Sunday afternoon and had dim sum with the girls. We could not squeeze into the clothes from Hong Kong. They were beautiful but way too petite for us. Even their extra-large was a challenge. I managed to find a beautiful double-sided warm velvet jacket that fit me. Borzena encouraged me to buy it. She knew I worked for a decent salary at the big company, so she would always say, 'Buy it Buy it. You have only one life.' I was on a tight budget and always resisted buying. At a vintage clothing store in Ventura City, I tried on two dresses from the 1950's and there she was, 'Buy them, buy them!' I bought them and wondered what I had just done.

Tiffany and Borzena's daughter, Alana came home crying from school one day. Every year the school hosted a Daddy Daughter Dance. It was advertised for weeks before the event. Some people rented a limousine and photos were advertised for sale after the event. The event was dreaded by any single mother. I wrote a letter to the school protesting about the drama it caused our children; the ones who were being raised without a father. The school never responded to my letter. I wondered if it was worth pursuing the matter with the district school board. Surely, we could not have been the only single parents at that school. Were we in the minority? I did not pursue it any further and waited the four weeks of build up and aftermath to die down. It was a painful time for me as my child cried everyday when she returned home.

'Everyone has a daddy. Everyone is coming to the dance except me. Waahhh.' Poor Tiffany; I tried to console her saying, Alana would not be going to the dance either, but this did not matter. Borzena and I decided to take the girls out that night to celebrate them as individuals and show our appreciation for them. It was a great distraction until the following day at school when photos were distributed for purchase and the pain started all over again.

Borzena would sometimes get invitations to interesting parties. 'Come with me to a fund-raising party at a big house in Brentwood. Who knows, maybe we will meet a rich man. It's Brentwood darling!' I was so excited. 'OK, I'm in. We should really be out there trying to meet a rich man,' We arrived in my red Mitsubishi Eclipse. Wearing trendy miniskirts and high heeled shoes would have been a great idea if we were to be delivered by a driver to the front door. However, we had to park far down the street and endure the painful walk in those beautiful shoes and the chilly night air on our legs. 'Don't worry darling, we look fabulous. Chin up and a big smile,' encouraged Borzena.

I paid at the door begrudgingly. I was a bit of a cheapskate parting with large sums of money for a miscellaneous event. Borzena did not have to pay because her employer at the clinic was one of the sponsors of the event. The large Mediterranean-style house was beautiful with a landscaped front of large palms and sub-tropical shrubs. The reception area led directly into a lavishly decorated room. Tables were filled with trays of finger food, dips, and other delicious morsels. We walked around smiling and exchanging pleasantries with those we met. It was a party of mostly well dressed beautiful women, and a few reluctant partners or husbands came along. It was all about cosmetics and beauty products. I should have known. Borzena met some of her wealthy clients from the clinic. They were all happy to see her and gave big hugs, even if their expressionless faces could barely smile.

Every ticket purchased entitled the attendee to a chance in the raffle. Several gift baskets were up for grabs. The first number was called and I looked with hope at my ticket–It was not mine. A second number was called, offering a basket of natural cosmetics made of fruit extracts. Suddenly, I realized it was my number. I screamed and ran up with my ticket to collect the hamper. It was a night well spent.

Hot Tub Party

The parties continued around Conejo Valley and in the San Fernando Valley; any event that promised gaining access to the wealthy were a draw for our group. In the end, we were a group of hopefuls aspiring to reach the wealthy but not quite getting there. We desperately wanted to catch the elusive and wealthy Mr. Right but never met him. We went to a Casino night fundraiser at a PWP friend's huge house. I knew absolutely nothing about blackjack or other casino games and so walked around gossiping with attendees and ogling this man's big house. He had a young girl friend who lived there too, so other hopefuls like me also stared at her and wondered why, why, why? Everybody loved going to Mona's house for a party. Mona had a big hot tub on the deck and the word around PWP was that people were known to go skinny dipping if they got really drunk. It was a party to go to, so I went.

Joanie knew where all the 'almost rich' people lived and which parties we should go to. One of her young friends, Glenn lived with his parents in the San Fernando Valley. One Friday, we got word that Glenn's parents were abroad on a trip. Before I knew it, a group of PWP friends were hosting a party at Glenn's parents' home because they had a pool and a hot tub. 'Bring a dish and your swim suit,' Joanie advised. 'You never know who'll show up.' Who was Glenn and why were we at his parents' home partying? I met a few random men but nobody I would be interested in. Joanie was eyeing a new prospect called Mike. He was an attractive stocky man with brown, curly hair. He did not speak much, but he didn't need to. 'I'm only giving up myself to serious contenders,' Joanie warned him loudly and anyone else in earshot. He knew where he stood, I imagined. But she stared at him a great deal that night. I believed she liked that one.

We partied in the pool and managed to squeeze at least fourteen into the hot tub. However, after a while I realized I was the only sober one and got bored with the nonsense conversations of the inebriated. I called it a night and bid them farewell. 'Have fun guys!' With Joanie entertaining and giving jokes, I knew the party would go on late. Thus was the life of party-goers around town.

The Land of Happy People

'Abre la maleta,' said the skinny customs officer as he stared at me. His co-workers stared even more. I had arrived in Puerto Plata, Dominican Republic after a long flight from Los Angeles to Miami, changing airlines to fly to Puerto Plata. I was tired and hungry and in no mood for games. The customs people, I suspected were trying to determine what language I spoke. They probably thought I was Haitian. A black Haitian was treated with scant courtesy in Dominican Republic where the population was a mixture of Spanish and African. I opened my bag without uttering a word. The officer moved the clothing and notebooks around, still staring at my face. His colleagues also stared. I was wearing a light green pantsuit with short sleeves. The heat was unbearable and I was glad I had worn light clothing. After a minute of quasi searching I had to speak up.

'Are you done?' I asked after he wasted my time. 'Aha ... Ingles, Ingles,' he confirmed to his buddies, and they sent me on my way. I made a note to myself, 'Never return to Dominican Republic where the customs people treat you like a criminal unless you are a confirmed tourist.' As I stepped through the exit, I looked around for a sign with my name. The owner of the farm I was visiting assured me his driver, Luis, would be at the airport to collect me. I looked around anxiously for Luis not knowing who I was looking for. The taxi drivers pounced, as is typical in any tourist country. 'Taxi? Taxi? Taxi lady?'

'No thanks,' I said in English. Even though I spoke enough Spanish to get by, it was evident one would get more respect as a foreign tourist than trying to blend in as a local. Within two minutes, Luis approached with his sign. He was a tall, skinny man with a long nose, light brown skin, and lips that formed a small pout. A good looking man by all standards, I thought I would interrogate Luis to find out his life story. 'Jenny Lee?' He asked to confirm. 'Hello. Are you Luis? Good to meet you,' I said and shook his hand. I wanted to thank him for rescuing me from the persistent taxi drivers who were convinced I needed help. Luis did not speak much English. This was fine for me since I wanted to practice speaking Spanish. We loaded my one large suitcase and set off for the hotel.

I had made a reservation online for an all-inclusive resort next to the sea and close to the town of Puerto Plata. It was convenient for getting to and from the airport. However, according to Francis, the owner of the farm it was far; at least one and a half hours' drive. Even though Francis tried to persuade me to stay at his "beautiful and elaborate" mansion on the farm, the thought of being stuck in the middle of nowhere and at the mercy of a farm owner was frightening.

We spoke briefly on the phone before my visit. The big company was sending me to conduct food safety audits of this new tropical fruit supplier in Dominican Republic. I was to inspect the farm, the packhouse and all their food safety documents to ensure everything was in compliance. We did not want any food safety issues as the Food and Drug Administration had started monitoring foreign imported fruit more regularly for pathogens. 'You ah can ah stay at my mansion at dah farm. Eet is safe. I have ten vicious dogs that are released every night to guard the area,' said Francis with confidence. This statement however, struck the fear of God in me. Who would want to be stuck on a farm in the hinterland and not be able to take an evening stroll because of the ten vicious dogs? Yikes! Was this man crazy? I feared for my life.

'No thanks Francis. I'll stay at a hotel in town.' 'But eet ees a long drive to zee farm. You will have to leave early to save time.' 'That's fine with me. I'm an early riser,' I assured him. When we got to the hotel, it was a completely walled resort with security at the gate. They opened the gate and we drove in. I checked in at the front desk and was directed to the building with my room. There was a series of buildings on the grounds. Some rooms were near the beach. Others housed the main dining area and other facilities. The main building at the front also had some shops and a private restaurant. All buildings were painted in white, beige and other light bright colours and the lawn and gardens with tropical shrubs I recognised from childhood, were neatly manicured.

Luis advised he would meet me at 6:30 am the next morning to drive to the farm. I would have to eat breakfast when we got out there. I bid him farewell and walked away to find my room. It was already nightfall, but I could see the tropical flowers and plants in the gardens around the swimming pool. They reminded me of my home country of Trinidad and Tobago. After leaving chilly California in the winter, it was good to get away to a warmer climate with warm sea water. My room was on the ground floor right next to the beach. That was what I had booked. Sadly, however, it was night and I had to go to bed for an early rise. There was no swimming for me that night. The room was basic, but comfortable. I turned on the air conditioning and within a short time, fell asleep.

I set my alarm for 5:30 am and was up in time to dress and get my paper work ready. It was too early for the breakfast buffet at the main dining hall. I had a little snack left over in my handbag, because I was quite hungry. Luis was already at the front desk at 6:30 am sharp waiting for me. People had risen early and were making their way to work as we passed through Puerto Plata. West of the town we entered more rural regions. The farm was located in the west of Dominican Republic, near the Haitian border.

As we drove, I tried to make small talk in Spanish. My vocabulary was limited to food safety words, just enough to train staff in hand washing. However, trying to keep a conversation about the weather, family, and politics during the long drive was a challenge. I observed people along the way. They swept away dirt and grime at the front of their homes. Even the yard was swept to remove stray leaves. Everyone appeared contented. One sight I would never forget was the mopeds. People owned more mopeds than cars. In fact I saw a whole family on a moped; mother, father and two small children squeezed in between them snugly. Nobody wore helmets. In the United States wearing helmets was the law. Were these people crazy? Did they know how unsafe it was to ride like that; especially with small children? I became really bothered by them.

However, everyone was smiling and happy. What were they all so happy about? They had no money for a car. The more I looked, people, seemed to have ready smiles and talked and laughed with each other as they passed along the roadway. What a difference it was to the environment I had left in Southern California. People there had large homes and luxury cars of every brand imaginable. And yet they always seemed to be in a hurry. People in Southern California always honked their horns impatiently at the slightest hesitation at a traffic light. For me it was incredible and moving to observe people with little material possessions really enjoying their lives. I made mental notes to enjoy whatever I had completely. In Dominica Republic, people were happy and they did not have half my possessions. If we could acquire a small fraction of their happiness, we would be on the right track.

After an hour on main roadways, we veered onto country roads and then onto a dirt road. Along the way, we passed a few sad looking black people in what looked like rags. Luis said they were Haitian migrant workers who crossed the border looking for work. They provided cheap labour for all the farms in the area. I could tell these people were not from Dominican Republic. They did not have the same happy, smiling faces. They had the look of pain and poverty. What a difference in such a small land mass. When we got to the farm, we drove through the big gates. We drove past a packhouse and farm buildings, and then we passed a white woman in a khaki outfit with tall boots. She waved at us and Luis informed me that she and her husband owned the farm. She was from France. That was interesting. Someone from France owned a fruit farm in the hinterlands of Dominican Republic. We then drove along another dirt road until we came upon a big house. It was a Mediterranean-style dwelling with whitewashed walls and a red tiled roof. As we entered the main doorway, we were greeted by a short, dark skinned man with big eyes and a bald head. 'Hello Jennylynd. How are you? Welcome. Welcome.'

'Hello Francis. Pleased to meet you.' Francis was of Ethiopian descent and had moved to Dominican Republic via Europe with his wife to start this farm. We had spoken briefly on the phone before my trip so it was good to meet face to face. We crossed the courtyard to the dining room. The central courtyard was still under construction. A beautiful tiled water fountain was being installed in the middle. I had hunger pangs and hoped something would be ready for us to eat before I collapsed. I was not disappointed. Francis led me to a dining room where the table was set and ready to serve a meal. 'Would you like porridge? Would you like eggs? What would you like? We employ the best chef in the country here! An award-winning chef,' he boasted. I found it hard to believe an award-winning chef would want to work at a farm house, however, for the right price, anything was possible.

'I think I'll have the standard hot breakfast thanks; eggs, sausage and toast if you have it,' said Francis. 'Yes we have everything.' He introduced me to Felix, the chef and then gave him instructions in Spanish. Felix disappeared to cook everything swiftly. The breakfast was ready in ten minutes and I ate ravenously. I had no idea what time lunch would be served and I was always hungry. When we finished eating, Francis said we would take a tour of the packhouse where I could audit operations and observe the workers. It was a short drive from the house. The workers were well prepared for the big bad auditor from America. Everyone looked crisp and clean and watched me with great suspicion. They were extra nervous and careful. All supervisors were well rehearsed and knew all the correct answers. A handwash monitor was stationed near the bathroom where workers were observed soaping and washing hands carefully before re-entering the packhouse. The monitor would give the employee a card. This card was presented to another monitor at the entrance to the packhouse. This was an excellent show for me and I wondered if they could keep it up after I left.

I walked around the area with my clip board looking for hygiene issues and observing the employees. They were well-dressed with overalls and hair nets and took great care to wash fruit before it was packed in cartons. I found minimal issues to report. As I took notes, Francis followed me all the way apologizing for any omissions and giving the employees the "evil eye". Poor them–I imagined the calm looking man may have had a crazy side to him. He took cigarette breaks to calm himself and I hoped the day would pass swiftly. After about four hours, we took a lunch break. It was back to the mansion for a feast. We passed a large hut which was the kennel for the big dogs. Good for the dogs. I was glad I didn't have to see them. At lunch time, a nanny brought around two beautiful looking children who hugged their papa and played happily in the courtyard. The boy and girl looked at me wondering who I was and we were introduced to each other.

The award winning chef prepared delicious fish dishes and vegetables. We dined heartily and I had difficulty standing up to return to work. "Are you sure you would not stay at the house?' asked Francis, 'The food is good.' I confirmed, 'That's fine thank you. I'm comfortable at the hotel.' It was always best to be independent of a client, I thought. We inspected the area outside of the packhouse and I then checked all the documentation for the packhouse and farming operations. The following day, we planned to audit the farms and observe farm staff. At 5:00 pm, it was time to return to the hotel. Luis appeared just in time and whisked me away for the long drive back.

When we arrived it was still daylight. Luis said he would collect me early next morning and he was off. The last few sun worshipers were lounging lazily at the pool before dinner. I walked briskly with my bag and my long hair blowing in the wind. At least a dozen white foreign men sitting at the pool watched me hungrily like dogs as I crossed poolside to go to my room. I imagined they were trying to secure a poor local for a night of sex. It was a frightening revelation. I walked swiftly to my room trying to avert the stares and winks. I vowed not to venture near the pool again for any reason. The local girls and staff in general, whether they were in the sex trade or not, must have had a difficult time beating off the tourists. "Sun, Sea, and Fun" included all options in the tourist's mind and I knew it well from strange situations in other countries where I was offered drugs as a tourist.

That night I planned to have a quick dinner at the dining room, alone, and then run straight back to my room. If any stranger approached me, I was to beat him off with my big handbag or a stick. I was not sure if I was too tired, or paranoid, or both. As I approached the dining room, I saw three skinny white girls in their twenties eating at a table with one free chair. 'May I join you?' I asked so I could belong to the group. I was a bit concerned about sitting alone and thus drawing attention to myself. 'Of course! Sit down. We have loads of space,' they chimed almost unanimously with strong British accents. They were flight attendants spending the night in Puerto Plata. The food was basic and some dishes over-cooked and of poor quality. It was different to the best food prepared by the chef during the day. I befriended the girls and we spoke about the differences of life in Britain and America. None of them had acrylic nails. I told them many of my friends in California said I needed acrylic nails to look beautiful. How could this be a priority? The girls were going out for drinks after dinner so I excused myself and went to the room. I was only able to stay awake for half an hour writing up my report and promptly went to sleep.

I set the alarm for 5:00 am with the grand plan of waking up early to take a dip in the ocean. My room was a few paces from the shore and I was determined to get a swim in the warm sea before spending the rest of the day at a farm. I jumped out of bed promptly at 5:00 am put on my swim suit and ran into the water. It felt beautiful and warm, like a tepid bath. The water was still. No wave rocked the ocean. The air was still and a few lights in front of the veranda of each beach front hotel room was the only sign of life. I must have been the only living soul in the water at that time. The security guard on patrol looked alarmed as he walked by to see what was happening. Had he never seen a woman in the water at 5:00 am? I came out the water, said good morning in Spanish and reached for my camera which was on the banister of my porch.

'Here you go. Take a photo of me,' I said, handing the astonished security guard my camera. I posed in the spotlight of the porch on the sand in my wet swim suit. 'Muchas Gracias!' I said, and went into my room to get ready for my day at the farm before he could ask any questions. I must have been a puzzling spectacle. Why madam why? His eyes seemed to say.

I was ready in time for my 6:30 am pick up at reception and greeted the morning with a new freshness after my dip in the ocean. The drive did not seem as long as the previous day. When we got to the "mansion" the chef was ready to take my breakfast order. Francis and his wife joined me for breakfast. I ate ravenously and after a few pleasantries we began our tour around the farms. The day was spent observing the placement of portable toilets and harvesting operations. Many of the field workers looked like the poor, sad Haitians I saw along the roadway. They were stranded souls hoping to make a meagre living, harvesting in the fields.

I asked Francis to show me how workers would use the portable toilets since I had not seen many of them placed around the fields. He muttered something in Spanish to the supervisor and workers formed a long line to enter the toilet. They then came out one by one to demonstrate how they could wash their hands. It was an elaborate show for me, but it was evident some of them had never used a portable toilet before. A number of people did not know where to find the soap and had obviously not received instruction on this. I told Francis they would have to step up on the hygiene for field staff. It was a vulnerable point in the operation since contamination of the fruit in the fields with dirty hands may not be removed even with adequate washing with chlorinated water in the packhouse. Francis was furious as I made notes about this point. 'It will be fixed,' he assured me. After visiting more farms and having lunch, it was time to head back to the hotel. My flight was the following afternoon so I had a morning to explore if I wanted. Francis said Luis would be available to take me around sightseeing if I was interested. Of course I was interested. We parted amicably and I promised to send a report of my findings on returning to California.

Next morning, I had arranged for a 10:00 am pick up. I had enough time to experience the buffet breakfast, as well as take a swim in the sea during daylight hours. It was a wonderful leisurely morning before checking out of the hotel. Luis collected me for a tour around Puerto Plata. He pointed out government buildings of significance. We visited the Amber museum. This part of the country was famous for amber and larimar, a blue form of amber. The history of amber formation and other displays were informative. When we got to the gift shop, I looked longingly at many of the beautiful pieces of jewellery made with amber and larimar. The larimar was particularly pretty with its soft blue colour. I held up a silver chain with three pieces of larimar to my neck and looked in a mirror.

'Isn't it beautiful,' I said to the store clerk who then brought out a pair of little earrings which she said would go really well with the necklace. 'I wish I could buy them,' I said, 'But I can't.' I was about to hand them back to the store clerk when Luis said in Spanish, 'Do you want them?' I smiled and he said that the boss said to "give her anything she wants." I could imagine Francis's big eyes trying to butter me up. I knew from an ethical standpoint I should not accept gifts of jewellery from the company's client. It could be seen as accepting a bribe. However, I so wanted the jewellery and had no money to buy it. 'Well,' I said. 'If it's OK with Francis, I'll take them.'

Luis paid the store clerk for the little chain and earrings and I put them on right away. I didn't think they were expensive but I never checked the price. Like a child, I was basking in the glory of my new jewellery. We then went near the waterfront and I spied a strange noisy machine on a pickup truck with a few people in line waiting to buy a drink. The man was putting stems of sugarcane into the machine and it was squeezing the sugarcane stems to get out the juice which was collected and served to customers. 'Do you want juice,' asked Luis. 'Of course. I'll try it.' I had tasted sugarcane juice many years before. The flavour takes getting used to but they served it with ice, so the drink was refreshing on a hot day.

After this we visited Fort San Felipe, the old Spanish fort at the waterfront. We took the tour of the fort and I had Luis take my photograph at various vantage points to capture the beauty of the fort. Poor Luis, he had to be agreeable to everyone the boss brought into town for a visit. He was a great host, however. I even got a picture sitting on a donkey when an opportunist selling rides on his donkey passed by to tempt tourists. The last stop before heading to the airport was the seaside market at Sosua Beach. We had to by-pass the exit to the airport and go east to Sosua. Behind the beach was a long line of shacks with artisan jewellery makers, artists, crafts people and other bric a brac. Everyone had something to sell. I eventually settled on a tiny coral necklace for Tiffany and we ran out of time. I thanked Luis profusely for giving the grand tour of the area and it was back to California. The first trip to Dominican Republic was memorable. I was to follow up and ensure that all corrective actions in my report were implemented.

Granny's Rule

My grandmother used to say, 'Never marry below your station'. We would laugh at granny's saying and tell her she was so old-fashioned. In reality she was right in her assessment of men and their egos. The Rules had said to open up slowly to men and this meant not inviting them into your personal space too early in a relationship because one would be judged in many different ways. I was learning about the fragility of the Californian man's ego by experimenting in conversations with suitors I met online. I found that if I told a man about my academic or work achievements, I would get silence, or a doubtful, 'Oh really?' I would never be asked on date.

One day I decided to assume the "Dumb blonde" role. I raised the pitch of my voice and giggled incessantly throughout a telephone conversation with a suitor. When asked what I did for a living, I said, 'Well, like, I work with food … uh, you know.' I then giggled again. I never said I was a Senior Manager of Corporate Quality Assurance with responsibility for food safety programs in divisions in South America and North America. That would certainly have killed the conversation and any potential for a date. My suitor after hearing the giggling said he found me to be a beautiful woman. He decided I was the kind of woman he really wanted to take out to dinner. He had never seen me, but deduced from my voice I was a beautiful woman!

I played along with the game and met a young fellow, Ted, for two dates. The first time for a simple coffee and a chat at a coffee shop on Westlake Promenade. The next occasion, it was for a drink at a local bar. I was careful to keep all new suitors away from my home for security reasons and to protect my privacy. Westlake had the reputation of being a wealthy neighbourhood. If the man lived in a dive, his ego would be bruised by seeing my townhouse in Westlake Village. Ted seemed like a reasonable man and we spoke cordially about life in Los Angeles and surrounding areas when we met. He lived somewhere in the San Fernando Valley and came out to Westlake to see me. Ted was 5 feet 10 inches tall with a medium length brown hair. He had no distinguishing features and could be easily missed in a crowd. However, he was pleasant and easy going so I thought he could possibly make a good partner.

On our second date I noticed Ted was well-dressed in a shirt and tie, with neat black trousers. 'So Ted, what do you do?' I asked, being impressed by his smart appearance. It was the dreaded question that had to be asked to ascertain whether a person was upwardly mobile or living off government assistance. 'Well', he said, 'Right now my day job is selling men's shoes at an upscale store in the Valley. But I'm taking acting lessons.' I was amused by the conversation and said, 'Oh really,' predicting what would come next. 'I'm going to be famous in Hollywood,' he said. Yes you and a million other hopefuls, I thought to myself. I thought about his words, 'My day is job selling men's shoes.' Then I said, 'Yes, I'm sure it's a really fancy shoe store.'

In the back of my head, I assumed his day job, was his job. I also kept hearing my grandmother's voice, 'Never marry below your station'. I tried to ignore images of my grandmother saying 'Station …' I also tried to ignore the fact that I could not see myself with a shoe salesman who might one day make it in Hollywood. Oh well, I decided to still go out with Ted. He was a nice man, however I continued corresponding online with a few other suitors just to keep my options open. The following week, Ted asked me to go out to dinner. He must have been paid that week if he was asking me out to dinner. I suggested the Olive Garden which had a moderately priced menu, in sympathy with Ted's supposed meagre pay-check. I really wanted to go to Macaroni Grill, one of my favourites on the Westlake Promenade. However, I knew their prices would have been a challenge. I felt since Ted and I had gone out twice before, I could let him pick me up at home. There should be no harm in this.

He arrived promptly at 6:30 pm as scheduled and I was ready. I only had to put on my shoes. When Ted pressed the doorbell I let him in and asked him to have a seat so I could put on my heels. He did not sit down. Instead, he decided to look at all my paintings and photographs on the walls and then my certificates. I forgot I had my academic certificates mounted and he had a good read. He seemed to turn green with shock when he saw my Ph.D. Certificate. It was obvious he did not know what it meant.

'Doctor of Philosophy? Oh Shit Doctor of Philosophy?!' he yelled. 'Yes,' I said calmly. 'Let's go now. I'm ready.' He continued, 'You mean you're a doctor of philosophy? Oh my God! I can't believe this. What was it like studying philosophy? You mean you're a philosopher?' He could not curb his excitement and I tried to guide him away from the topic. 'Well, I did not really study philosophy,' I told him. 'Oh shit,' he said. 'I did not know I was out with a philosopher!'

I wanted to say, I did not know I was out with an idiot. He missed the lower part of the certificate that said Food Science. However, this was written in Latin, so he would never have understood it anyway. I asked him to change the subject during dinner, but could tell he was visibly shaken. When we got back home after dinner, Ted gave me a hug and said, 'Take care.' I never heard from him again and I never called him.

Bad Romance

Ms. Red Car Long Legs returned to the drawing board of

internet dating. This time I was determined to meet a professional man. The criteria were simple enough: a man who was well-travelled , who had many university degrees and would not be bothered by my academic qualifications and job. I had to meet a professional and give up on the idea that a good-looking guy would be happy with me no matter what. The male ego was fragile. While perusing DateMaker.com, I came across Matthew's profile. He was an engineer with a prominent company and he lived in Santa Monica. His story seemed to offer potential. I thought maybe we could be attracted to each other simply because we were foreign professionals. He highlighted that he was British. After exchanging phone numbers online, we chatted briefly a few times and decided to meet. I was to look for a tall white guy with black, curly hair and glasses. I told him to look for a tall black girl with long hair.

We arranged our first meeting at the Starbucks Café in the Barnes and Noble bookstore on Westlake Boulevard. I hoped there weren't too many tall white males with black, curly hair that day at the store because I was not prepared to walk up to each, and ask if he was Matthew. I was going to try to do The Rules with this prospect, but could not promise myself to be patient. I arrived in the parking lot at the Westlake shops ten minutes early so I sat in my car for the short time to calm my nerves and practice 'acting coy and pretty'. It felt worse than a job interview. At least with a job interview, there was the prospect of an increase in salary and work responsibilities. With the dating scene, the prospect of meeting Mr. Right and potential husband seemed out of reach and close to impossible. Did every date have to be a potential husband? It was a tough question to answer, but every single woman I knew was looking for a potential husband, so I felt I should also be looking for one too.

I walked around the book shelves next to the café pretending to look at books while scoping out the clients. I spied a tall white male with curly black hair, bushy black eyebrows and glasses. He wore a black leather jacket and was a good "Matthew" candidate. However, I remembered from The Rules book we should also let the man make the first move. I decided that instead of running up to him with a big hello, I would smile at the wind and look approachable. He looked over at me and I smiled then continued looking at a cobweb on the shelf. Would he ever come over to say hello? What was he waiting for? My palms were sweating. Engineers had a reputation of being either socially awkward or too wild. I wondered which he would be. The website had a lot of single engineers.

Eventually the curly-haired fellow came across. 'Hello. Are you Lindy?' he asked. 'Yes. Are you Matthew? I wasn't sure,' I said. I shook his hand and he awkwardly suggested we sit. 'Would you like a cup of tea?' he asked. 'Yes thanks,' I said. We found seats near the window and he went to get our tea. I checked out his body. He was about six feet tall. If I wore high heels I could still look up to him, so that was a bonus. He looked physically fit; no beer belly or double chin. And he had a full head of bushy hair. Well, in my mind he qualified from a physical standpoint as husband and baby making material. The next test was to see if we had anything in common and could have a decent conversation. I struggled to control my nerves. Remaining calm in front of a potential bed buddy was extremely important.

When Matthew returned with our tea, we spoke about our British education. That was one thing in common. Like me, he had completed Cambridge Ordinary level and Advanced Level exams in high school. We agreed that the British exams were way better than the America high school system and that was our first bonding. Matthew sang bass with a Classical music choir in Los Angeles and I told him I sang soprano with the Ventura Master Chorale. We could actually talk about singing and upcoming concerts! For me it was a match made in heaven.

I threw caution to the wind, forgot The Rules and talked about my whole life history in two hours. My new best friend asked me out to dinner the following week. I accepted willingly. I even gave my address so he could come and collect me. Such was the comfort I felt with this total stranger. With past prospects I would always meet them a few times at venues before trusting to let them see where I lived. He looked nerdy and he looked safe. Matthew said he would look for a lovely restaurant in the neighbourhood and get back to me. During the week, I forced myself not to call his house, but waited patiently for his phone call. Wednesday he called to say he had made reservations at the Boccaccio Restaurant at Westlake Lake, and he would collect me at 6:30 pm. I accepted graciously and as soon as I hung up the phone, started planning what I would wear for my Saturday date. How was I going to comb my hair? What shoes should I wear? I was way too excited! But he was good looking. I had to look fabulous too!

I decided to wear my dark navy velvet dress with spaghetti straps. This would be highlighted with diamante necklace and earrings, voluptuous curly hair and high heeled sandals.

I put on just enough make up as the icing on the cake. I made sure to drop Tiffany at the babysitter's early so I could get ready and relax. When the door bell rang, I paused and took two deep breaths. I didn't want to look too anxious. 'Hello, good to see you,' I said, acting casual as I opened the door. 'Wow! You look fabulous,' he said. 'You dressed up just for me? You look amazing!' He was excited by my outfit. He probably liked the view of the cleavage. I wondered if I had overdone it. However, it was too late. 'OK, let's go,' I said. We walked towards the curb and I saw he had a little convertible. 'Oh what a cute car. It's perfect for driving up the California coast!'

He gallantly opened the passenger door for me and I climbed in; the man not only had a great looking car, he also had manners. What more could a girl ask for? We arrived at the Westlake landing and looked for parking. I had always wanted to eat at one of the restaurants at the Lake, but felt I could not afford it. It was more romantic to go on a date. We walked up to Boccaccio's and he opened the door for me. I smiled, put my nose in the air and walked in. He had pressed all the right buttons thus far. We sat near the window. It was early spring and a bit chilly that evening, so all dining was still indoors. We would have to return in the summer when it was warm enough to sit out on the patio. There I was, planning life ahead of me.

When the menu came I had no idea what to order; continental dishes and Asian fusion; it was all too confusing. 'What's a Bento Box?' I asked. 'Oh, it's an assortment of Japanese dishes,' he said. 'OK. That's what I'll have,' I said. Even though I was perpetually hungry, I didn't think I could eat a great deal while looking at this man in front of me. He might have been a potential husband, and father of my next child. I tried not to stare too much and examined a dumpling and the occasional rice grain in the Bento Box. He had a traditional continental dish and we enjoyed our dinner. We spoke a long time about work and living in California in general, and then it was time to leave. We were among the last ones to leave the restaurant.

Matthew delivered me to my front door and before I knew it, he planted a big kiss on my lips. It took my breath away. I was in love. I wanted him so much. 'Good night. Thanks for dinner,' I said, trying to sound relaxed while my heart skipped a few beats. I fumbled while unlocking the door and hoped he would run along before I changed my mind and jumped on him. 'OK. Good night. See you again soon,' he said. I ran inside and locked the door swiftly. Oh my God … oh my God … who could I call? I had to call someone with my story. I had to tell somebody. It was the best date in ages. After he left, I went to collect Tiffany at my friend's house and gave her the highlights. She was happy for me and asked how well I knew the guy. 'I don't have to know him,' I said. 'He's perfect!' And so our romance began. After three dates I had fallen for him completely. I wanted more than a hug and a kiss, and I knew he did too.

Matthew suggested I come over to his place one evening to hang out. I was excited by the suggestion because I knew what that meant … It meant going on to the next step. Should I wait to get to know him better? Should I follow The Rules I had learned so well two years before or should I just take the plunge and let fate deal with it? I decided to take the plunge. I was starved for attention and I was getting it finally. I arranged with my friend's teenage daughter to babysit Tiffany overnight in case I needed extra time. I didn't tell anyone else about my adventure, not even Joanie. In case things did not work out favourably, I did not want everyone feeling sorry for me.

I dressed casually and drove over to Matthew's pad in Santa Monica. After locating the apartment building and parking, I could not find the apartment. I walked around the garden looking at numbers. Finally, he came out to see me walking around. His place was up one flight of steps and I had no way of calling him. He acted a little awkward and apologized for an untidy place. 'I'd promised to clean up before you came. Please forgive the smell. I know the place smells like bloke,' he said apologetically. 'What does smell like bloke mean?' I asked. 'Oh, I must have pissed on the toilet seat. Nobody's here to remind me to turn it up. Tried cleaning but the smell can't come out,' he admitted.

I made a mental note that while at his place I would only use the toilet if it was absolutely necessary and always lift up the seat and squat. Yuck … the apartment of a bachelor was usually notoriously filthy. 'Can I get you something to drink?' I looked around the tiny bachelor pad. It was one big room with a kitchenette at the back and a sofa bed to one side. He had a computer desk and chair and a tiny wall unit with a stereo and some books. A large closet held clothing, linen, and I imagined household supplies that could not fit in the kitchen cupboards. The bloke's bathroom was behind the front door and the room opened to a small balcony overlooking the street.

He offered me some chilled juice and he had ordered pizza which came eventually. We sat on the sofa bed for a while chatting, and then began to kiss. That sofa bed was a little hard and uncomfortable, so Matthew suggested we sit on the carpet. 'Oops, that carpet's a bit dirty. Wouldn't want you to ruin your clothes,' he said. 'Let me spread out a blanket.' He spread a sheet and a blanket on the ground and we progressed to the floor. It did not take long before Matthew had his way with me. He pulled off all my clothes and we made passionate love. The floor however was not comfortable. But, looking at the collapsible sofa bed, I imagined that was not comfortable either. We ate a few slices of pizza and before we knew it, we were grabbing at each other again, this time more passionately, and less awkward than the first time.

Eventually, I said I had to go home. It was getting late. He suggested we go to the shower and I agreed without thinking. This delayed departure for at least another hour as we made love passionately in the shower. I shrieked and screamed as if we were in a world all of our own. 'I really must be going now,' I said, drenched in water. 'I have quite a few things to do tomorrow.' 'OK, if you insist,' he said begrudgingly. I confirmed, 'Yes, I must.'

I had to tear myself away so as not to linger too much. I quickly got dressed, gave him a big hug, and headed for the front door. As I was leaving, his neighbour was smoking a cigarette and leaning on the railing of the balcony that joined all the upstairs apartments. He stared at me as I left. I turned my head to avoid his gaze and walked swiftly to my car that was parked on the street in front of the building. Matthew came downstairs with me to the car and gave me another hug. 'Don't mind him. He's a bit nosy,' said Matthew. 'He must have heard me screaming,' I said. 'I don't like that. I won't come back here,' I said. 'Don't worry about that bloke. He's harmless,' said Matthew. I felt a bit naked having the neighbour listen to my raunchy screams. We would have to find an alternative and I did not want him at my home either. I had promised myself not to introduce my child to any boyfriends. That was one Rule I was sticking to.

I planned to have Matthew visit me while I was at hotels for conferences. We would be on neutral territory at splendid hotels and never have to worry about the neighbours. Two weeks after our rendezvous I was participating in an event at a conference in Long Beach. The program organizers covered the cost of my hotel room and meals. I was even allowed to bring a guest to the dinner dance on the closing night. Long Beach was not far from Santa Monica, so I asked my new beau to accompany me to the dance and he could certainly stay over if he liked. Of course he wanted to stay over. We enjoyed the dinner and enjoyed the dance party. A live band covered Beatles music expertly and I introduced Matthew to a few colleagues. At least I did not have to be alone like in most of the previous gala events. We disappeared close to midnight as the party was winding down and went to the room.

It was perfect, with a large, comfortable king-sized bed. We had fun all night and could make as much noise as we wanted. I imagined he was tired when he went to work that day. I was required to participate in a few meetings next morning and did more observation than talking until it was time to drive home to Westlake Village in the afternoon.

The next meeting that month took place in San Diego. My aunt was visiting from Florida and in return for getting her a ticket to come out to California, she would help me by babysitting Tiffany during the three days at the Conference.

Because I was part of the organizing team, I got a free hotel room if I wanted. My company also gave me a hotel room because they sponsored a symposium I had organized. With two rooms, I could easily have family in one and invite Matthew as a guest. I was getting more and more creative in planning these rendezvous. We made plans so that I would leave a key for him at the front desk. When he arrived after work, he could settle in the room. I was busy with meetings until late in the evening.

I had again orchestrated a night of pleasure. He did not refuse. I was not following The Rules and was taking the lead in coordinating our relationship and never stopped to think what effect it could have. When I travelled to Latin America, I missed him intensely, especially since I stayed at some of the finest hotels. I was usually stuck alone on a king size bed. I decided I would try to get him to take vacation time when I was having my next expedition. 'Hey Matthew, I have to travel to Oahu to visit some farms next month. Do you think you could get time off from work? If you buy your own plane ticket, you could stay with me,' I said. 'Oh that sounds splendid,' he said. I was very excited. 'Of course it's splendid! We'll be in Hawaii together. It'll be amazing!'

He promised to see if he could get a few days off. When my air travel was booked by the company, I gave him the information to see if he could get the same flights. He was not able to get on the same plane for the outbound journey; however, he could get a seat on the plane returning to Los Angeles. He joined me at the hotel in Oahu that night and we had a pseudo-honeymoon experience that first night. I had a rental car for visiting the farms, and woke early to find the location. With many road maps and instructions from the local manager, I found the site easily.

We visited one farm after the next and I took copious notes. It was not easy to concentrate knowing I had a red-blooded man sitting around all day doing nothing but waiting for me. I wanted to get back quickly. 'See you guys tomorrow,' I said at 5:00 pm sharp. Matthew and I planned to go to a traditional Hawaiian Luau; dinner was going to be late. When I got to the hotel, I saw he was a red as a lobster. He had been sitting in the sun all day at the beach near the hotel and was burnt all over and cranky. 'Aloha,' I said cheerfully. 'Ouch. Ouch. Don't touch me,' he yapped. 'OK, sorry. What were you thinking? Do you usually sit all day in the sun?' I asked. When some people arrive in a tourist destination, all logic and reasoning disappears.

We changed into floral Hawaiian clothes and within a short time the tour bus collected us for Germaine's Luau. According to the brochure this Luau was the most fabulous in Oahu and not to be missed. They had to drive around collecting tourists from many hotels. Eventually, we got to the site of the Luau. We saw rows and rows of wooden benches and a stage up front. Many tourists from the US mainland were yapping away about being in Hawaii and being excited. My guest however had a bad attitude from his burning skin. He also did not like the tourists and called them common, loud Americans. When the time came for the meal, the entertainer explained over and over that the roast pig was cooked in the ground and seasoned with sea salt. This was served with a special rice noodle. Each picnic bench was called to collect a meal. The lines were long and Matthew became even more disagreeable. When we finally sat to eat, we realized the meal was bland with no distinguishable flavour. He was upset. We had chits for free beer so I gave him my chits so he could drink more. He barely ate the food and complained about the lack of flavour. The beer calmed him a little bit. I bought both our tickets to console him. I should have really let him pay for his own ticket, but he was too upset.

The next day after work, we planned to drive around Honolulu in the hills and around the city to see what we could see. We fought about the way I was driving. He obviously did not like my slow pace. I never drove quickly in an unfamiliar city. Things were not going well. We had an extra day on Saturday to travel around the island before flying back to Los Angeles. I was determined to see as much as possible, since I was not sure when I would be able to visit Hawaii again. We had maps of the island and set off early. My idea of an interesting trip was to hop from beach to beach. He wanted to sit and chill out at one beach all day. I wanted to grab lunch at a drive-through and eat in the car while driving to the next beach. 'We only have one day to see everything!' I screamed. 'We don't have to see everything. Woman you're crazy. Stop the car! Stop now! I'm not eating in the car. 'But … but ….' I hesitated. 'I refuse to eat in the car,' he said. 'Let's sit down at the park bench over there and eat like civilized people!' He was angry with me and I was naive enough to wonder what his problem could be. We had so many squabbles on the trip that I wondered if it was worth it. However, I was happy to have seen a good deal of Oahu, even though it was at a frenetic pace.

When we got to LA we went our separate ways since our cars were parked in different parking lots. We hugged and I said 'See you soon.' He replied, 'Thanks dear.' I hoped he was not too disturbed by all the fighting the past few days. A brief meeting on a date was never the same as a trip abroad. An extended trip was really one of the best ways for people to get to know each other.

A wonderful couple I knew from the University alumni association was hosting a summer pool party and invited me over. All their friends were other couples and I seriously wanted to arrive with a man so I would not be the odd one in the crowd. I invited Matthew to join me that evening at the party and hoped things would work out fine. My friends lived in Valencia and I arranged with Matthew to meet at my house. I would drive my car over to Valencia so he wouldn't have to be too stressed with driving. However, that may not have been a great idea since he was annoyed at my slow driving as usual. When we found parking near Norma and Jacob's townhouse, we strolled in for introductions. 'Hi guys, this is Matthew,' I said. 'Hello Matthew,' said Norma giving him a good stare and evaluation in a few seconds. He appeared a little self-conscious, which was to be expected. 'You can change into your swim suits and head over to the pool,' said Jacob. 'I'm preparing some burgers to put on the grill.'

As we changed into swimming gear, Matthew admired their beautiful townhouse and furniture. They had bought some elegant furniture and he may have been a little jealous. 'What do those two do?' he asked. 'They're engineers like you,' I said. 'Hmm,' he said deep in thought. The sun in Valencia was dry and hot. As we sat next to the pool, two other couples arrived and we yakked for a while about the weather, our jobs and other details. Matthew was not too talkative. He just looked at the other couples and acted antisocial. He then remarked the sun was too strong and he didn't like it. 'We could go in the shade under the umbrella if you like,' I said, trying to cheer him up. The others noticed his brooding and discomfort.

'In England on a sunny day, it's absolutely perfect. Not too hot, not too cold,' he boasted. I thought it rained a lot in England he had come to California to escape the rain. He was just being difficult. After we ate, he continued his disagreeable behaviour. 'Would you like to leave,' I whispered to him when the others were deep in conversation. 'Yes, I don't like your friends.' I couldn't understand why he wouldn't like them. They were all young professionals, upwardly mobile, and ambitious. He appeared tortured. 'Well Norma and Jacob, thanks so much for inviting us. We're going to head back now. It's a long drive you know.' Norma had been observing my companion closely. As a good friend, I knew she would call me the next day with an evaluation.

Matthew complained on the drive back that my friends seemed arrogant. He found many reasons not to like them. His behaviour was irrational since these people were quite simple and agreeable. The problem was all in his mind. He had low self-esteem and could not relate to his equals. It was a problem to watch. When we arrived at my home, I asked him if he would come in, but he refused. 'I'm tired and I'm going home now,' he said. 'Well, suit yourself,' I said, and let him go on his way. This was my first attempt to integrate Matthew into my regular circle of friends. I had never met any of his.

While speaking with him during the week, I told him I would be planning a big birthday party in a few weeks and hoped he would come to that. I usually invited everyone I liked to my birthday dinner and dance. His response was a careful, 'We'll see.' And we left it at that. I did not hear from Matthew for a week and grew worried. I tried not to call or run after him, but could not help myself. I hoped I did not scare him off trying to micromanage our relationship, but then, maybe I did. One evening when I sat reading a book, feeling sorry for myself, the phone rang. It was Matthew. 'How have you been Ms. James?' he asked. 'Well, keeping busy as usual.' I tried to sound cheerful, even though I was moping around the house and missing him. 'So when am I seeing you?' he demanded. 'Someday soon I hope. What do you have in mind?' I wondered with curiosity. 'It's summertime! I quite fancy driving up the coast with my convertible top down!'

'Sounds exciting. When do we leave? Where are we going?' I was ecstatic. I also fancied driving on Highway 101 with the wind blowing in my hair and the convertible top down. It was the stuff one saw on television. 'Let's go to Monterrey next weekend!' he said. 'Sure I said. When would you like to pick me up?' As he spoke I started to wonder who would watch Tiffany for the weekend. Arrangements had to be made. I just wanted to get away with my lover.

'I'll meet you at 9:00 am on Saturday and we'll drive through Big Sur and check out the scenery,' he confirmed. 'See you then,' I said. I was bouncing off the walls ... things to do and places to go ... I had to set the plan in motion. My bags were packed five days in advance. But what did I really need. We were staying just one night and driving back down the following day. It was enough. I was nervous and clinging when I saw Matthew. I didn't realise how much I missed the physical closeness. I was lusting over him and my behaviour was irrational. As we drove along the way, he seemed a bit distracted. We had the car top down and the air was hot. It was so hot in fact with the sun was beating down on my head. I asked him to close up the car.

'But you said you wanted to drive up the coast in a convertible,' he complained. 'OK. Don't worry. I'll try to cover my head.' I covered my head to try to keep the peace and not complain, but I could feel some tension starting. The constant din on the highway was also annoying as we drove at high speed in the convertible. It might have been enjoyable at a slow speed in chilly weather but was definitely painful for me. I complained again. 'The noise is bothering me. My ear drums will burst! Please close up the car!' I shouted. Matthew became upset. 'Close up the car. Close up the car. You're acting like an old bat!' I became very upset. 'Thanks a lot. Just what I needed to hear,' I said. 'Well it's true. Look at that couple. Look at that one. They have the roof down.' He pointed to other couples passing us in the opposite direction. I wasn't sure how they did it but I was uncomfortable. He pushed the button and closed the top. What a relief it was for me.

'Now we can hear the music,' I said. As we got to Big Sur, the views were spectacular. I was happy we drove on the side away from the precipice, on the edge. Matthew was driving fast and I was close to having a panic attack. I feared driving over the edge in the haste to go nowhere. I knew if I complained, I would get the old bat story again, so I looked away from the view sometimes. 'Suddenly he pulled aside for a rest stop and we cuddled while taking in the view and leaning on the side of the car. It was certainly beautiful looking at the calm Pacific Ocean. He then suggested we go for a short hike up the nearby trail. I agreed without thinking. I was just calming down from the mad drive on the coast road. As we got out of full view of passing cars, we kissed passionately. 'Do you fancy doing it here, right now?' he asked. 'What? Right here? Suppose someone catches us.' I quivered with anticipation. 'Nobody will come. Our car is right there,' he explained. Before I had much time to think about it, I let spontaneity play out and we had fun in the bushes. We thought we heard some people approaching and had to come to an abrupt end. We would no doubt have to finish what we started when we got to the hotel in Monterrey.

As soon as we arrived that afternoon at the little hotel, we checked into the room locked the door and jumped on each other. The love making was mad and desperate. It had been quite a few weeks since our last adventure. We then fell fast asleep only to wake up when it was dark outside. 'I'm so hungry; I could eat an ox,' I said. 'So am I. We better get dressed and go somewhere for dinner.' We looked around the room for our bags but could not find them. 'That's funny, I thought I brought them upstairs from the car when we got here,' said Matthew. 'Well, they're not in the bathroom or anywhere in the room. Guess they must still be in the car.' Matthew got dressed and was about to go down to the car to retrieve our luggage. When he opened the door, there were the bags in front the door where we had left them. We were in such a hurry to get naked and hop into bed, that we forgot our luggage at the door. It was indeed funny and we had the first hearty laugh of the whole day.

'A hot shower and change of clothes are in order,' I said and went to the bathroom. We had the dilemma of where to have dinner. I suggested going to Carmel, since I remembered many cute restaurants the last time I was in area for work. He complained about not having a lot of money. I told him it didn't have to be expensive. I was sure they had many options. We walked on one of the main streets in Carmel looking at menus and eventually decided on a tiny place that served one fixed menu every day. 'That's easy,' I said. 'No choices and no fuss.' Matthew was not looking happy when the bill came and I did not offer to pay. I had paid for several other outings when we went out in the past and expected this weekend trip to be his treat. Maybe I had misread his invitation. We walked around briefly and returned to the little hotel.

'I have a gift for you,' he announced. 'A gift? Wow, I love gifts! Let's see it … let's see it …' He pulled out a white box from his bag. I was excited and carefully opened the package. It was a black and red naughty negligee set; thigh high stockings, a tiny bustier, a little bra and a g-string. I was so excited to get such a sexy gift but it looked a bit tiny. I had a lot of curves so I wondered how I would look in this. 'Put it on,' he said. 'Let me see you.' I was able to put on the stockings, panties and the bustier. However, the bra was a size "A" and I was size "D". It could not fit and would probably burst. 'Everything's fine except the bra,' I apologized. He laughed heartily. 'Stand facing the wall,' he said. I stood against the wall and he laughed again. 'Your breasts fall to the ground. They don't stand up.' I was so hurt at that comment. Not everyone had the plastic doll's figure and breasts, and I certainly didn't. I took off the ensemble and put on my little negligee which fit perfectly. 'Don't touch me you,' I screamed at him. 'You're so rude. I hate you!' He tried apologizing but I felt extremely offended.

We went to sleep without speaking and when we woke next morning it was time for a short sight-seeing trip around Monterrey and then the drive back to LA. 'Are you still mad with me?' he asked. 'Well, I'm not pleased,' I said. We had a quiet breakfast and then drove to Cannery Row, stopping for a stroll and tour of a historic site near the Monterrey Pier. We then started the drive back home on Highway 101. This time, we drove back with the car closed. He had bought a new cell phone. It was the latest toy for many professionals. Suddenly his phone rang. He seemed to be speaking in codes with someone. I was sure it was a woman, but tried not to get too jealous.

'OK, I'll see you later. OK … uh huh. bye.'

He hung up and did not tell me who it was. In the meantime my mind wandered on the possibility of his sleeping his way around Santa Monica. This was possible since I did not know him well. The following week, he did not call me at all and I did not bother calling him either. If he was genuinely interested, he would reach out. He knew I was planning my birthday party on the Saturday night. I had told him I would be cooking a lot of food and having some friends over and I had invited him to the celebration. On the morning of the party, he did not call me, and I imagined our relationship was truly finished. I had many wonderful friends who all came to the party. Luckily, most of them did not know he existed so I did not need to explain his absence. Only one couple had met him and he was a bit quarrelsome at their house. After the party, when I had cleaned up and was about to go to bed, I decided to check my email messages and I saw a message from Matthew. It said, 'Happy birthday Ms. James.' I never heard from him again.

Joanie Marries Bozo

Mike, who attended the impromptu party at Glenn's parents' house, had a soft spot for Joanie. He didn't mind the loud bursts of expressions, and lack of privacy, and her open character. Mike started following us around to every PWP event even though he had no children. The group had planned a camping trip for parents and children up north at a lakeside campsite and Mike came with us. It was Tiffany's first outdoor camping trip and many in the group owned big tents. We did not have to worry about camping gear since we had many people to share with. Our group rate included entry fees to the camp site, meals, and snacks. It was a good get away from the suburbs. Some members of the group also had boats and skidoos and promised to provide rides for members and kids for a small contribution for gas. What an exciting trip. I had not gone camping for a long time, and certainly never with so many people. We travelled in a caravan of cars meeting at the site. Some had arrived earlier and set up a few tents.

The kids can sleep here if you like and showers and toilets are in the building down the hill 'said John, our fearless leader. 'Tiffany, would you like to stay in the children's tent? No mommy, no … I'm scared.' I consoled her, 'That's fine hon. You can stay with me.' We had been assigned spaces but many people roamed around to various friends' tents and certainly did not stick to the schedule. Joanie promised I could come to hang out in her big tent. She had room for extras. We were lucky. Her tent also had a skylight since part of the top could roll back so one could see the sky. The desert lake was large and provided many hours of entertaining swimming and riding on water crafts. One man in the group, Frank had a big skidoo. Some women didn't like the way he hugged them when they asked to ride on it with him. 'He's a slimy wretch. Look out for him,' said one woman. Forewarned was forearmed; I didn't bother to ask. I just looked on. There was no life guard on duty anywhere. "Swim at you own risk" said the sign. I was going to take minimal risks. Another person offered a short ride to the middle of the lake and back. That one I decided to hazard and took one trip out and back. It was really fun and I wished I owned my own craft for that short period.

We conversed around the camp site telling stories after dinner and eventually people wandered off to their various tents to sleep. I heard the rowdy commotion in Joanie's tent and went across to investigate. Mike was hanging on close but, just looking on as she told jokes. 'Five dallah, make you hallah!' And everyone laughed. 'What's that,' I asked. 'What are you talking about?' She explained, 'That's a prostitute with a foreign accent.' She screamed again, 'Five dallah, make you hallah!' And everyone laughed. 'Wait ... wait ... there's a full moon tonight,' observed Joanie. 'Moonlight special. I give you five dallah hallah for tree dallah!' The group exploded with laughter. The moonlight special was particularly entertaining. With Joanie on the floor, I doubted we would get any sleep that night. After one hour of entertainment, Tiffany and I went across to our assigned tent to try to sleep. I didn't do well sleeping on the ground with a sleeping bag. But, at least it was quiet.

After the camping trip, Mike and Joanie were inseparable. I

passed one day to visit her and Mike was there. From the looks on their faces, I knew I had interrupted something really important so I left quietly. I no longer had my buddy, Joanie to hang out with. One day Joanie called to tell me she really liked Mike. He was studying to be a home inspector and had the potential to make money. 'But is he making any money now?' I asked her. 'I thought you told me you only liked guys with property and a big job.' She seemed so smitten, she was willing to forget all the training and coaching she had given me about men with money and where to look for them. Mike had caught her heart. 'I'll make him wait a few more weeks to see if he's serious!' she said. 'Are you sure? If you're madly in love with him, just go right ahead,' I said. 'No! No! I'm holding out,' she screamed. 'That's fine. Suit yourself,' I said.

I wondered how she was coping with the fact that he had no real money. She met his family and felt more comfortable with him. A few weeks later, she announced to me and to a few others that she thought he was serious. She told everyone she let Mike have his way. We didn't need to know this, but we congratulated Joanie. She called me screaming one day to announce Mike proposed and she said yes. I was so happy for her. I knew she wanted to get married again and he was a good-looking guy. Joanie immediately started planning an economic wedding. The dress would be purchased on the internet. She had loved Westlake Inn for the reception and would take their economical menu. All her friends would help put up the decorations. The wedding was to be that September close to her birthday.

One fine evening she called sounding a bit distraught. 'I broke up with him!' I could not believe my ears. 'What?

What are you saying?' I asked. 'I'm calling off the wedding. He's stupid. He's a bozo. I won't marry a bozo!' She explained. I was trying to make sense of the situation since she was crazy about him just a few weeks before and had spent a lot of time planning the wedding. 'He's a bozo, what was I thinking. He has no money. He's studying, for crying out loud. I have my own house. Can you imagine? He doesn't have a house,' she lamented. Well, we all knew that before. Why did the fact suddenly hit her? Joanie broke up with Mike for a month and moped around barely able to speak. She was miserable and not her usual cheerful self.

However, after six weeks, Mike was back on the scene. He had begged his way back into her heart. She said she didn't mind waiting for him to finish school. He had to promise to work really hard to finish on time. While they broke up, he also went out with another woman to drown his sorrows. She may have become pregnant with his child. How could Joanie take him back? I would never have accepted him, especially with the talk of a child expected. As they say, "Love is Blind". I imagined Love was also really crazy and confused to put everything out of focus to accept such a complicated situation. But, however, if Joanie was open and willing to move on with her wedding, I was prepared to support her.

'He's back with me and he still wants to get married,' she said. 'Are you sure you want to do this?' I asked. 'I'm sure. I've waited a long time for this,' she said. 'Well, I'll sing for the wedding!' I said. Déjà vu! There I was, singing the Ave Maria at another wedding and wondering if the parties actually loved each other or were just staging a wedding. I rehearsed with the organist and choir members of a Catholic

Church in Thousand Oaks. We went through the songs for the wedding mass and my solo, just to be sure everything was in place. We decided who would stand where. The choir was to perform at the side of the church and keep an eye on the organist who was seated in the balcony.

Joanie made a beautiful bride. Her makeup was done just right. Her blonde hair was curled and decorated and she wore a lovely ivory gown, purchased online for $150. 'Nobody would know,' she had told me with a wink. She probably told countless others in our group, 'Nobody will know!' Mike looked dapper in his rented tuxedo. The reception at Westlake Inn was a hit with a delicious meal. Her friend, Leon, was the DJ and he did a great job keeping us dancing for hours. Eventually, it was time to go home. The happy couple planned to honeymoon at the hotel for the weekend. It was Joanie's fairy tale come true and I was happy for her.

Another Parent Without Partner was hitched!

Speed Dating; the Final Straw

Internet dating had proven futile for Ms. Red Car Long Legs. Every man I had met did not meet my strict criteria, which I kept redefining as I went along. Even when friends tried to play matchmaker, nothing constructive had happened. I was not lucky to meet a reasonable man by chance and had almost given up on the species. However, Borzena convinced me I was young and beautiful and needed to get married again. I had to find another means to meet people. It was 2004 and the "Speed Dating" phenomenon had become popular in Los Angeles. This was supposed to be better than finding random people on the internet since you actually met in person. I went online to find a Speed Dating event and there was one coming up in Pasadena.

'Do you think I should drive out all the way to Pasadena just for this?' I doubted the value. 'Yes you should Lindy,' she confirmed. 'You have to try it. You never know your luck. If you stay at home, you can't meet anybody.' That was true. 'But it sounds scary. Suppose I meet some crazy men? I'm afraid to go.' Borzena re-assured me, 'Don't worry. I will go with you. I won't participate. I'll just sit at the side and watch.' What a relief! Will you? Oh thanks so much ... That would be a huge help,' I said gratefully.

We decided our daughters could stay together when we drove off to Pasadena for a few hours. We would not be away for long. She was to sit on the other side of the bar and give me certain signals if a man was acceptable, or not, based on his appearance. We worked out some secret head and eye movements. It was all funny and childish. When we parked and walked into the big sports bar, we were ready with our codes. I registered at the door and Borzena quickly went to the side to buy a soda and get settled for monitoring. Several women and men walked into the side of the bar for the event. As each man walked around, I gave Borzena a stare to assess whether or not he looked suitable.

A nod to one side meant just ok. A lowering of the head meant no way. A wink meant yes. The organizers explained that couples had five minutes to chat. At the sound of the bell, the men would move to the next woman for five minutes. At the end of the night, we were to put a check mark next to each person we wanted to meet for a date. The organizers promised to send us an email with the matches the following day. A racial mix of men came to the event: white, black and Hispanic. I gossiped animatedly with those who liked to talk and endured the five minutes of boredom with those who had social challenges. Half of the time I forgot to look at poor Borzena who was trying to give me signals. She sat bored on the other side of the venue also trying to ward off suitors who came around.

The event ended after an hour and a half. It was tiring to talk to so many men. I saw three who were successful professionals. Others looked like players out for a good time or quiet introverts requiring work to get out of their shells. As we drove back to Westlake, Borzena and I compared notes on who I wanted to date again. There was one black professional who was quite attractive, and two white men I wanted to meet again. Next day, I eagerly ran to my home computer after work to see who had added me as a likely match. The email from the organizer came around 7:00 pm. I took a deep breath and opened it … I breathed again when I read the email …

'We're sorry you have no matches at this time. Please join us at our next speed dating event in two weeks!' The words cut like a knife: NO MATCHES AT THIS TIME!

What had I done wrong? Why didn't anyone like me? Borzena had said I looked beautiful? I was skinny with long curly hair. I wore the cutest mini outfit. Not even the black man selected me. I cried for at least half an hour out of self-pity. I called Borzena to complain and get comfort. She said I should not worry about it. The men at the event were stupid not to choose me. I would just have to try something else.

Was I not good enough for anyone to love? What had I done to deserve this? Those men at the speed dating were not as educated as I was or even earned my salary; yet, they did not want me. That day, I decided to give up the chase and drown myself in work. If the relationship game was not working out, then at least I could be the best at my career. I did not want my life to depend on the random selection of strange men. If I was to meet Mr. Right, we would meet by fate. Other than that, I was determined to be a successful career woman.

11

HIGHER GROUND IN THE INDUSTRY

Brodie's Floaties

One day while attending a large industry event, I saw a group of twelve people come on stage to be honoured for participation in the Industry Leadership Program. Each person was a senior manager for the company he or she represented. The audience screamed for them as they received their plaques and got handshakes from the sponsors and other dignitaries. I saw one black man in the group. This was great encouragement for me. At least the industry had some diversity. I was determined to speak to him after the ceremony that followed. Every Industry event was full of food and drink. I pushed my way through the crowd and eventually met Michael, a skinny brown-skinned guy with large eyes and glasses. He had a short afro and his suit was hanging on him like a sack. He needed to eat more food in my opinion. He was not even eating the good food as it floated around him. All he was doing was chatting. His wife stood next to him smiling. She was also a tiny woman with a short afro.

'Hello! Congratulations on your achievement!' I approached with noise and fanfare and my hand outstretched for a handshake. 'Thanks so much,' he said quietly. Many people passed to shake his hand. I stuck around asking the million dollar question. How did a black man get accepted into the program? Should I apply too. We spoke for a while about his company and his history in the industry. I then told him I was thinking of applying for the Leadership Program. 'Go ahead and do it Jennylynd. You'll make loads of connections. It would be the best thing for your career!' he explained. 'The people in the program will be around in the industry forever. Many of them worked for their own family businesses for years. They all know each other,' he said. 'I will,' I re-assured him.

The following week, an email was circulated by the organization announcing a search for the next group of industry leaders. Even though I was new at the company, I did not hesitate sending in my application. If accepted, I was going to be one of twelve in the whole United States. I would also be the first black woman in the program which was irresistible. I was vain and power-hungry, and I knew it. The small problem of asking my new boss time off to participate in program was a bridge I would have to cross later!

I was happy when an email came saying that I was short listed amongst all the applicants and would have to do a telephone interview with an industry leader. I was bouncing off the walls but had to focus on what I would say when I was called. A woman I had met the year before at one of the industry conferences called me for the interview. At that conference, I had congratulated her on her award and spoke with her a few minutes to find out about her business. Over the years the art of networking and schmoozing with big wigs had become one of my greatest skills.

I sailed through the interview with many examples of why I would be a good industry leader and why I wanted to participate in the program. In fact, I had only worked in the industry for three years, compared to the years put in by some applicants who grew up in the business. However, I was passionate about my work. A few weeks passed and I kept the anxiety of acceptance to myself. Will they take me? Will they? Will they? Finally, an email of congratulations came. I had to send an official response from my boss to confirm that the company would give me the time needed to participate in this program. On some occasions, I would need four days' time off to visit sites and participate in workshops around the United States. I walked sheepishly to my boss' office to ask for permission to participate in the program. This of course should have been done before an application was ever sent. However, I did not want to "jinx it", as the saying goes.

My boss looked a little annoyed when I showed him my acceptance as I babbled about making up the time away from the job by working harder when I got back. He said he couldn't stop me from the doing the leadership program. It was an important one, so I could go ahead. It was the first sticky situation I managed to find myself in but things worked in my favour. A month later, I was on an all expense paid trip to El Paso, Texas, a border town with Ciudad Juarez, Mexico. Our leadership group was to meet for three days of training.

I arrived at the small hotel and met one of the participants at the check in. We shook hands and went to deposit bags in our respective rooms. As we walked across the courtyard, three other men stood near the water fountain. 'Are you here for the leadership program? Are you? Are you?' Everyone was excited to be there. One or two already knew each other from being in the industry. I hurried to my room to put down the bags, and returned to the group. As I joined them, two ladies were chatting with the group. We then heard loud laughter as a young woman came into the courtyard walking on her hands. 'What the hell! Who is she?' asked one of the men. Most of us were in shock. This woman had certainly made a grand entrance and nobody could beat that. 'Hi, I'm Clare,' she said when she stood on two feet, red-faced. 'I'm from California!'

'Well I'm Jennylynd and I live in California too!' I said. The leadership program had participants from Texas, North Carolina, Washington, Arizona and other areas with big agricultural enterprises. I imagined they wanted to spread the resources around the country. Clare was tall and fit with muscular shoulders and arms. She had long brown hair and pretty face. There was Frank, a skinny European with a distinct accent. He compared his thin arms to Clare's and started laughing. 'I have to watch this one. She'll beat me up!' Clare confirmed she had a black belt in martial arts. Bradley was quiet young man from the East Coast. His family owned a big business. Doogie was a short Irish lad with brown hair and blue eyes. He chatted and joked with some of the louder men in the group and was immediately one of the gang. Burt was a bald young fellow with glasses. He was of medium height and medium build. He was quieter than some others in the group. They threatened to get him drunk to see his true colours.

Sam Brodie owned a produce sales company in the north. He was a tall, family man with blonde hair and a serious face. He looked mature for his age and observed the antics of the noisier, younger members of the group. He was sometimes amused, but mostly shocked. Joe was a tall skinny fellow from Texas. He had black curly hair slicked to one side of the head with gel. He was loud and determined to make friends quickly. Claudette shared a room with me. She was an older woman who appeared fit and exercise-conscious. She had tidy black hair and thick dark eyebrows. She was polite and reassuring to everyone. 'I will sleep out on the sofa, she said. I snore loudly all night. I thought about this and said it would be fine with me if she wanted to sleep out there.

Mike was a red head and a serious family man with glasses. He was pale and turned beet red when any outrageous suggestion was announced from the group. His family owned a big company and he was destined to be president later in life. The loudest was Charlie. He was a tall ginger with a moustache and beard. 'What happens on the road stays on the road!' He yelled at the top of his lungs when he spoke. His every second sentence was a joke and I wondered out loud why he spoke so much. 'I'm in sales! In sales yah gotta know howdah tawk.' And he sure knew how. His eyes were wild and he was on to the next joke. He could look at anyone in the crowd and find something to joke about. He was sharing a room with Sam. Poor Sam, I thought, he would have non-stop jokes and they would all be about him! Cynthia came in late. She was a pale, skinny woman with medium length, brown hair. She was in sales and travelled frequently to Europe on company business. She missed the initial introductions with the gang.

We had to rise early for a breakfast meeting and a full day of workshops with the course facilitator. The program was daunting. Nobody could hide in a corner because there were only 12 of us. We would be forced to speak and participate all day. I suddenly became terrified of the prospect of facing these people everyday. What would they think of me? They all appeared confident and self assured. Who was I compared to them? Would I be able to measure up? I was not usually shy, however at that time, I felt like retreating into a burrow to hide. The first day was full of introductions and determining why we were in the program and what we hoped to get out of it. I had to get my story straight in my head so I could express it to the others. I could not reveal that I saw program graduates on a stage at the Industry Conference and decided I wanted to be there too next year. They would think I was crazy! I created logical and plausible reasons for participating in the program.

At 5:30 pm we were released. 'Let's go across the border!' shouted Charlie who knew the town well. 'But how would all of us get there? We don't have a van,' I said. 'We just have to walk over,' said Charlie. 'Woo hoo! Look out world here we come.' We walked across the border to Ciudad Juarez. The two security guards just looked at us and didn't say anything. Americans crossed the border on foot every day to party, get drunk and walk back. They were quite used to the sight of us. There was nothing to ask. 'Let's go to this bar! No let's go to this one!' The team was going wild and I could see us separating into several groups. There was no way twelve people could stick together with so much to see and do. Some of the program managers also came with us for fun. I decided to stick close to Clare to see what other wild antics she would do. 'Belly to Belly! Hey I'm going in there,' she said.

From the open partitions to the street we saw a mural of a fat Mexican cowboy facing a fat American cowboy. Their big bellies were labelled with country of origin as they had a face off; hence the name Belly to Belly. This bar had a mechanical saddle that one could ride to simulate a rodeo. I was wearing a mini skirt and felt a lady like me could not possible ride the bull. Clare was also wearing a short skirt. Before we knew it, Clare was on the mechanical bull screaming at the top of her lungs. She was strong so she could hold on with one hand and not fall off. The guys were cheering for her in disbelief that she would even venture on that saddle.

'Clare is wild! She's dah best!' Close to 12:00 am things started to wind down, as it should, because this was the middle of the week. 'I think we better walk back now,' I said, trying to be the voice of reason. 'We have an early morning.' Some in our group would have partied all night. I did not have my passport or work permit and hoped walking with this wild group we could all be perceived to be Americans. It worked. I walked in the middle of the gang. At any rate the US immigration inspectors only stopped Mexican-looking pedestrians. My roommate was sensible and already asleep when we got back. She snored loudly on the living room sofa of our suite and I hoped that the bedroom door was enough to keep out the din.

Next morning at our workshop, a few hung-over faces greeted our instructor. She was ready to roll and we had to get with the program.

The instructor pointed arbitrarily to people in the group for quick answers to questions. On one occasion when she pointed to Frank, he could not think of an answer and so just said, 'Woof', like dog. We all collapsed with laughter. It was one o our group's standard jokes for that trip. We had to prepare presentations on various topics on the spot; write for a few minutes, then read to the group. It was an intense few days of workshops. The dinner party at the end of this session also involved intense partying. Many people got drunk. We had a dining room at the hotel all to ourselves and there was no need to walk far away. Burt got drunk and stood on a chair dancing and singing. His new buddies had vowed to see his true colours and he showed them, as he howled at the moon.

Our next meeting included a few days in Monterrey, California where we visited a tree farm and had lunch in the middle of an orchard. The meal was exquisite and so was the service. It was my first time experiencing such an elaborate picnic. We explored a large packing house with an electronic eye that sorted products based on colour. On this trip we enjoyed a few hours of team building at a gymnasium with rock climbing and a flying trapeze. If anyone had told me I would be climbing up a wall with a group of managers for training, I would not have believed them. The flying trapeze was the most frightening. We had to grab the swinging trapeze when the instructor released it, jump out, and then swing ourselves back to the platform.

'Oh shit!' said loud-mouth Charlie. 'Ah aint doin' that.' The guide said, 'Don't worry; we have a net below to catch yah if yah fall.' Charlie continued, 'Ah don't care about any friggin' net. Ah aint doin' that!' Everyone stood staring up at the swinging trapeze and the long fall below. Even Clare was quiet. 'OK. Who's first?' asked the guide. I suddenly got the courage to step forward. 'I'll do it.' I surprised myself. What was I proving? Well, nothing ventured, nothing gained and I felt there was everything to gain. I climbed up the ladder to the high platform. The instructor then released the trapeze and instructed me to grab the bar when it returned to the platform, swing out with it and swing back to the platform. Without giving it too much thought, I jumped and grabbed the bar. The weight of my body made the ropes of the trapeze swing far out. Then as if by magic, the flying trapeze and I were returning to the platform. I just had a few seconds to stick out my feet and get onto that platform before the trapeze, like a pendulum, swung back out again. I focused and bingo, I jumped onto that platform. It was a similar experience to my Cloud Forest Adventure in Costa Rica.

The group below cheered loudly! 'Good job Jennylynd! Woo hoo!' I felt so proud of myself. It was like climbing the highest mountain. Everyone slowly went one by one to try the flying trapeze. I suddenly had more courage than ever before because I led the pack with this exercise. I knew I could finish the leadership program. I had proven it to myself.

A few months later, we met again to participate at a Conference in Washington D.C. It was my first time in the nation's capital and I was determined to see as much as possible outside our meeting hours. During the day we had workshops on crisis management and speaking to the media. We were even filmed and critiqued on imaginary news reports. As the gang planned which bar they were going to hit that night, I told them I was going off to meet a friend that evening so they were not to look out for me. 'Jennylynd are you snubbing us? OK, be that way! Go off on your own,' yelled Charlie for everyone to hear.

An old friend from a previous job lived in DC and she knew where the best dancing could be found that night. She passed by to collect me and we were off. We danced at a crowded club with three floors of fun. I had to drag myself away knowing I would be tired the following day during workshops. I managed to keep my eyelids open all day because we visited the Chambers of some important government senators related to the Industry. It was a little unnerving being there because it was shortly after the incident when letters were found in a few government offices contaminated with anthrax. We were assured that everything was safe once more. All bags were being checked as we entered the building because of extra security.

I stayed alert too because I had planned to take the night tour of Washington DC. I thought if I could not see the place during the day, I have to see it by night. All the beautifully lit monuments were spectacular and I took pictures in the night. This tour went on for hours and just as I was about to fade, we were done. I went back to the hotel and fell fast asleep. One more day of workshops and I had a chance to explore Georgetown for an hour with another friend. The beautiful old Victorian buildings and the expensive shops were a tourist's dream for exploration. We visited a street which seemed to have a hundred ethnic restaurants.

'Everyone lives in Washington, D.C.,' said Anita. 'It's the capital city. What would you like to eat?' I thought carefully and said, 'I want something I've never had before.' She said, 'Well, my favourite restaurant is Ethiopian. Would you like to go there?' It sounded quite exotic. 'Of course!' And so we rushed off for an Ethiopian dinner. We sat on the floor on large cushions. The picturesque decor was an adventure in itself. They brought a large flat-bread which I learned was from fermented dough. We ate this bread with various sauces. The flavours were like nothing I had tasted before; strange spices and new flavours. This dinner was a great ending to my Washington D.C. visit. I wanted to return to Washington another time since there was so much to see and so little time.

Another session was planned for our group a few months later in Delaware. I was excited to be arriving in one of the oldest parts of the country and wondered what amazing experiences the program managers had planned for us. I studied the programme and saw it included clay shooting. Would we actually be shooting? I couldn't wait! We were whisked away to a big farm and assigned rooms in two adjacent houses. These were modern country houses with aluminium siding. It was hot that day, but thankfully the buildings were air conditioned. Our house had a pool table on the main floor and bedrooms upstairs and downstairs. I was exhausted from travelling and went to my little room to take a short nap. On the program it said we would have a barbecue at the river.

I must have fallen into a deep sleep. After waking up, the place appeared extra quiet. I freshened up quickly and went out to the living room. 'Charlie? Sam? Anybody?' The house was empty. I walked out to the roadway. I had no key, so just closed the door. We were on a huge farm, so perhaps nobody but our group was staying there. I went to the house next door and tried the door. It was open. 'Hello? Hello? Anybody here? Cynthia? Clare? Anybody?' There was silence. Where the hell was everybody? I started panicking. Where could they have gone? I started walking down the road to an old wooden farm house we had seen when we were driving in. Surely they had to be over there. Maybe the barbecue was near the house.

'Hello? Hello?' I said as I tried the door to this farm house. This door was unlocked too. I peeped in and stared at the old walls. This house looked a bit frightening. I had visions of myself being pulled in and chopped into bits by the insane farmer who lived within. I closed the door quickly and ran further down the road in the direction I thought was close to the river. Eventually I heard some voices. 'Hello? Hello?' I ran and ran and eventually I saw members of our clan sitting in little groups near the river chatting, and one person preparing burgers.

I screamed out, 'Hey! Nobody told me you were leaving the house. That was scary man. I fell asleep and nobody missed me. How could you? How could you leave me?' People turned around in disbelief. 'Oh you were not with us? Sorry Jennylynd.' Charlie came around to give me a hug. His eyes searched to make a joke about the whole incident. 'You! Don't you dare laugh at me! I was frightened. I couldn't find you guys,' I said. 'Don't worry, there's nobody around here,' said one of the program managers. 'That's just it. Suppose there was somebody around. Just suppose!' It took me a few minutes to calm down. Then I remembered I was hungry. I grabbed some food and took deep breaths. Two romantic couples had formed in our group. They were cute to observe as they sat separately from the rest of us.

The next day I was ready for my clay shooting class. We drove in vans to another part of the farm and got instructions on how to hold a rifle and how to aim at clay ducks as they were fired from a machine. This was another extreme team building exercise. I had never in my life come close to a gun, even if it just had pellets. The firing rifles made really loud bangs and we wore noise reduction ear muffs. We each had two or three chances and took turns at shooting. I got my first taste of hunting. It was a great skill to be able to aim and shoot quickly. Some people in our group had done this before on their family farms. For me, the little Caribbean girl, I felt I was light years away from my small town back in Trinidad. The experience was exhilarating.

In the evening we were treated to a baseball game in a big stadium. It was an American tradition not to be missed with hot dogs and mustard and the works. The excitement of going to the game was more interesting than watching the game itself. My first big stadium baseball game was punctuated with stories of "Brodie's Floaties". Charlie had us falling over with laughter as he described how his roommate, Sam left some floating matter in the toilet when they shared a hotel room. He carried on, rolling his eyes as he explained in detail how Brodie's Floaties wouldn't flush! Much to Sam's horror, we had a new joke for this trip. Who could remember the baseball game? Too many jokes were passing.

'But what happens on the road stays on the road!' shouted Charlie.

The next day after a workshop, we attended a fancy dinner held in our honour at a beautiful historic house in Delaware. It was the icing on the cake of all the extravagance and honour bestowed on us in the leadership program. Everyone dressed in their best dark suits while I wore a colourful red tie-dye skirt suit from Trinidad with gold fabric puff paint. 'Oh my God Jennylynd! I need sunglasses to look at that suit!' yelled Charlie. 'You're just jealous you don't have one just like it,' I said. I had caught him off guard. He didn't know how to answer that one.

A few months later in the summer, we had our last set of workshops and team bonding experiences. We were on stage standing at our graduation ceremony, just where I had dreamt I would be the year before. I represented the group by singing the US National Anthem. My friend Jenna and Tiffany were my guests at the award ceremony. They were in the audience to cheer me on. As new Leaders, we faced the admiring industry professionals and we were called forward one by one to receive a large plaque and a leadership pin.

Two couples had matched up in this program before our eyes: Clare with Bradley and Frank with Cynthia. I was not even aware what was going on as we travelled periodically during the year from one city to the next. Some of the participants were married, but the single ones were actively looking for partners; and what better place to find one? We were a group of people with the same industry bond. I could not see myself getting together with Burt, the last single man left in our group. He was about ten years younger and not my type. I did not think I was his type either. We all vowed to remain friends and stay in touch forever after graduating from the program!

A few weeks later while checking my mail back home, I got an invitation for Clare and Bradley's wedding in Palm Springs. This was going to be big affair. Clare's family owned vineyards in the desert near Palm Springs. He was from the East Coast and she was from California. One person would have to move. Clare was going to be transformed from a Tomboy into a dainty bride. I looked forward to seeing this. 'We're going to another wedding Tiffany!' I said. 'Another wedding? Wow!' she said. It was a fairy tale wedding, complete with the bride arriving on a horse-drawn carriage ... Lifestyles of the rich and famous.

Alpaca Steak with Quinoa

I flew to Lima, Peru and stayed overnight. My work assignment was to visit operations in the north in Sullana and Piura. However, I arrived early to take a planned three day detour visiting the ancient Inca cities of Cusco and Machu Picchu. Even though the company was not involved in my plans, I managed to enlist the help of Norma from the Costa Rica office to contact a tour guide in Cusco to plan tours for me. I kept this detour quiet in case the big bosses tried to stop me. Imagine a young woman travelling around the Andes by herself. They would have been afraid of liability issues for the company. It was Fourth of July in the United States and everyone was away for the long weekend. So I felt justified in taking time to explore Cusco. Tiffany was visiting her grandmother in Poland that summer and I promised to call them on arriving in Cusco. After flying to Lima and staying overnight at a quiet hotel in a wealthy city district, I arose early for the flight to Cusco. The Lima airport was huge and imposing. Everything was written in Spanish; all the signs, bill boards, and notices.

Many foreigners were also en route to the Andes. I saw many Europeans with back packs and camping gear so at least I was not alone. My Spanish lessons paid off in finding the check-in counter and getting onto the correct plane. Views from the aircraft were spectacular that morning as we traversed the snow capped Andes. I felt like I was at the centre of the Universe. The sun broke through some cloud cover and welcomed the morning as we flew close to a few summits. Everyone on that plane was a blurry eyed tourist from one country or the other. After landing, the early morning sun hit us in the eyes as we boarded a shuttle bus for downtown Cusco.

According to my email instructions, my personal tour guide, Fabian Zapata was to meet me when the shuttle arrived in the main town. As we alighted from the bus, we were greeted by a mob of vendors selling dolls, jewellery and trinkets. I could not resist and bought a rag doll which depicted an Andean woman with two long braids, carrying a baby bundle, and corn and potatoes in a sack. She was cute and I was sure Tiffany would love her. Fabian Zapata approached with a sign showing my name. 'Hola. Buenos dias,' I said in my best Spanish. 'Hola. Jennylynd?' he asked. 'Yes it's me. Can I just take a few seconds to see the jewellery over here?' An aboriginal woman in full costume opened a tray of miscellaneous jewellery which was too tempting to ignore. She showed dangling earrings made of metal and semi precious stones. These were accompanied by matching necklaces with elaborate wire bending. 'I'll take this one and that one,' I said. I had changed some money at the Bureau de Change in the airport so I had Peruvian currency in hand. It would have been too expensive trying to haggle with US dollars.

Fabian rushed me along, 'You will see many of these things

in the town. Let's go,' he said. 'That's true,' I agreed. We hopped into his little car and he spoke in English with a strong Peruvian accent. He looked like a pure Spaniard with no hints of indigenous blood, but one would never know. Fabian explained that I was to go to rest in the hotel to get acclimatized to the altitude. Cusco was 11,000 feet above sea level. I was to drink the Mate de Coca tea offered at the reception in the hotel. Mate de Coca was made with leaves from the Coca plant, the same one used to make cocaine! The descendants of the Incas and the Andean people chewed on coca leaves all the time. It was said, to combat altitude sickness. Being a person who was always fit and in good health, I wondered if this was necessary. I also wondered about chewing on coca leaves all weekend and returning to the United States the following week. Customs and immigration dogs would sniff me out and I could be arrested for having cocaine in my blood. Imagine the plight of the simple travelling food scientist!

It was July, but the air was cold and almost zero centigrade according to the thermometer. I had walked with a warm jacket so I was prepared. In addition, a warm wool sweater and socks were on my shopping list for the town. When we arrived at the little hotel, I wondered if it was an elaborate house converted into a hotel. Fabian said again, 'Get some sleep and I will meet you in the afternoon.' I said thank you and went to my room with a cup of Mate de Coca. The room was small with a tiny bed on one side, a dressing table and chair and the tiniest bathroom. It was a basic motel, but this did not matter. I was paying just for a place to sleep two nights. After all, I was anxious to explore. Laying down for a nap, I jumped up within half an hour.

Was I crazy? I was at the centre of the world, and I was taking a nap? I needed to get cracking and explore the town. And that is what I was going to do. When again would I have the opportunity to travel to the ancient Inca capital of Cusco in Peru? I got dressed in some warm comfortable clothes and put on my walking shoes. I enquired at the hotel lobby for a map of Cusco. The attendant showed me where we were located on the map and I asked for the closest markets to buy souvenirs. Her English was perfect. I set off to find the craft markets and immediately got a mild headache and felt nauseous. I tried to ignore the discomfort since my goal was to explore and shop. The quaint narrow streets and little shops were beautiful. Then I found a building that said 'Mercado Artesenal'. In there, vendors sold CDs of Andean music, paunchos, socks, art and other miscellaneous items. I bought a few items and realized my head was spinning. I just had to sit down. The only problem was that I was in a strange market where everyone spoke Spanish.

'Please give me a chair! Somebody please! Una silla! Una silla por favor,' I yelled. I was about to collapse as the space revolved around me. A man saw my distress and brought me a chair. It must have been a common sight; collapsing tourists suffering from altitude sickness. I sat there for a while and watched the world spin as I caught my breath, what little was available. 'You OK lady?' he asked. 'Yes I'll be fine thanks,' I said gasping. After about fifteen minutes, I felt strong enough to move. However I also realized I was hungry. It was a long time since dinner the night before.

I walked to the nearest restaurant which was two doors down from the market and sat down again. The place was empty, but they were open for business. I looked at the menu in a daze while translating in Spanish. Then I ordered a light soup. My stomach may not have kept down a heavy meal.

I chatted with the waiter and told him about my near collapse from altitude sickness at the market a few moments before. He suggested that I rest. Why was everyone trying to get me to rest? As I finished my soup, an indigenous woman walked in from the street and spoke loudly with all the waiters. She also greeted me vociferously. She carried a tray covered over with a white cloth. The waiters started motioning to me to taste something.

'Cuy! Cuy!' they said in chorus. 'What?' I had no idea what they were talking about. Everyone knew I was visiting from America. 'Cuy! Cuy!' they said again. 'Trata lo!' Just then, the woman removed the white cloth to reveal what looked like six big barbecued rats. Their eyes and teeth were looking at me. 'Cuy!' They motioned for me to try it. I looked in disgust and the creatures smiled back. 'No gracias. Nada para mi,' I said. I was not going to taste the ugly looking critters; not for love nor money. She did not accept no for an answer. The woman took her grubby fingers, with nails full of dirt and broke off a piece for me to taste. By that time, all the waiters in the restaurant were at my table looking with delight and egging me on to try it. I looked at her finger nails and remembered all the food safety practices I was preaching to people on the farms. Wasn't I in Peru to do inspections of farms? If the altitude sickness didn't get me, the cuy or her dirty finger nails would certainly finish me off!

I took the generous offering and put it in my mouth chewing away vigorously. Everyone was over-eager to know what I thought. 'Bueno. Delicioso,' I said. In fact it tasted just like any piece of chicken, except it was brown and the animal's head looked like a rat's. I had been forewarned that a local delicacy was roast guinea pigs. Villagers would keep guinea pigs under their beds in remote mountain villages, fattening them with potato skins. This was one of my first big culinary experiences in Cusco, Peru. I survived and thanked my hosts, then walked slowly back to hotel to get a nap before my tour guide picked me up. There was to be no more wandering around until I got some rest!

Later in the afternoon, Fabian drove me to the collection point for a pre-paid tour of the city of Cusco. The Incas built so many amazing structures of solid stone: temples, houses, terraced agricultural sites and other building along the sides of mountains. Spanish invaders could not destroy the structures, so in many cases, they built on top of them. The area was steeped in ancient history. Many interesting people were also on the tour. I met a family from Holland that day and spoke with them during the break. I also met a young man from Grenada on the Cusco tour. His mother had married a French man who was a diplomat currently stationed in Peru. I spoke to everyone possible, and asked them to take my photo at places of interest.

One American family with two young boys took the tour around Cusco and I later spotted them at various sights around the town. The locals would have been able to point out new arrivals and could surely spot when we left. A Russian man called Alexander was serious about chewing his coca leaves. 'I don't want to get altitude sickness,' he explained. 'Good for you Alexander,' I said. The mountain people spoke a language called Quechua and only spoke Spanish if necessary. They also knew how to haggle in English to sell to tourists. On the tour around Cusco we came across many women dressed in traditional costumes. They wore brightly coloured dresses with layers of wool shawls and large flat hats. They walked with costumed children begging tourists to take photos for a few "nuevo soles". The children looked so adorable and they sometimes carried a little lamb. I was sucked into the tourist trap, at first, and paid to take photos with them. So many archaeological sites and so little time ... A few tourists told me they would be doing more tours of the area in the following days. I had only one more day left before going to work so I had to cram in a day trip to Machu Picchu before leaving the mountains.

On returning to the hotel, I decided to take a short walk around the town looking for a good dinner restaurant. Greeters stood in front of all the restaurants welcoming visitors. Not knowing where to go, I walked into the Paititi restaurant and took a seat. 'Dinner for one,' I said, as the waiter looked around to see if anyone else was coming. He presented the menu and I looked in a daze at the selection. 'I want to eat something I've never had before,' I told him. He suggested I try the Alpaca Tupac Turin. It was grilled alpaca steak with a cake of quinoa – a rice like dish with vegetables. 'Oh my God, you actually eat alpaca? But they're so cute,' I said, trying to decide if I could be a savage and eat the poor little alpaca. 'OK. I'll have that,' I decided.

Peru was famous for different coloured maize and potatoes. It is said the European colonizers were first introduced to potato when they invaded Peru. However I had never seen such beautifully coloured potatoes in my life. Only a few varieties may have left the Andes. In addition I had never heard of quinoa and promised myself to research it when I got home. The meal came with multicoloured corn – purple, white and yellow. I also ordered the national drink, pisco sour, a cocktail made with grape brandy, lime juice, syrup, ice, egg white and a dash of Angostura bitters. When the meal was placed in front of me, the smell of the alpaca was revolting. It was strong and gamey. I was determined to eat the whole meal but had to hold my breath to block out the strong smell. The meat was tasty and chewy, just like any steak. I sauntered back to the hotel full to the brim and ready for a good night's sleep after the day's adventure.

The next day, the plan was an all day trip to Machu Picchu, the lost Inca City. The Vistadome train to Machu Picchu left at 6:00 am. There was Fabian early in the morning to take me to the train station. Even though I paid for this service, I wondered how many other people poor Fabian had to shuttle around in the morning and night. The train was packed with tourists. Some adventurous folks preferred to hike along the ancient Inca trail to get up to the mountain. This was a gruelling hike taking several days with guides. I preferred to sit in comfort and take in the view on the Peruail train which had large windows and a glass ceiling for a panoramic experience of the Andes. These were the highest mountains I had ever seen. Some peaks were covered with snow. There were also many farms along the way.

Light refreshments were served on the train which made a few stops. At the terminals, vendors rushed to the train windows selling trinkets and boiled corn. I was amazed how large the corn grains looked. The corn was also a strange white colour, a variety not typically seen in North America. The end of the train line was at the town of Aguas Calientes, the closest access point to the historical site of Machu Picchu. Many hotels and restaurants lined the streets and tourists walked everywhere. Happily, some of us had bus passes, because it was a gruelling one and a half hour trek up the steep roadway to Machu Picchu. We followed a tour guide to the bus. This was a frightening drive further and further up the mountain. The precipices lunged down the side of the mountain on either side of the narrow roadway. Sometimes a bus could be seen descending and have to pass us on the other side. I had to close my eyes in order not to panic. When we got to the top of the mountain, we disembarked at a modern visitor's centre. The bus tour guide told us to relax and sign up for one of the tours offered at the site. People milled around ticket booths trying to decide what to do. I also saw the Russian, Alexander, the American family, and some other travellers who did the tour around Cusco the day before. The complex looked huge with many terraced buildings and walking around with a map while tired would do nothing for me. I decided to sign up for a guided tour for a few hours. It was a short wait and enough time to socialize with other solo travellers.

I met an Irish lad visiting from Cork in Ireland. He showed me where I could rent a locker to store my bags until the tour was finished. He said he had taken six months off work to tour the world. He got a cheap worldwide ticket on Quantas Airlines for 1300 euros. The only requirement was to make a stop in Australia. Not a bad place to stop, I thought. The tour of the facility was to take us walking around the large compound. It was up steps and down steps. I marvelled at being at one of the Wonders of the World. How did the Incas build this amazing structure? Our tour guide was emphatic with his descriptions of the ingenious architecture, the terraced gardens, and the sophisticated irrigation channels. It was all too amazing to comprehend. Most of the descriptions were speculative however, since nobody really knows what went into the construction of Machu Picchu. Some llamas strolled around the complex providing great photo moments for tourists. The tour guide warned that a llama could spit on you or kick you if he was in a bad mood. I tried not to touch or irritate them, but I got close for photographs. We even saw a two week old baby llama. He made me regret feasting on alpaca, a close cousin, the night before.

After being immersed in ancient history for a few hours, it was time to leave. The tour guide on the bus on the way down from the mountain to Aguas Calientes made a pass at me as I tried practicing Spanish with him. 'Get outta here buddy,' I finally said. 'I'm just trying to speak Spanish'. Tour guides were probably propositioned by visiting tourists looking for a partner for the night. Anyone was fair game. We had half an hour before the train came back to collect us for a three hour ride to Cusco. I walked around Aguas Calientes looking at the hotels, motels, market places, and restaurants. I was sure they did a brisk business all year round. I wandered around a street market trying to decide what to buy.

'This one good price,' a girl said as she showed me a scarf. The label said llama wool, but I had my doubts. I did a bit of haggling and when she would not reduce the price, I started walking away. She ran after me to make the sale. After that, I bought two blankets which had the lingering smell of a wild animal. I knew for sure they were made with llama wool. However, there was no space to pack these purchases. I had brought just two bags on this trip as hand luggage. Packing would be an adventure of rolling and squeezing everything to shrink its size.

On arriving in Cusco, Fabian was waiting at the train station to take me back to the hotel. He had booked a buffet dinner for me at the Inkanata restaurant which offered a folkloric show of song and dance for tourists as we dined. Fabian promised me the best buffet including roast guinea pig. He was surprised when I spoke about tasting the little animal the previous day. He also suggested going dancing as a local club afterwards, since I was leaving the next morning. This Fabian was working overtime, but it was fine with me.

After dinner we went to a disco called Ukukus, downtown Cusco. The music was rhythmic and a live band of musicians of African descent called Los Negritos played drums, guitars, and a wooden box instrument which kept the rhythm. I was so surprised to see them since I had only seen people of European descent or indigenous people. Fabian told me that black people lived in some coastal regions of Peru. The cigarette smoke in the club was blinding and we danced until I was too tired to go any more. The music was similar to Meringue and unlike folk music from the Andes with pan flutes and drums. As Fabian took me back to the motel, he suggested he could also stay for the night.

'No thanks Fabian,' I said swiftly. 'Just drop me off.' Again I had the shock of being propositioned. This good looking tour guide may have been used to having his way with the ladies who came on vacation. He provided all services. 'Buenas Noches Fabian!' I yelled as I ran into the hotel. 'See you in the morning.' I had to finish packing my bundles of souvenirs for the early morning flight back to Lima. My two wool blankets stank of the smell of llama. They surely needed a few washings. The dolls, jewellery, wool scarf, wool socks, CDs and tons of costume jewellery bulged out of my two small bags. Even when I tried sitting on the bags to close them, they would not zip up. I had a small crisis on my hands. I would have to travel with half-open, bulging bags like street vendor. That night I slept like a log. The fatigue was intense but I was satisfied in the knowledge that I trampled on holy terrain of the ancient Incas.

'Farewell Fabian,' I said at the little airport. 'I'll keep in touch'. Goodbye Cusco. Goodbye Machu Picchu … I stared with longing at the snow capped mountains as we flew away from the Andes to the coast. What an action-packed few days. When again in my life would I ever have the opportunity to visit that part of the world? On arriving in Lima, I had just a few hours that Sunday morning to catch the LAN airlines flight to Piura in the north of Peru. This was where work started on Monday morning with the company's staff. All flights had been timed carefully to make the connections. The airlines within Peru were sophisticated. This flight also carried passengers who were continuing to Spain. I was surprised at the luxurious service in comparison to flights within North America. They served red and white wine with a full dinner on a one and half hour ride.

I was collected at the Piura Airport by Max, the tall Dutch regional manager for operations in this part of Peru. He was an amazing Adonis and I had to pinch myself to focus on general company business and stop staring at his body. He gave new meaning to the words "tall, dark and handsome". We drove to the Rio Verde hotel in Piura to check into our rooms. Max warned me not to drink the water; it could make me sick. 'I use bottled water even for brushing my teeth,' he said, 'and I take these carbon tablets every time I visit this area.' Using only bottled water appeared to be a bit excessive and I definitely was not going to take the strange pills. However, I would be careful not to swallow the water. 'What time will we have dinner?' he asked. 'There's a dining room at the hotel and another manager will join us.'

I wished I was having dinner alone with Max. We were going to be joined by Ian Wong who was the Chinese manager for the Peruvian operations. He was third generation Chinese in Peru. A few years before, Peru had a President of Japanese ancestry, Alberto Fujimori. I found this mixing of cultures very interesting. From outside Peru, one would seldom hear about the fusion of cultures.

We met for dinner at 7:00 pm and discussed the course of work over the following two days. Early the next morning we drove to Sullana. It was amazing to learn how people lived in the Provinces around Piura and Sullana. This part of Peru had desert type terrain. It was dry and close to the ocean. It was supposed to be ideal for organic farming. Some homes in villages were made of mud and straw bricks. The people tended to be short, so the doorways looked tiny to me. Fences were made of straw and bamboo. There was no running water in some villages, but they managed by using river and canal water nearby. Truck borne water was brought in for drinking. It was a rough life. The company provided jobs for hundreds of people in the region so this helped increase their purchasing power. One could see the difference in lifestyle for those who were employed by the company. They would be able to buy bricks to build a small home and they would also have electricity. The average salary for common labourers was 16 soles or $5 a day. Most people in the area farmed and lived off the land. Children at a school near one of the company's warehouses ran to look at me when I visited. They were fascinated to see this tall, black woman in their village. They waved at me and I waved back taking some photos.

At lunch time, Ian took a group of us to a local Cevicheria restaurant near the company's office in Sullana. Many variations of ceviche graced the menu: king fish, shrimp, black conchs, squid, and octopus etc. "cooked in lime juice". I was not sure which one to get so I got a mixed batch. Throwing caution to the wind, I ate and drank everything. We drank Pisco Sour and I also tried a drink called Chica Morada made from purple corn. We stuffed too much and had to return to farms for visits in the afternoon. At one of the farms, the owner presented me with a plastic wrapped silk red rose. It had a tiny white teddy bear with a red bow-tie attached to the stem. He felt honoured that a manager from America was visiting his farm. I vowed to keep that rose forever. It was such a beautiful gesture. He was taller than the others and showed more European features mixed with indigenous blood. The man was dressed in his cleanest and sharpest clothes for my visit.

After seeing several farms we learned about all control measures implemented to ensure workers maintained safe food handling practices. Supervisors removed faucets from taps at hand wash stations every evening after work since they were afraid they would be stolen. It was a chronic problem described at operations throughout the region. Since we feasted on typical Peruvian food during the day, Ian suggested we sample local Chinese food for dinner. We were taken to a grand Chinese restaurant in Piura. Chinese food tastes different in every country, being adapted to local tastes. This was a delicious change.

In Piura and Sullana, the typical form of transport was the motor taxi. This was a motorcycle with a two-seater carriage perched on top. These were pretty, and seats came in many colours: red, blue, yellow, etc. They were said to be imported from Thailand and China where people used bicycles instead of motorcycles to transport passengers. Max told me a joke about his first adventure on a motor taxi. He was big and tall compared to the average Peruvian. As a result, he caused a motor taxi to keel over onto its side when he sat in it. The taxi driver couldn't understand what happened when this "giant" caused his taxi to collapse.

That night, I had serious case of food poisoning and was unsure what could have caused it. It may have been from the hotel breakfast when I used milk from an un-refrigerated container in my cereal. It could have been water from the swimming pool which I inadvertently swallowed while taking an early morning swim. I certainly ate and drank a host of different food while out on the road that day, so the illness could have been caused by anything. All the way on the plane back to the Lima airport, and on the way back to California, my stomach churned. I groaned and shivered on the plane and hoped for a speedy recovery.

Visit to Guayaquil

Guayaquil, Ecuador was one of the most important South American bases for the company's operations. I arrived in Guayaquil late in November, to visit farms and do inspections. It was close to Christmas and some shops and vendors had started their holiday sales. Guayaquil was a major port city located on the western bank of the Guayas River which flowed into the Pacific Ocean at the Gulf of Guayaquil. The city was the commercial center of the country, with more than half of the companies in Ecuador based there. It was the most highly populated city in Ecuador with over two million people. I visited Ecuador to learn more about the company's operations and was charged with ensuring food safety practices came close to the evolving requirements in North America. Alberto, the regional manager, was at the Guayaquil airport to collect me. It was Sunday afternoon and his wife also accompanied him. They were relaxed and ready to entertain. They suggested I check into the Hilton Colon Guayaquil, leave my bags, and then we would do some sightseeing around the town. It was a brilliant idea and I jumped at the opportunity. Guayaquil was the typical expansive South American city. Sunday afternoon was relatively quiet around the Hilton hotel but I was advised not to go out alone at night. We saw a mall near the hotel and walked through briefly. They then drove and parked near a large craft market, Mercado Artesanal. This was the largest market of its kind in the city. It was said to have over 200 booths with vendors selling indigenous crafts, jewellery, and paintings.

I felt like a child in a toy store as we entered the massive market. My hosts had no idea I would spend hours shopping. I bought a beautiful embroidered, aquamarine wool poncho. The aboriginal women wore hand-embroidered cotton blouses with long sleeves. I explained in my broken Spanish I wanted one of those. They had to look for an extra large to fit me. I was fat by the standards of these petite people. I bought embroidered clothes for Tiffany and jewellery and anything else that was conveniently pushed into my sight as we walked around. A wooden bracelet, a leather belt, a nativity scene carved into a calabash ... everything was unique and new and I planned to keep all my treasures for years.

'Jennylynd are you finished?' Alberto and his wife watched the shopping *American fool*. 'Wait. Not yet,' I pleaded. We haven't gone to that side yet!' We wandered over to another side of El Mercado. I wished we had more time. However, we had to go to another area before everything was closed for the day. They were anxious to show off a modern part of the city. As we left the market, I wondered if I could have shopped some more. I had only travelled with a small suitcase of working clothes. I was going to have to buy a travel bag for all my new trinkets. We then visited a new part of the city called Malecón 2000 (dos mils). The Malecón was a restoration project of the historic Simón Bolívar Pier. As we parked the car, I saw a wide boardwalk with shops and performance pavilions. Everyone was excited about Malecón 2000, built to commemorate the new millennium. We ventured into the nearby mall. All merchants used US dollars, which was a revelation to me. 'What ever happened to the Ecuadorian money Alberto?' I asked. He explained the country had recently given up its currency. Any old currency note was like a souvenir. Alberto gave me a few pesos for my collection. I had started collecting money from every country I visited.

'Wait, I need to check out a few shops before they close.' Alberto and his wife were good-natured and patient with me. Walking into a store selling leather jackets, to my surprise the merchandise was less than half the price of jackets in California. I had to get one! I must have tried about six black jackets before settling on one that was just the right price, a mere $35! I could not believe my luck. We then visited an old part of the city called Las Peñas. It was a neighbourhood in the northeast, an artistic centre of the city. We had to park and walk up the steps to get into the old city. Brightly coloured concrete homes and box shaped buildings could be seen as we started our hike. As we got higher into the old town, the architecture was decidedly Spanish colonial. Many of the area's 400-year-old houses had been converted into art galleries and I heard that notable artists owned studios in the area. Some buildings were losing plastering, but they were magnificent with balusters and elaborate carvings. Wooden shutters hung precariously at the sides of the windows. This artist colony was so beautiful and I wished we had more time to wander through the narrow lanes looking at the little shops and visiting cafes. I wished to return to Guayaquil just to explore Barrio Las Peñas.

It was said crime rate was so high that all farms, businesses and hotels had extra security. This was no fun for someone like me who liked exploring a city on foot. I had to stay inside the hotel until someone came to collect me and chauffeur me from place to place. Early next morning, I ate at the extensive breakfast buffet and then Alberto came to collect me. We visited the company's main office, then the port to view preparation of product to send in large ships to Europe. A great deal of produce at the port was inspected and containers stuffed into the hold of large ships for many weeks' journey across the Atlantic Ocean. I was in awe at the large scale operation and how much food was moved from one part of the world to the next to feed millions of people.

We visited two nearby farms, later that day, where I conducted food safety inspections at the packhouses. The good people who worked in operations were always happy for input to try to improve. As Alberto drove me back to the hotel that night we were caught in Guayaquil rush hour traffic. It was the craziest driving I had seen to date and it was terrifying to watch. We would weave in and out of lanes. The roads went from five lanes to two in a matter of less than a mile. Everyone was in a hurry and chaos reigned. Alberto was not bothered; he was used to the driving conditions. On a few occasions I covered by eyes with my hands only daring to peek out occasionally. He laughed at me. 'What 's wrong Jennylynd?'

'You're driving fast,' I said, out of breath as he swerved left to avoid being hit by another driver who swerved into our lane. Crossing the big city at rush hour took ages and it was dark before we came close to Hilton Colon. I observed a few black people as we drove around the city. Most of them were poor. All the black women wore their natural hair. It was not chemically processed as in other countries. I even saw a street child begging for money at the road side. It made me sad.

'Alberto, where did these African people come from? I did not know you had black people in Ecuador. I thought it was only Spanish and indigenous people.' Alberto told me Afro-Ecuadorians were descendents of formerly enslaved Africans brought by the Spanish when they took over Ecuador. They made up just a small percent of the population; maybe four per cent. Most of the one million or so Afro-Ecuadorians lived in the northwest coastal region called Esmeraldas and Valle del Chota, in the Province of Imbabura. Many also lived in Quito and Guayaquil. People associated them with the *marimba* music. Most people in Ecuador were mestizo with mixed Spanish and indigenous background. But some like Alberto also had a bit of African blood.

It was close to 8:00 pm and students were well-dressed in their uniforms, in the streets in droves. 'Why are so many high school students out here at this time?' I asked Alberto. 'The schools are overcrowded,' he explained. The city had to move to a three shift system to accommodate all the students in the existing school buildings. 'What? You mean some will be on the road late at night?' I asked. 'There's the early morning shift, an afternoon shift, and then a night shift,' he said. So at any time day and night students could be seen all over this tough city. On the whole, people in Guayaquil did not smile or look contended like those in the other Latin American countries I had visited. I wondered if life was unbearably hard for them. I assumed all Latin Americans were happy, dancing people like the music we heard on the radio.

I was thankful to get back to the hotel and rest after the long day on the road. The lobby had many armed security guards, which was a bit worrying. Going directly to my room, I planned to order dinner from the room service menu not feeling ambitions enough to sit in the restaurant or bar by myself. A black woman sitting alone at night in a hotel bar was just not a good idea in any city. The menu had many local dishes so I ordered seco de chivo, a traditional Ecuadorian goat stew, served with arroz amarillo (yellow rice) and patacones (fried green plantains). When dinner came I stuffed myself while flipping TV channels. It was relaxing. Every morning I would join all the hotel business people for the elaborate breakfast buffet and pig out before leaving for a day at the farms. I felt guilty about the excess eating and would vow to return to sensible portion sizes and exercise on my return to California.

On another trip we visited two independent farms in Zona Guaga. These were contract growers and we had to determine if they upheld the same standards as the company's farms. These growers had farms in remote areas well outside Guayaquil. Alberto drove with me almost two hours outside Guayaquil to reach the farm. It was clearly off the beaten track. After entering security gates at the main entrance from the highway, we took dirt roads for what seemed like an eternity before coming to another set of gates. I saw a small zoo near the entrance with animals in large cages: monkeys, tropical birds, llamas and other creatures. 'You mean to say the owner has a zoo on the farm?' I asked Alberto. 'Yes. He's a rich man,' he said.

As we drove for more miles, I wondered when we would ever reach buildings and see people. We drove through fields and eventually went past some ragged wooden housing. 'That's where the workers live,' said Alberto. I looked at the wooden shacks and my heart sank. Then we came up to a large packing house. As part of the audit we were supposed to look at hand wash facilities and toilets. Little was available for hand washing; an old bar of soap sat next to the tap designated for the staff. I asked to see the toilets and was again disappointed at the poor conditions. In some cases, no toilet paper was provided. What would they use if there was no toilet paper? I asked to see the living quarters out of curiosity. They had no electricity; each room had simple beds with cupboards to store personal belongings. The scene brought back images depicted in books and shows about slavery. These were indeed slave conditions and all set up so cheap fruit could be shipped to

North America and Europe. I felt ashamed to be coming from the north, like some kind of hero, while poor people were being exploited in a Third World country. I was going to insist the owner improve toilet and bath facilities for the workers when I put together my report.

'Meals are provided for them,' said the local supervisor proudly. I wondered what sort of meals they would get. Lunch time came and I was able to observe firsthand what workers were fed and what we were served for our lunch. Of course we had the best fruits and vegetables served with our meal. Packhouse workers stared at me as we sat a few tables away from them. I was the fancy manager from America. I smiled and said hello while scrutinizing their meals. They were served a large bowl of rice with one ball of meat in the middle and a lot of sauce. 'They love rice,' the contractor's supervisor told me. Every day we give rice. I was quite fond of rice, too, but this was not a nutritious meal. I was surprised this country did not use corn as a staple as in other parts of Latin America. I could not wait to leave the farm and had visions of being ambushed and not being able to escape through the two security barriers with its heavily armed guards. I thanked God when we got out of the area and went back to the urban madness of Guayaquil. The deplorable conditions there were slavery re-visited.

The following day we were scheduled to travel north to a desert region in order to observe organic farming. A company jet was ready early in the morning to whisk us away to the region. We then had to drive an hour inland to reach the farms. As usual, all the staff was friendly and cooperative as we did inspections. Happily, staff facilities were more generous than those witnessed the previous day.

Workers were treated more humanely. The local managers took us to a dining room where a wonderful feast was prepared by a lady who was chief cook for the plantation. Caldo de bolas was served. It was a typical soup from the Coastal region in Ecuador. Made of green plantain dumplings stuffed with meat and vegetables, this was served in a beef broth with corn and cassava.

We had to stay overnight in the area and drive back to Guayaquil the next day since no airplane was available. I did not mind. It was my opportunity to enjoy the beaches of the Ecuadorian coastline on the way back. We passed many beaches admiring the coastal towns. I had no idea so many scenic beaches existed since we had only traveled inland or downtown Guayaquil up to that time. We stopped in La Manta for lunch along the way. A US naval base was stationed there, so it had stimulated restaurant and hotel business. There, we feasted on fried fish with cassava and vegetables and of course fresh fruit juices. As I left Ecuador, my head was spinning with details of the many places I had the privilege to visit and the many new friends made. Arriving in Los Angeles was indeed a surreal experience after visiting the hinterland of Ecuador. My bags were laden with souvenirs and treasures waiting to be opened.

Guns at the Gate

'Jennylynd we have a melon grower in central Honduras and we really need you to go out there for a visit,' said my boss one fine day in our California office. 'That's no problem,' I said while the brain was ticking away trying to plan babysitting. This was always a dilemma with every trip. All the other travelling managers were men with wives who took care of their children. I would never dare murmur about not having childcare. As the only female manager in our department I had to prove I was as capable as any of them. 'Someone has to do a food safety audit to be sure they're meeting the GAP standards,' he said. 'Sounds like a challenge. I'll be right on it,' I said.

I had planned a visit to the office in Costa Rica that same week and would see what arrangements could be made from there to visit Honduras. I contacted Rudolpho at the San José office and he knew about the melon grower. 'We could easily pop over for a one-day visit if we took the company jet,' he said. 'OK will see you when I get to San José!' I said. I packed my typical farm visit outfits with a small upgrade for the trip to Honduras. We were to leave San José early in the morning on a four-seater jet bound for Tegucigalpa, the capital of Honduras located in the middle of the country. I had never heard the name of the capital city before. It was embarrassing when my boss mentioned the name, so I had to search the internet to learn about where we would be landing. The one hour journey was to take us from San José, over the northern part of Costa Rica and the full length of Nicaragua. All I knew of Nicaragua from childhood were stories of revolution and fighting. I hoped and prayed we did not have to make any emergency landing over there. We would then fly over Honduras and into the capital of Tegucigalpa. Then we would go by jeep to the grower's farm in the middle of a rural district.

Rudolpho collected me at 6:00 am from the hotel and we went immediately to the light aircraft terminal at the airport. 'We'll get breakfast on the plane,' he explained. 'They give meals when it's a long flight'. I didn't understand how anyone could serve a meal on such a tiny craft, but waited to see what would happen. El Capitan and his assistant, after a few greetings, took off for Honduras.

El Capitan's assistant asked what I wanted to have for breakfast. I look up to see him hunched over with a short list of options. The menu included a continental breakfast with fruit and yoghurt, or a hot breakfast of ham, eggs, toast, and gallo pinto. Not knowing when the next meal would be on this trip, I selected the hot breakfast and so did Rudolpho. Our attendant hunched his way to a small compartment at the back of the jet. He removed the neat breakfast portions and placed them on trays in front of us. I thought he was brave to move around without a seat belt. I also noticed there was no toilet on the tiny jet. I silently hoped the trip was short enough and I would not have any emergencies. With that in mind, orange juice was ordered instead of tea.

The breakfast was quite delicious for a small airplane menu and we ate and talked all the way. They pointed out when we had crossed the Costa Rican Border and were flying over a big lake in Nicaragua. How exciting to see Central America in all its glory. As we stared at the terrain, it was not too long until we crossed the border into Honduran airspace. Rudolpho explained that El Capitan would take our passports into the office to have them stamped. Then we would have a chance to enter the terminal and be greeted by a local manager who was waiting for us.

I closed my eyes while landing, still not being used to looking at a runway as close as touching distance. The landing was bumpier than a big airplane and one could feel every pot hole and crack in the tarmac. We waited patiently for El Capitan to negotiate stamping the passports in the terminal. Rudolpho gave me an update of the melon grower and mentioned there were safety issues. Things were a bit dangerous. How dangerous was "a bit dangerous" and what did he really mean? I knew some parts of Central America were considered unsafe, but I had no experience with this reality, and welcomed my first visit to Honduras with the excitement of a small child on a field trip. El Capitan was to return to Tegucigalpa to collect us at 5:00 pm sharp.

When we safely exited the terminal, we were greeted by a driver who held up a sign with our names. I carried a clipboard and long check list to evaluate food safety programs at the grower's fields and packhouses. 'Hola! Como estais? I'm Jorge. I'll be your driver to take you to the farm!' said a tall stocky gentleman. 'Nice to meet you Jorge!' we said. We boarded his jeep and fastened the seat belts. He said we should lock all doors, the area we were travelling to was in the forest and dangerous. That was the second reference about danger and those people had me genuinely afraid for my safety. We by-passed the large city of Tegucigalpa and headed into a rural zone.

After driving for an hour or more on rural roads, we then continued onto an unpaved road into the forest. Jorge drove at top speed talking about not slowing down because of bandits. He even mentioned he had a gun under his seat just in case of trouble. 'A gun?' I asked with trepidation.' 'Well ah… yah never know,' he said casually. Well in fact I did not want to know. I wanted to go quickly, do the inspection and get out alive. We finally approached our destination with tall, chain-linked fences crowned by barbed wire, and an even taller gate manned by armed guards. A number of poorly dressed people of mixed Spanish and indigenous descent stood in front of the gate. I wondered why they were loitering near the premises. 'Looking for work,' Jorge explained. 'We always have many people in front looking for work.' As we approached, the security guards opened the gates cautiously and let us in. As the loiterers approached closer, the guards closed the gates. I wondered silently if they were looking for work or looking to invade. It was a bizarre situation.

The owner of the farm greeted us joyfully and took us on a grand tour of the packhouse. We saw the area where fruit was washed and heard about the woes of using well water in the area. The water had to be recycled. Judging from the colour of the water, I wondered how long he could safely recycle it. I took copious notes on the sanitation of the facility and the staff, making a list of recommendations. The host then invited my colleague and me to have lunch. The lunch tables were at the front of the packing house and in full view of the "job seekers" at the gate. I did not feel comfortable munching on sandwiches while the desperate people stood outside the gates observing us. In a normal situation, I would linger to learn as much as possible about the company's clients, but uneasiness filled the air. Rudolpho and I felt we had gleaned enough. A great deal of work was needed to raise food safety standards at this operation. Many of the questions I asked were fielded or avoided leading us to suspect the owner had a lot to hide. The employees were not dressed in protective gear as one would see in other food operations.

'OK. I think we've seen a lot,' I announced by 3:00 pm, keeping an eye on the clock. We had to drive back through the bush to Tegucigalpa and I did not want to be caught anywhere close to a potential war zone in the dark. 'That's it?' asked the owner. 'Yes, that's enough for us today. I'll send you a report by email and our company's supervisor for this area will be in touch.' The owner said, 'Gracias señora! Gracias.' With that, we drove out under the glaring eyes of the loiterers at the gate. 'And goodbye to you too,' I thought. Rudolpho and I heaved a sigh of relief as we left the area. We could not wait to get back to the airport where El Capitan would be waiting for us with the company jet.

When we got to the airport, we had at least half an hour to spare so I decided to comb a few shops for souvenirs before they closed. I bought a Honduran folk dress for Tiffany and a straw doll of a little paysano sitting on a donkey laden with fruit. 'Come on Jennylynd. Come on. El Capitan is waiting,' said Rudolpho. 'Not so much time to waste. If we leave earlier it's better,' said Rudolpho. With that, we left Tegucigalpa looking down at the expanse of urban sprawl which I never got to visit.

Buen Provecho

I had to return to Honduras to visit company farms and packhouses on the Caribbean coast a few months later. The trip was going to involve a series of layovers and changing of planes to get to the town of La Ceiba on the coast. When I looked at the convoluted journey, I was happy to have four days locally for recovery before flying out again.

I flew from Los Angeles to Toncontin International Airport, in Tegucigalpa. From there I had to fly on a local plane to San Pedro de Sula which was in the north and closer to the coast. By the time I got to San Pedro Sula, I was surrounded only by locals. There were few, if any tourists in this part of the country. The local flights were filled with business people and traders flying around the country. Wearing modest clothes, I tried to blend in. The Honduran population was cosmopolitan in some areas, so it should not have been obvious I was visiting from "America". I always tried to hide in case someone had an unfriendly bias against Americans.

The last leg of the journey was on an air bus from San Pedro Sula to La Ceiba. I wondered why the travel agent referred to the flight as an air bus but thought nothing of it. We boarded a small plane with a big belly in midday sun. It was hot and humid that day and everyone was perspiring since the little airport was not air conditioned. The airbus was also hot. I fastened my seat belt, and waited to be airborne so the craft could cool down. Nobody was strict about overloading like in North America. Passengers had brought everything they possibly could onboard. As we lifted off, the little plane groaned and rattled. I looked at my neighbour who sat calmly, pulled his cap over his face and leaned back to get a nap. How could anyone sleep through that heat?

The air bus rattled and rattled. There was no cool air. In fact it got hotter and we flew lower than what one would expect for a plane. I could see tree tops. Surely, this was too low. It reminded me of old newscasts of planes carrying soldiers at war who would jump out with a parachute. The other passengers were comfortable and I tried to focus and think happy thoughts. With every rattle I thought the sides of the jet and the doors would fall off, or we would crash. I held onto the arms of my chair, closed my eyes and prayed for myself, my child in California, my family, and for everybody.

In the middle of the prayer, we started our descent. I could not wait to walk on the ground again. It was the longest twenty minute flight of my life. As we touched down every inch of the plane rattled noisily. Passengers grabbed their belongings from under the seats and in the overhead compartments, making a mad dash across the tarmac for the small terminal. When we entered the terminal, I went to baggage claim to collect my small suitcase. I hoped it would arrive after changing planes so frequently. Thankfully, my suitcase came and I rushed out to the front of the small concrete terminal to see who had come to collect me. I was supposed to look for someone with my name on a sign.

Sure enough I saw a stout fellow holding up a name card. 'Hola ... Yenneelee?' he asked. 'Hello Juan. How are you?' I held out my hand to shake his. Juan was a tall, mixed race man with a round jovial face. He wore glasses and mopped the sweat off his forehead with a handkerchief. The humidity was high and so was the excitement in the airport as people went in all directions with associates and family. Juan was dressed in his company T-shirt and long khaki pants. 'How was your flight,' he asked with a Honduran accent. I assumed his accent was typical of the region. 'Oh it was interesting. I thought I would die in the air bus, but no big deal.' Juan did not understand my English sarcasm and so did not laugh at my half joke. 'I will take you to the visitor's housing to put your bags, then we go to dinner,' he said. 'Thanks, that would be great,' I said.

I forgot I was hungry on the airbus. And thankfully I had

not eaten or else I may have brought everything back up. However, when firmly planted on the ground, my insatiable hunger returned. We drove through the streets of La Ceiba which was near the coastline. All the while, Juan pointed out some of the main landmarks in the area. We finally came to a complex of concrete and wood buildings. Waiving to security at the gate, we drove into the company's compound with many buildings to serve the region.

Visitors' housing reminded me of 1950s buildings on old agricultural stations throughout the former British colonies in the Caribbean. La Ceiba was on the Caribbean coast, so the similarities were astounding. Juan gave me a key for the front door of the building and a key for my room. 'There are other bedrooms in the house. Maybe another guest will stay here later. I'm not sure,' he said. 'What? You mean other people share the house?' I asked a bit concerned. That was not too comforting. I would be sure to lock my bedroom door when I turned in at night. 'You can eat anything you want in the kitchen for breakfast.' He opened the fridge to show me some fruit, bread, butter, cheese, juices etc. I assumed there was no lavish hotel breakfast at this joint. We were leaving at 6:30 am next morning to visit farms.

As I put down my things and came back to the living room, we were joined by two other regional managers. We then all went into the town for dinner. 'Yenneelee, what would you like to eat?' That was my favourite question and I was famished. 'Let's have typical Honduran food. I want to see what it tastes like,' I said. 'Well, there's pupusas, pan fried pork chicharrones, fried plantain, and tamales,' he explained. 'Yes everything,' I said. 'And fish too.' Juan smiled at me, probably thinking *La mujer esta loca* (the woman is mad).

When we got to their preferred restaurant we had a table waiting for us near the door. The manager was expecting us. Juan ordered a bit of everything as I requested so I could taste the best of Honduran cuisine. It was delicious, especially the freshly-fried fish! Anyone who entered the *restaurante* told our group, 'Buen Provecho.' This was similar to *'bon appetit'* or *'enjoy your meal'*. It was a sign of respect for our party. All the managers would answer, 'Gracias.' By the fourth *buen provecho*, I had given up and focused on my meal. The Honduran population was too well-mannered for me. Nobody went unnoticed or ungreeted.

After dinner, everyone shook hands again and promised to meet the following morning to visit the farms. Juan asked if I wanted to drive around to see the town. I declined and asked to do that the following evening after work. As I settled in my small but comfortable room that night, I set my alarm for 5:30 am so I would have time to shower, dress and have a bite to eat before my host collected me at 6:30 am. During the night, I was awoken by a trampling back and forth.

Swish swash, swish swash ...

A wave of panic overcame me. Someone was in the house. Who was it? Was this person also visiting from the US? Was it a burglar? We certainly had a lot of security around the complex. I doubted a thief would get in but I had nothing of much value for a thief to take. I wondered if I had remembered to lock my door. I rose ever so quietly out of bed and walked to the wooden door. As I approached, I heard the same noise

Swish, swash, swish, swash …

Someone passed by. He probably went to the kitchen.

In the dim light, I saw the key was still in the lock and breathed a sigh of relief. I had locked the door in my tired state before getting ready for bed. I pulled out the key and peeped through the key hole to see if I could spot the other inhabitant of the house. Fortunately or unfortunately, he had gone into his bedroom and closed the door. I could not fall asleep readily that night. It was a little disturbing to know I was sharing the guest house with an unknown person.

When I was finally deep in slumber, the alarm sounded. Yikes! Time to get up! I had a quick shower and got dressed in my long khaki trousers and khaki coloured long sleeved shirt with a colourful scarf. It was my standard farm outfit with ankle high work boots and a company cap. I then cautiously went to the kitchen to fix a small breakfast of cereal and fruit. I looked around the living room to see if there were signs of the other inhabitant, but did not see anything. Sitting at the small table in the kitchen, I ate slowly. Eventually I spotted a little clock on the wall which showed the time as 5:00 am. How could that be? I had set my alarm for 5:30 am. Maybe the clock was wrong. It was then I realized my error. I had changed time zones and did put my alarm enough hours forward. I had awoken too early and would have to wait another hour before Juan came to meet me. That was so disappointing. I was actually in a deep sleep before the alarm sounded. The best remedy was to go back to the room for a little rest while I waited. I locked the door and lay on the fully made-up bed in all my farm gear. My eyelids were heavy.

'Yeeneelee ... I am so sorry Yeeneelee ... Eet ees time to wake up!'

Again I had fallen into a deep sleep and was awoken by a knock on my door. It was Juan who had come to collect me.

'Oh my God ... Sorry Juan ... So Sorry ...' I apologized as I rushed out of the room a bit rumpled but ready to go. I told him I had awakened too early and drifted back to sleep again. At any rate, we locked all doors and were off. We visited farm after farm that day as I took notes and made recommendations. The sun was scorching hot and the air humid. It was a tough day on little sleep. I was happy when we were done for the day and off to another restaurant for dinner. This time, I was prepared for every *buen provecho* as people entered. The next day was more of the same. This part of Honduras near the coast was happier than the first area I had visited in the forest. The people appeared cheerful and the population diverse.

On the last day in town I had arranged a trip to the vast ancient Mayan ruins of Copan before flying off to California. Juan recommended I hire a taxi for the day since it was a long drive to get there and back. It was almost a four hour drive to Copan Ruinas. Copan was close to the Guatemalan border. I was used to long drives in California so this was manageable. The Copan ruins, one of the most important sites of Mayan civilization were not excavated until the 19th century. It is thought the complex was abandoned in the early 10th century. No one knows why. The Mayan city of

Copan was composed of a main complex of ruins and several nearby complexes around it. The Ceremonial Plaza was the focal point of the main complex with a stadium, pyramids, sculptures monoliths, and altars. The Hieroglyphic Stairway Plaza was also a famous monument from the Mayan culture. I had done some research in advance and anxiously looked forward to the visit during the long drive through the countryside and towns.

When we finally approached the entrance to the complex, the driver said he would give me an hour and a half to tour the complex but we had to head back to make it to the airport in San Pedro Sula to catch my flight out. As we neared the entrance, a tall, dark and skinny black man approached the car and said in his best English that he was a tour guide. He was quite good looking. I knew he was probably just hustling for a few dollars that day. He said he would be my personal tour guide and take me to see all the most important areas in the complex. Since we were pressed for time, I agreed to hire him for an hour or so. The taxi driver went off for a rest and I was transferred to the care of José. I struggled to maintain a casual conversation with him in Spanish, and he promised to show me everything in my time limit of one hour. José said I looked like I was from Roatan. 'Where is Roatan?' I asked. 'Roatan is an island in the Caribbean Sea just off the coast. We have three islands: Roatan, Utila, Guanaja. Many of the Honduran people on the islands are black people,' he explained. I was always interested to learn about the people who looked like me in any Latin American country I visited.

José suggested that since I was a black woman I could say I was from Roatan and then pay the local fees to get into the complex and the museum. 'Nobody would know the difference,' he said. I was ready for the challenge and we walked casually to the entrance chatting about life in Roatan in earshot of security. Half of what José said in Spanish, I did not understand. But, he was quite loud and he mentioned the word Roatan several times. 'Sí. Sí,' I said. When we were finally in the complex, we walked from one structure to the next. I read the plaques which were written in Spanish and English. My tour guide explained a few facts about the site. There was a main plaza where it is said the Mayan played a game similar to basketball. The ball was shot through a hoop. I felt transported many centuries back in time. It was a wondrous and serene location. We joined an onsite tour with an English speaking guide who explained about the human sacrifice that may have taken place on a large stone resembling an altar. The Hieroglyphic stairway plaza was protected with a roof to prevent further deterioration by the elements. The guide explained how anthropologists were trying to decipher the language inscribed on the staircase. The pyramids were impressive and we went upstairs and downstairs checking out the sights. My personal guide took my photograph at various locations and explained any details that the on-site tour left out. I did not dare do the tour that went underground to see the succession of pyramids. The tour guide explained that each monarch built his dynasty on top of the previous dynasty. I would have felt claustrophobic going underground.

We ran out of time quickly and had to return to the main entrance to meet the taxi driver. Giving my guide José a generous tip, I ran to the waiting taxi, and we were off. The deal with the taxi driver was to take me to the airport at least one and a half hours before my local flight. I would pay him

$100 when I was safely at the airport. 'Don ah worry,' he tried to reassure me in broken English. 'We have ah time. We have ah time.' I was too worried to accept his casual attitude. I had a plane to catch and changes to make too. It was going to be 10 hours of flying and a layover in the San Salvador airport. I was very worried. We got to the airport in San Pedro Sula fifty minutes before my scheduled departure time. I paid the driver quickly, jumped out and grabbed my bags, making a mad dash to look for the correct departure gate. There was only one gate at this small airport so I had no chance of making a mistake. On this trip, returning to California, I did not have to take an airbus. We boarded a small jet and headed to Tegucigalpa. From there I walked around to find the departure gate to San Salvador. In San Salvador I had a long lay over and quite a few notes of money from Honduras. Looking at snack counters and little souvenirs, I wondered about spending the few remaining pesos. Approaching one woman at a snack counter, I explained in my rudimentary Spanish that I wanted to buy a snack and spend my Honduran money. 'What was it worth?'

She looked at the money and then looked at me with a slight laugh. 'No mammy,' she said. She may not have been familiar with the currency. In any case, I was not in a position to spend my cash. I had to use a credit card at the fancy bar in the airport for a snack and juice. Listening carefully to the Spanish language announcements, I stuck close to my departure gate so as not to miss the flight from San Salvador to Los Angeles. Nobody wants to be stuck in an airport overnight. At last it was time to leave. I settled in my seat and eventually fell fast asleep. I was surprised to hear an announcement about approaching Los Angeles. The day's adventures had worn me out and I was actually able to get rest on the plane.

When we landed at LAX, every limb ached. I still had to get the shuttle bus back to Westlake Village, then head straight to bed. My entry back into the United States was not smooth however. I had forgotten the visa card with my work permit printed on it. I had removed the card for safe keeping a few weeks before, placing it in one of my many envelopes at home and never returned it to my passport. 'Where are you coming from?' asked the immigration officer. 'Honduras,' I said, as the cocky Asian immigration office looked me over and looked at my passport. 'What were you doing there?' he continued. 'I was on company business. I went to inspect the company's operations,' I confirmed. 'Where is your visa card? What kind of visa do you have to work in the United States?' he grilled. 'I have an O-1 visa. Can't find my card today,' I said shyly. He went on showing off because he had the authority to do so. 'Oh, sorry. I must have forgotten it. My passport is stamped though. I go to South America for work all the time.' 'But you have no proof of your status in the US,' he said. 'But I've worked here for years. You can see it on your computer. I own property and I've been here for many years on different work permits,' I pleaded. 'You know I can put you in the interrogation room,' he threatened. 'You should have your documents with you,' he said. 'Sorry, I thought I had it in the passport,' I said.

I had a Canadian passport, and technically, Canadians were supposed to be able to enter and leave United States without a hassle. This immigration officer, I was sure, was letting me know he was in charge of the situation and I was at his mercy. After entering and leaving the United States for work on numerous occasions, it was the most embarrassing incident for me. I wondered what would become of me. I was too tired to fight and hoped he would back down and just let me through. The man ran from one desk to another. I was sure my whole life was on his computer screen and there was no need for the charade. Eventually he returned. 'OK. We will let you through this time, but don't forget your immigration card again.'

'I won't,' I said humbly and ran to the exit to collect my bags. What a silly man. I hoped to never meet the likes of him again. He ruined my enjoyment of touring the ancient Mayan ruins and travelling back in time that day.

12

CHICKEN GUDGEONS

Weapons of Mass Destruction

Borzena attempted internet dating and always had stories about some of the men she met—who was suitable and who was not. She was graphic in her descriptions of some of the characters, but I knew it was all in jest. She wanted a father for her daughter; a man who would be a reasonably good provider. Borzena planned to keep her cosmetology business, however—married or not. She liked her financial independence. 'He is a loser wid ah small penis!' she said after dating a macho man from one internet site. 'What? Why are you saying this,' I asked. 'You haven't even gone that far yet!' She said, 'I just ah know eet. I just ah know. I don' ah like him.' Finally, one evening Borzena called me with a story of meeting a man in his forties who had never been married. We wondered out loud why he had never committed in the past, and would he be willing to settle down with a single mother.

Borzena said she would continue to go out with him and see what happened. Eventually, on a Sunday afternoon, Tiffany and I were invited out with Dan, Borzena and her daughter for a stroll and dinner at our favourite Thai restaurant in Ventura. Dan was skinny with a broad smile, large green eyes, and bald with glasses. He had a great sense of humour and didn't mind the little girls being noisy sometimes. He had a lot of patience with all of us.

When Borzena's daughter had first communion at the Catholic Church, Dan agreed to host the after party at his home. Borzena wanted to invite all her Polish friends and others, and her home was too small. Dan owned a lovely home on a hilltop in Moorpark. Tiffany and I drove up the winding hill to his house. As we approached, the simple split level home built against the rocky hill, we saw the beautiful layers of his cactus gardens landscaped into the hill. Lucky Borzena, I thought, admiring the landscaping. At least he is good at gardening. We found parking down the hill then enjoyed the view overlooking Conejo Valley, as we walked up to the house.

Borzena had decorated the open living room and prepared a table full of treats for the occasion. She fussed getting things ready as people arrived and admired the beautiful view. Furnishing was simple as one might expect with a bachelor: a table here, a sofa there, some chairs and other trimmings. Borzena winked at me, 'I will fix this place up if he lets me.' I smiled back. 'Well, we'll see,' I said. 'Hosting this party is certainly a big step in that direction.' An assortment of her European friends came to the party. As people drank, discussions became deeper and turned into arguments. Not wanting to be left out, I jumped into a discussion about the poor soldiers sent into Iraq to fight Saddam Hussein. 'I think it's absurd,' I said with conviction. 'There are no weapons of mass destruction. It's just an excuse to go and steal the oil.'

A German woman, Hilda, jumped to the soldiers' defense immediately. 'What are you saying? American soldiers are losing their lives,' she shouted. 'It's rubbish,' I continued, as her face got redder and she prepared for a heated argument. 'Why should people lose their lives for oil? There are no weapons of mass destruction. It's a fabrication. A hoax!' I got louder to match Hilda's tone. 'You! Where are you from? If you do not support our soldiers you should get out of this country! You are anti-American!' she screamed. Hilda had missed my point completely. It was not a matter of not supporting the soldiers. I felt sorry for the soldiers being killed for a cause which I felt was not worthy or justified. 'You should get out of America!' she wailed.

Her accent was thick and punctuated compared to mine which was, at the time a neutral Californian twang. I wondered who sounded more American. I was about to tease and tell her she was not even an American, but decided to leave it there since one could never win an argument about race, politics or religion. 'And one day I will leave America!' I said. I left the scene, moving to a friendlier group on the balcony, before I got punched for having an opinion. It was unbelievable that anyone in the country who dared to oppose the government's strategy would be seen as traitor. In a real democracy, both sides of an argument would theoretically get a hearing. However, I felt there was no democracy. The general public had been brain washed and whipped into a war mongering frenzy by the media. The climate was: You're either for us or against us.

This war mongering and hate, came and went in waves while we lived in the United States. Every year, a new enemy was declared. It was a new enemy for people to hate. One year it was Muammar Gaddafi. Another year it was Osama Bin Laden. Merchants made Osama dolls you could beat up if you got into a rage against him. That year, it was Saddam Hussein. I wondered who it would be in the future. War, war, war … people seemed to derive a strange pleasure from the country's going to war. I could not understand the psychology behind this behaviour and I could not accept it.

Perhaps Hilda was going to get her wish and I would get out of the country!

Stranded in Dublin

We packed feverishly for our trip to Dublin, Ireland that Christmas. I had booked 10 days in Dublin, Ireland so I could meet with Cathal, a former Irish boyfriend from County Kerry. We had met in Trinidad a decade before when he was in the country on vacation, staying with a family friend. We managed a long distance relationship for a year until it fizzled out. Cathal had visited us in California that summer. We wondered about the possibility of re-kindling the old spark that had brought us together many years before. Even though his behaviour was a bit odd, I was still curious and wanted to spend Christmas with him. I wanted to see his country, Ireland, and learn what the attraction for Ireland was all about. Many people idolized the idea of visiting Ireland or Eire. One of my best friends, Gary, boasted about his Irish ancestry. He would probably never go to Ireland for financial reasons, but he was jealous when he heard we were travelling to Ireland for Christmas.

Borzena advised I should not go. 'That man is no good for you Lindy. He is horrible. You will not have a good time.' She met him while he was visiting us in California and observed his behaviour. Never listening to anyone, I bought our plane tickets anyway. With money in my pocket, and several credit cards, I reasoned I could always go to a hotel, or in the worst case, buy tickets to return home if things go badly.

Cathal had promised us lodging at his sister's house in

Dublin. She was going to be abroad for Christmas holidays and we would have the house to ourselves. Knowing his character and his aversion to providing more than the basics, I bought groceries and packed as much as I could in large suitcases. Europe was known to be extra expensive and I had no intension of spending more than necessary. I bought a turkey, a ham, cans of tuna, and some dry goods. We had enough for our first few days in Dublin. I also imagined everything was going to be closed for the holidays and we would not have the luxury of picking and choosing goods as we did in California.

We left on an overnight flight to Dublin on December 22nd 2003. It was a 10 hour flight from LAX; a long and torturous journey if one could not sleep. I bought a few magazines for the journey and could barely flip through them because of the excitement. What was Dublin going to be like? Would it be cold? I took a large trench coat with an inner lining. According to weather reports it rained a lot but temperatures were usually mild. We arrived early morning and the little old airport appeared to be a shadow of the busy LAX we left behind. All weary travellers passed effortlessly through customs and immigration. Nobody was fussy. 'Happy Christmas to ye!' and they sent us on our way. I always thought it was 'Merry Christmas', but 'Happy' was the Irish version. We collected our massive suitcase from the carousel. Knowing I was transporting the Christmas turkey and a leg of ham made me a little anxious. However, I was not going to hesitate. 'Anything to declare?' asked the immigration office. 'Nope.' I said confidently.

One sign stated a ban on importing meat into the country. Well I planned to cook mine right away so I wasn't importing. That was my logic. I pulled our monster suitcase resolutely through the green area and away we went. It took some time to read signs, adjust to the damp, grey air, and determine where to find airport buses. Eventually we were able to locate the Air Coach bus that would take us to Dublin's Southside. Cathal told me about a bus from the airport that would bring us close to where his sister lived. From there he would meet us and we would get another bus to the house. My hair had been coiffed to perfection. It was long and straightened, with neat curls at the ends. I touched up my makeup after the long journey and touched up my smile.

We alighted from the bus and took our suitcase from the hold as Cathal arrived. I gave him a big hug and he shrugged slightly. He did not look happy. 'What's with the big suitcase? Did you come to stay for good?' he asked. 'I wanted to bring everything we would need,' I explained. 'Tomorrow is the last day for stores to be open so I hope you will buy groceries,' he said. Well nice to see you too, I thought. The man was already complaining about buying groceries. He was the same one who would not buy anything when he came to visit us and was annoyed when I did not cook him dinner every night.

We had a long walk from the bus stop to the house. Cathal complained of having to drag my large suitcase across the pavement. I told him I would roll it if it was a problem. Tiffany walked ahead with purpose. This was the first of many arguments on our trip. We crossed a bridge over a river, went down one street, and then turned down another. Finally, we were in front of a small mid-terrace house. The grey colour of the house was matched by the other grey and brown houses on the street. The colours matched the grey sky, and everything blended into one. There was a small concrete patch in front the house. One shrub grew there but I could not tell what kind of plant it was. The neighbours had mostly weeds out front.

When we got into the house, Tiffany and I were exhausted with jet lag and hunger. We walked into the small dark house, which had two bedrooms and a bathroom upstairs. We could hear a muffled conversation somewhere. I later realized it was coming through the walls. There was a cold, damp feel to the air. Cathal instructed we were to keep all the doors closed to keep in the heat. The radiators were on a timer and only came on a few hours at night. We had to save energy. The dark entryway had a bicycle. As we moved around the obstruction with my huge suitcase, we entered a small dark living room. A little Christmas tree, about 4 feet tall, stood near the window at one end of the room.

'My sister put up the tree for Tiffany before she left. I would not have bothered. I guess Christmas is for children,' he muttered. Cathal showed us the kitchen at the back. A few small cupboards and a counter top were next to the stove. It was narrow enough for only one person at a time to walk through. I could not see a refrigerator. In California, one would always see a large stove and refrigerator in every kitchen. 'Where's the refrigerator?' I asked. 'In Europe the refrigerator is small. It's under the counter,' he said. Sure enough, I saw a small fridge, enough for one person's food, under the counter. 'You'll have to buy food. Don't think you can use my sister's things,' he said. 'Don't worry. I brought tons of groceries,' I confirmed. 'Harrumph" he muttered. 'I will still show you where the grocery is.'

With that, Cathal took our bags upstairs. I got the large bed in one room and Tiffany had the tiny bed in the other room. He said he could stay with me or sleep on the sofa, whichever I preferred. Well, what a predicament. I had flown 10 hours non-stop from California to Ireland and was already feeling rejected. I smiled and kept a thoughtful face. Cathal gave instructions about keeping the shower curtain wide open after showering so it could dry and not get mouldy. Then he announced he was going to the pub for dinner and would call to check on us later. Was I in some strange nightmare from which I would awaken and realize it was all a bad dream?

No, this was reality and I had to find a way to deal with it. The man was going for dinner by himself and we had just arrived. My instinct was to pack up and find my way back to the Dublin airport with my little girl. Borzena had warned me not to come and she was right. The man could not even spend the first evening with us. He ran to a pub to drink and hide. Oh well, I had a hot shower, opened some cans of tuna and packs of crackers from my luggage. After our little supper we went to sleep off the jet lag. I was awakened by some muttering about going to bed too early, having to stay up late to overcome the jet lag ... Blah, blah, blah ... I fell asleep again.

The next morning I could barely pull myself out of bed. Why was I so tired? The time difference was 8 hours with day light saving time. The sun had managed to peep out slightly from behind the cloud cover but it was still 3:00 or 4:00 am in California. By the time I dragged myself out to the kitchen, it was close to noon and I was met by a grumpy face. 'You will miss the whole day. What are you thinking? It's going to get dark by 4:30 pm,' he complained. I could not emphasize enough that arriving from another time zone made it difficult to stay awake. He said he never got jet lag and we had to go to the grocery. I had unpacked the meats and tried to cram them into a corner of the small fridge. The turkey had to be left outside to thaw. There was no space. My dry goods: cans, packs of crackers, rice, and noodles fit neatly in the cupboards. I guessed we would need fresh fruits and vegetables, breakfast meat, eggs and perhaps some chicken. We got dressed, had a light snack from our stash, and then followed Mr. Grumpy to the shops in Ranelagh.

I walked around the supermarket like a zombie, not being used to the brands and the currency exchange. Everything was more expensive than California. What did we possibly need for a 10 day stay? Better to be safe than sorry. Nothing was going to be open for days. We wandered around the Swan Shopping Centre for an hour and then it became dark as night at 4:30 pm. It was time to return home. I started planning the Christmas dinner and wanted to go to midnight mass on Christmas Eve. In 2003, Christmas was still a quiet time in Ireland. All shops were shut and there was not much to do. Cathal was not a church goer and could not understand my desire to go to midnight mass. I had marinated the turkey all day and put it in the oven for the time we were going to be out.

We arrived early at the Church of Ireland in Ranelagh. Unfortunately, we were the only ones there and Cathal was distressed. Eventually, a few old people filed in and the service started. They were happy to have us since very few people came to church. After this it was back home. The boredom set in and we were off. We argued about everything and nothing. Christmas Day I rose early to cook the typical Christmas feast from my menu list. I put the meat in the oven and tried to find pots in the tiny kitchen to cook some stews and a rice dish. I prepared breakfast and Tiffany came down. We opened gifts and exchanged pleasantries. He did not like the bathrobe I got for him. It looked cheap and he already owned a bath robe, which he seldom used. He had got Tiffany some toys, which she liked. Santa Claus had also come the night before and left Tiffany a baking kit. We would certainly have to make some bread rolls using the rolling pin, and tiny bread pans. Cathal gave me a Gucci wallet and he had put 20 euros in it. He said it was good luck to give a wallet with money already in it. I was so sour, I did not appreciate his gift. In hindsight, it was probably a wonderful gift, since I used it for many years afterwards.

As the hours wore on, jet lag kicked in again. Everything was cooked and I went back to bed. Cathal woke me up wondering when we would eat because he had promised some friends round the corner that we were going to visit. He did not want to be late. Rush, rush, rush. 'If you don't want to be late for your appointment, we could possibly eat after coming back,' I said. He really did not have a fixed appointment time. After all, this was Christmas Day. 'If you're not going for a specific dinner time, then what's the rush?' I asked. He just wanted to torture me. He said, we could possibly eat and then head over. I ate my dinner with little appetite. He ate heartily complaining that he was usually a vegetarian and did not partake of meat dishes. My guess was that he seldom bought groceries but would eat whatever someone gave him.

We got dressed in Christmas finery and had to run behind

Cathal to keep up as he rushed the few blocks away to visit friends. The couple were pleasant and we chat about life in California, had some Christmas pudding and learned more about Ireland. I felt a heavy weight on my shoulders from not having enjoyed the Christmas Day of my dreams. The day after Christmas was called St Stephen's Day in Ireland. I was determined to have some fun on the trip, so asked Cathal to take us downtown to see the sights. We walked round and around downtown. Everything was closed and few people were on the streets. We managed to walk into one building on O'Connell Street that had an animated Crèche with dolls dressed up to tell the story of the Nativity. Tiffany truly enjoyed the display. While we were there I spotted brochures advertising a trip to County Wicklow; buses left from O'Connell Street. Since I wanted to see some of Dublin and the Irish countryside, I decided to avail of this company's planned tours. We would do the tour of Dublin City one day, and a full day trip to Wicklow County on another day.

Cathal announced he already knew County Wicklow and would not be going with us. That was fine with me. It was good to get away from him and the little house and see some of Ireland before it was too late. The day trip proved to be enlightening as we visited the Dun Laoghaire port with ferry boats leaving for the United Kingdom. The bus drove down the coast, and then to Avoca where we visited the Avoca Hand Weaver's factory and show rooms. Elaborate knitted wool sweaters, scarves and other clothing were available for sale. We were encouraged to buy a typical Irish lunch in the tea room, leek and potato soup, served with brown soda bread. It was a welcome treat on a cold dreary day. The most interesting part of the trip for me was a visit to Roundwood to see an ancient Norman tower and hear the history of Medieval Ireland. The tour was a full day well-spent.

Cathal did take us walking around Dublin to see some of the sights that opened up after the extensive four day Christmas break. We could never walk fast enough for him. He was 6 feet 4 inches tall and with his long strides we were always behind. He had no time to wait, and would walk far ahead, look back every now and again, to see if we were following. I was tempted to duck into a store or alleyway to hide, just to see if he'd notice we were gone.

I should not have come on the trip, but it was too late. I tried to enjoy mini tours with Tiffany which we took on our own. We learned some of the history of the city and Ireland, and enjoyed the last few days before it was time to return to California. I wanted to taste Irish stew which we'd heard about in shows. We were also tired of eating Christmas leftovers, so Cathal recommended a restaurant downtown and begrudgingly showed me how to find it. He said he was not hungry himself and would not eat. However, when he got to the restaurant he complained about the expensive food and made quite a scene. It was difficult to eat our stew which turned out to have more potato and dumplings than actual meat. It was an unpleasant experience looking at his sour face while trying to eat. I was sure that if I had bought the stew for this self-professed vegetarian, it would not have been as bad as he decided it was.

However, my funds were near the end, so I could not pay for him too. He in turn decided to sit and watch us eat with a sneer on his face. The other patrons in the tiny restaurant were astounded. Later that night, he professed that he loved me but was not sure what to do. He presented a tiny diamond ring he had purchased in a second hand shop and said the ring meant a lot to him. It must have been someone's old engagement ring. There was engraving on the inside. I had no idea how to respond. His actions were contrary to his words. He had ignored and insulted me from the day we arrived and then suddenly he was professing love. It was the behaviour of a mad man. I said thank you and graciously accepted his gift.

I was unsure what the gesture meant but there was certainly no future with such a tyrant. He would demand that I support him. We started packing to fly home in peace. The next morning the airport bus arrived at the terminal with ample time to buy breakfast. Thankfully, our suitcase was lighter after Christmas. Leftover turkey and other food were left in the refrigerator in case Cathal's sister wanted any on arrival from her trip later that day. Unfortunately, we were not going to have the opportunity to thank her for accommodating us.

As we arrived at the airport, Cathal rounded up at least a dozen luggage trolleys and I wondered what he was doing. People had put in a one euro coin to release a trolley from the stack in order to carry luggage. Trolleys had to be returned to a bay in order to retrieve the one euro coin mechanically from the handle. On leaving the curb, many had not bothered reclaiming the euro. If one was patient, it was possible to collect "a few bob" as he put it. Tiffany and I had gone upstairs for breakfast after checking in luggage and getting our boarding passes. Eventually Cathal joined us with his huge tray of sausages, eggs and other food. He had managed to collect enough money for a full Irish breakfast.

He beamed at his free meal and forgot his staunch vegetarian path for that moment.

When we went through the security check point, he gave a huge sigh of relief as he waved goodbye. His onerous duty of taking visitors around was done. He did not have to worry about this woman and her child. His body language said everything words did not say. I was relieved to get away from him and return home. We went up stairs and then downstairs following signs for the US immigration check point. In the airport, once you crossed a certain line for flights to the United States, it was symbolically like entering America. The US laws ruled on that side of the line. I had applied to renew my Canadian passport with which I travelled, but the application sent in the mail from California had not yet been processed. My plan was to travel back to California on my Trinidadian passport and just show my old recently expired Canadian passport which contained a stamp with the US work permit. My Canadian passport had expired on January 2nd and we were travelling on January 3rd. From my logic, everything should have been in order, but that was not how the situation unfolded.

We reached to the security check point and showed our tickets and passports. The US immigration officer started with small talk about what we were doing in Ireland. We said we had come for Christmas holidays. We talked for a short time then he said, 'Ma'am your passport has expired'. I feigned ignorance, 'Really. Well I have another passport. I have dual citizenship'. He corrected me, 'You can't use that. Your work permit is only valid for the Canadian passport.' I protested, 'But what's the big deal. It just expired yesterday.' US immigration officers had a knack for being exact and following rules. 'With no valid documents, you cannot enter the country,' he said. 'You can't be serious,' I said. 'Yes I am. Take these two away and remove their luggage from the plane,' he said to one officer who was waiting at the side.

'Come this way ma'am,' the officer motioned. I felt like a common criminal. Tiffany and I were being removed from the flight. How could this be happening to us? What was I going to do? My credit card was almost at the maximum and I barely had enough euros left to buy a few meals. I could not believe it. My mind was fuzzy as I tried to make sense of our plight. I called the Canadian Embassy in Dublin and they were conveniently closed until the next day. I then called the home of Cathal's sister, even though I loathed having to face him again. She had returned from her trip early that morning. I explained the situation to her and the fact we were stranded at the airport. She was a kind and reasonable woman and said it would be no problem for us to return to the house and stay until I could get my passport sorted. Life was not finished for us.

Again we boarded the Air Coach bus and travelled to South Dublin. We were already familiar with the route to the house and knew which buses to take to reach Milltown. What would Cathal say when he saw us? How long would it take to get a new passport? Would I have enough funds to last another week in Dublin? What would I tell the people at my job in California? I was supposed to return to work in a two days. How would they respond? Would they be lenient and assist? Would they be uncompromising? I had so many unanswered questions.

Cathal's sister asked us to relax, get changed and not to

worry about anything. It was such a relief. He was out somewhere roaming the city and not anywhere near the house. She told us about her holiday in Cuba and showed some photos. I waded through the mountain of Christmas leftovers and made a meal. Cathal got home around 8:00 pm after his day on the town. His jaws dropped when he saw us. 'What are they doing here?!' he cried. His shock was priceless, but we had his sister's good sense and reasoning to protect us from him.

The company was sympathetic. The HR department sent a letter directly to the Canadian Embassy concerning my employment and another one for me to present to US immigration in the airport. Passports had to be processed at their UK Office and sent in by courier. This took two days. I should not have expected it to be easy. After four days of wrangling back and forth with the Embassy on limited public hours, I was able to get my passport and book new flights back to California on a second credit card. This was a bit of life drama we would never forget.

Quest for European Experience

No sooner had I returned to California, than my boss asked me to fly out again to visit growers in the north of Costa Rica. I hadn't been to that part of the country and it was a different type of adventure, interacting with growers of Chinese descent. We also had to contend with wild winter winds that blew the company jet in circles as we tried to land on a rural dirt road. I closed my eyes in panic, while Ruldulpho prayed to the saints, and El Capitan cursed the weather. It was then off to the mid-winter deep freeze at the port of New Jersey, followed by Southern Hemisphere summer in Chile. I discovered the terrain and crops were similar to California. Visiting the port city of Valparaiso, with its colourful hill-side buildings, narrow lanes, and street elevators were a welcome diversion from the serious industry tours. And we still managed to squeeze in souvenir shopping at seaside markets on the Pacific coast and the impressive Mercado Antesanias de Las Condes in Santiago.

My life should have been complete, with frequent journeys to interesting foreign sites and auditing farms off the beaten track. However, my inquisitive character was always seeking to do more and experience more. I looked critically at my comfy life and surroundings in Southern California found reasons to become dissatisfied. Some women appeared to be dying to be beautiful. They were in a state of constant starvation to be skinny enough to meet the mark of imaginary approval. The skinny legs were accentuated with false breasts and artificially tanned, leathery skin. The bleached, blonde hair with extensions, false nails and false eyelashes were considered necessary to look like the doll that men craved. Chemical peels to bring out young flawless skin and skin bleaching for an even skin tone were the order of the day. Botox injections to reduce wrinkling, formed expressionless faces. It was a high price literally and morally for women to pay to find the ever elusive "Mr. Right".

I was not prepared to alter my body significantly, even though I had altered my food consumption to remain skinny. I started to despair and had low self esteem because I had no steady boyfriend. Feelings of being ugly and unloved plagued my thoughts. I could never be considered beautiful without these outer transformations to look like the doll in the magazine. What would become of me? How could I survive the prime of my life with natural beauty and without a husband? I so wanted to have another child before my biological clock expired. The poor state of my dating life indicated that having another child with someone desirable could possibly never happen. After wallowing in self pity for a few weeks, I decided it was time to make a move. I was going to move to another country with a rich culture; a place where looking like a doll did not matter. I wanted a place with real people so I could be my true self. The search for a new job and new life had begun.

Every year the Company's European Quality Assurance team would meet for an update from all divisions. That year, the meeting was held in Prague, Czech Republic. It was a beautiful old city, and prices were reasonable compared to other European cities. I was invited to Europe to speak about my work conducting Good Agricultural Practices audits in Latin America. Representatives attended from Sweden, France, Germany, Belgium, and the United Kingdom. My colleague, Rudolpho from Costa Rica and I represented the Americas. I was so excited to see Central Europe. The journey was long from Los Angeles and I tried to sleep but it was not easy. With a 10 hour time difference, I didn't know if I was coming or going. 'Stay awake as long as you can,' one colleague advised. 'It's the only way to adjust.'

The hotel was spectacular; a mix of modern and old world. Even though we checked in at the street level front desk, we had to take the Funiculaire, a small elevator with glass windows, up a tiny hill to get to the bedroom level. This was a unique part of this impressive hotel which was perched against a hill. One could see a lovely view of the city when ascending to the bedroom level. I examined the quaint furniture in the room. All fixtures were tidy and modern, compared to the standard American hotel; and everything was small. There was a lot of wood and steel. The toilet flushed with the push of a button. There were no handles. The shower was an enclosed glass case with water spouting from many apertures on the wall. What was this? A standing spa? I had to take a shower right away to experience the enormous toy, and of course, to wake up.

After the shower, I decided to walk around the neighbourhood to get some dinner. The first meeting was scheduled next morning and my presentation was scheduled early in the session. I had asked at the front desk about a good place for dinner and they suggested a few restaurants nearby. I walked around and looked at the menus and admiring the architecture: ancient buildings interspersed with one or two modern buildings. One restaurant offered cuisses à lapin (rabbit legs). I had never tried rabbit legs and gravitated toward this meal for the experience. It was my opportunity to find out if I would like the exotic meat. The food was tasty and many seasonings were used even though I could not determine which ones.

Next morning, our meeting began and there was no shortage of food: two hours of presentations, then a tea break. Two more hours of presentations were followed by a lunch buffet, then another two hours and it was afternoon tea. All presentations were a blur, except my own. I was able to find energy, despite being hopelessly tired from jet lag. My presentation focused on Good Agricultural Practices in our operations in Latin America and what we were doing to bench mark the ISO 9000 programs to ensure they matched the US hygiene requirements. I had promised to give some of the presentation in Spanish, but gave up. Everyone seemed to speak English and at least four other languages effortlessly. During the breaks, I spoke in English and fumbled with the French and Spanish to try to fit in. It was amazing how these Continental Europeans had learned so many languages. We met in the lobby at 6:30 pm when we were taken to a banquet hall in a large medieval building for a grand dinner. The venue itself transported us back in time.

As I contemplated the advantages of living and working in Europe, it finally hit me like a lightning bolt. I should apply within the company for a job with one of their European divisions. There was nothing to lose. I was looking for opportunities to expand my knowledge in the food industry. Foreign travel, whether, it was good or bad, always had a romantic draw for me. Travel was the spice of life. During the second day of meetings, I dared myself to approach the Vice President of the European QA Division to ask for a job opportunity. He was a stern looking, yet friendly German. He ran the meetings with *German Precision* and I wondered what he would think of my request for a job. My boss was one of his good buddies. He would probably run off to tell him right away. I didn't care. My plan was to also tell my boss on returning that I wanted to work with the European division.

Determining how and when to ask Hans posed a small dilemma. After hemming and hawing all day, I decided to pull him aside during the afternoon tea break. Time was running out and we would all fly our separate ways at the end of the day. 'Hello Hans, I have something to ask you,' I began. 'Sure. Let me hear Jennylynd,' he said casually. In the meantime, I was quaking nervously. 'Well … I'm interested in joining your QA team here in Europe,' I managed to blurt out with much effort. He looked at me in disbelief. 'Uh … ah … well … ahm … you know.' His discomfort was evident. He may have supposed everyone wanted to live in America. Who would want to work in Europe? Well, all Americans wanted to visit Europe, that's who. I carried on with my monologue and watched his body language. He was still surprised. 'Do you have any openings for someone with my experience?' I asked. 'Well, let's keep in touch,' he said. 'I will think about it and we can discuss this in the future'. Well, he did not say an outright 'No'. In my mind this meant yes or maybe. I was definitely going to pursue the matter further.

I flew back to Antwerp with Lucia, the QA Manager of the Belgium Division to have meetings with two managers from the port of Antwerp. They controlled the coming and going of our company's ships at their port. We had the exciting opportunity to board one of the big ships that arrived from South America, checking out the controlled atmosphere storage equipment. This helped preserve fruit quality on the long journey across the Atlantic. Lucia did a presentation for the port managers on the inspections conducted in warehouses when fruits were offloaded.

I again enjoyed the romantic notion of living and working in Antwerp. Her job was not exciting, however. She supervised the inspection of fruit and wrote reports daily. However, the old city seemed exciting to me. When it was around 12:00 pm the port managers decided they would stop for lunch. I asked if food would be brought in so we could work and eat.

This was a typical corporate America question. They all looked at me in alarm. 'Non!' was the abrupt and loud answer I received. 'Non! We go to lunch!' I had been used to the working lunch in United States and had no idea what to expect in Belgium.

We drove a few miles out of town to an impressive old mansion that was converted into a restaurant. It was packed, but we had reservations and the owners knew monsieur, one of the port managers. Lunch was a three hour affair with various courses accompanied by wines and liqueurs, and Lord knows what else. Did they always eat that much everyday or only when visitors came? Who drinks many glasses of wine in the middle of the day with a meal? Well, perhaps all of Belgium, France, Italy, Spain, Portugal, and many other countries where everything seemed to stop for grand lunches. Monsieur asked for a special carafe for the wine to be warmed to room temperature and I learned the virtues of having different types of wine with different courses. I ate heartily and sniffed the wine in the glasses presented to me. The mineral water was delicious!

At 3:00 pm the big feast was finished and we had to go back to work. How could I keep a straight face and work for the rest of the afternoon? They had to be kidding. Mercifully the afternoon session was short since most of the material was covered in the morning. After leaving the port offices, Lucia, our company manager delivered me to the hotel and promised to collect me later that night for dinner. More food again, I mused? I would surely gain 10 pounds on a one week business trip.

I enjoyed the beautiful old hotel with lavish bath robes and complimentary fluffy slippers, but my stomach was on the California clock and dictated it was past dinner time. Sure enough, I was ready to eat on cue. It was mussel season in Antwerp, and pots of mussels were the rage in some of the restaurants. We looked at posted menus and my hostess explained any part of the menu I couldn't understand. That night I ordered garlic mussels. I will never forget the tasty food in Antwerp. Everything was seasoned to perfection. We strolled around the town after dinner taking in some of the sights and shopping for lace souvenirs. I probed relentlessly about living in Belgium and my hostess graciously answered as many questions as she could. Then we happened to pass a sign for a Jamaican restaurant. I was curious and had to go in to say hello. The proprietor was a Jamaican woman who had moved across from London and had married a Belgian. I said hello, established my Trinidadian roots and engaged in small talk. It was an enjoyable ending to the evening.

The next day after work, we had dinner at a restaurant in a de-consecrated old church. I guessed the general population was no longer religious like North Americans, where going to church was an important activity. It was the first time I had seen a business being run in an old church building. The thought was novel and almost irreverent coming from a Bible wielding society. Again the flavours of the Belgian cuisine were like an explosion to the palate. Many herbs, garlic and onions were used to flavour the meal. My flight was early next morning, and as I boarded for the long journey to Los Angeles, images of jetting around Europe and speaking in tongues, floated in my mind. It seemed romantic and I was determined to make something happen.

Chicken Gudgeons

On Mother's Day in United States, Sunday 9th May, 2004 I was all the way across the Atlantic in a small hotel in St Margarets, County Dublin, eating chicken gudgeons. All I could do was place a telephone call to my little girl and reassure her mommy still loved her and would be home soon. Reflecting on the past few weeks, it was interesting how this situation developed. When I returned to California from the Czech Republic, I pursued a few members of the company's European QA team repeatedly, to see if they could find me a position. Hans suggested asking one or two persons I had met at their regional gathering, to see if they would want to do a temporary exchange with me for US experience. One manager in Sweden expressed interest and I immediately started looking at the cost of living, prices of apartment rentals or purchases, day care centres and other details of setting up life in Stockholm. I even spoke to one African girl from a trade association who said her sister was living and working in Sweden, and doing very well in her career. Her sister had a senior managerial position at a bank, and was married to a Swedish man. Well, if she could do it, I thought I would be able to survive and thrive too.

In the end, the Swedish manager pulled back her offer since she could not imagine living in America. I was devastated for a day. However, I regained my energy and decided to pursue my own opportunities. The United Kingdom had a large fresh fruit and vegetable industry and the County of Kent was considered the garden of England. I sent my resume to the CEOs of many reputable companies and also contacted recruiting firms in the UK. I read an article that said if you wanted a senior position, never speak to HR; always go to the CEO. And so I did. I went online to find the CEO of my Company's equivalent in the UK, and sent him an email note and resume.

What a surprise it was when he responded saying he would forward my details to the relevant department. I was flattered that a man of such importance would actually open my email, read it, and pass it on. These people had good manners. I submitted copious material in an application for a work permit in the UK, sending original University certificates for evaluation. I must have been crazy to send my original certificates across the planet. At the time, it was possible to apply for a work permit as a professional entering the UK, even before securing a job. All the authorities wanted to know was that a person had the potential to get a job and a permit was issued. I held my breath for a month until my documents were returned with a work permit valid for two years. What an amazing country, I thought. It was not so easy to get into the United States, whether educated or not.

Visit to the UK

I had a UK work permit and then what? I searched for a way to use that two year privilege so it would not run out. Chasing UK businesses when they had their own nationals to employ, was not easy. Because the economy was moving along fairly well, companies were open to hiring foreign nationals, if their skills fit the job. I signed up with a fresh produce recruitment firm based in Suffolk and arranged to meet and speak with the CEO and head recruiter. I then applied for numerous jobs from UK websites in the fresh produce industry. I managed a telephone interview with the Operations Manager of company based in Cambridge, then arranged an onsite visit around the same time as the other meeting. Next, I booked flights, hotels and train rides around the country and, of course, paid for my job search travels. I was a woman on a mission and remained focused on my self-appointed task.

I even talked my way into visiting a business in Cantebury, Kent to investigate their plant and have conversations about opening a new role for me. Travelling around the UK was interesting, but salaries proved to be a great deal lower than California. And with the high cost of living, I wondered how people survived. I even started looking at property prices in Kent to see which town I could afford to live in and buy a home. Home prices were more affordable than Southern California, but they matched the lower salaries.

I arranged to meet Matt, the suave recruiter from Blue Hare Industries, at the Manchester train station. We then drove to a nearby meeting room at the Village Inn for a discussion about my background and the work Blue Hare Industries was doing to place qualified food scientists in the fresh produce industry. Matt appeared to be in his mid 30's. He had a full head of brown hair, deep blue eyes and was dressed in a smart shirt and tie. He was of medium build and seemed quite knowledgeable about all the fresh produce companies in the UK. He knew who was hiring and who was not. He had a post available for a UK expatriate in South Africa, but would not consider hiring me for the role. Imagine my boldness, wanting to be hired as a UK expat! Well, why not? I applied for any job within the scope of my skills. It was hard to imagine someone of his youth commanding the industry. However, from what I was told, ageism was rampant in the UK and it was in my best interest to appear really young to get a managerial role. Some jobs even prescribed an age range. This was something one would never see in the United States. In the US managerial roles tended to be offered to persons with more worldly experience in their 40's and 50's. It was a different part of the planet.

After numerous pleasantries and the promise to keep my resume on file, I was delivered to the train station to catch a train to Cambridge for a job interview. On reaching the company, the head of QA and food safety greeted me. He was a middle-aged man with a plain face and bald head. He explained the company's operations and I chimed in what I knew from studying their website with great care. I tried to imagine myself living in the small English village near the factory, but that would not suit. I then asked which were the big towns nearby and where did the average staff member live. The village was surely boring; however, one might have been able to commute from a bigger town.

Everything was going well until he asked what salary I was making in California. That was the beginning of the end. I should have known that the highest one could make as a food scientist was £40,000. I had no business explaining my high salary at the multinational company was $90,000 and that it fitted well with the cost of living in California. This was too much information. His countenance changed and I was out of the running for the job.

Leaving for California empty handed was sad, but at least I had a better idea of what the English countryside and job prospects looked like. I also had the opportunity to visit a dear friend, Joyanne, in Wokingham, near Reading. She and her husband had coached me for the interviews. I practiced my speeches and formulated structured answers to the predictable questions: 'Why do you want to move? Where do you see yourself in 5 years? Tell us about your background. What can you do for our company? It was the same question in each location with small variations on the theme. I tried to imagine myself living in the English countryside. But realistically, I would have felt lost in the bush. Perhaps it was best not to get the job. I had loved the bright lights of California. Even the suburbs were close enough to the action, if one was prepared to drive. At some of the UK companies, the most exciting events for miles around were cows or sheep crossing the roadway. Not the ideal life for a city girl.

I returned to California from my UK visits dejected, but continued sending out applications. Then one morning I checked my email and a message had come from a fresh produce company based in Dublin, Ireland. They had seen my application for a job in their UK office and decided to contact me for a role coming up in their Dublin office. That was very interesting. A fresh produce company in a city? Not just any city, but Dublin Fair City! Right away, the opportunity presented hope for European work experience. I answered 'Yes, I would be willing to interview for the role'. We went back and forth to plan the ideal time when HR could call me for a telephone interview. Dublin was 8 hours ahead of California time, so I had to wake up early in the morning for them to conduct an afternoon interview. This was no problem for the opportunity of a lifetime. I was prepared to wake up early.

The call was arranged for 5:00 am one fateful morning in April 2004 with HR and a technical manager. We spoke for almost an hour about my academic background and my work experience with the companies in California. The technical manager was excited about my international experience and hoped I would fit into their business. The HR manager's voice was warm and friendly. Her accent was not typical of what you would hear in shows about Ireland. The roll of the "r" was less pronounced. She went through the usual HR questions and then promised to get back to me with a follow up. That follow up was a personality test, where I had to answer a series of questions. As I answered the questions I wondered what they would glean from the information. I had to be truthful, but was I to try and second guess the traits they needed? In the end, I put whatever came to my head and left the rest to fate.

Within a few days, an email came asking when I could fly to Ireland for a face to face interview. Well, I had to thank my lucky stars. They were serious about me and my dream was coming true. I found every piece of information about the company and studied like a maniac. Reviewing the job description a thousand times, I prepared a concise Power Point presentation about my skills addressing each and every role in the job description. Practicing the presentation backwards and forwards and in front of a friend was critical. I applied for a day off to fly to Dublin, Ireland and back for the interview. My friend Joanie was to keep Tiffany for me again, over the weekend.

The plan was to leave Los Angeles on Saturday night, get to Dublin Sunday morning, and rest all day Sunday. I was already familiar with Dublin airport from my trip over the Christmas holidays. The interview was on Monday morning at 9:00 am. This interview, however was actually taking place at 1:00 am California time. How was I going to stay awake? Reluctantly I had to resort to coffee, a beverage that never touched my lips. Drastic times called for drastic measures, and caffeine was certainly going to be needed. I was then scheduled to fly back to Los Angeles on Monday evening to get to work bright and chipper on Tuesday morning. My internal clock would have to take the shock treatment.

The Irish company paid for the airline tickets and booked a room on Sunday night at a small hotel in St. Margarets, Dublin. I was to take a taxi from the airport to the hotel. According to the exact and well-spoken HR coordinator, Lisa, occupancy was low that day and I could be accommodated with an early check in. It was great news for me. I was going to sleep all day to recover from the jetlag. Lisa then explained the limited menu available from room service. She said she could pre-order my lunch and dinner so I did not have to worry about this. The company would cover the charges. 'Well,' I asked. 'What's on the menu?' She said proudly, 'They have spaghetti cabonara and chicken gudgeons.' I asked nonchalantly, 'What are chicken gudgeons?' The prospect of some strange chicken concoction in an unpalatable green sauce was not appetizing. The dungeon of a chicken, or gudgeons of a chicken ... My mind strayed as my hostess, equally puzzled that I did not know the dish, proudly announced to The American, 'Well, they are pieces of chicken breast dipped in a batter and fried'. I responded, 'Well, chicken gudgeons it is!'

They sounded like chicken strips to me. I curious as to where the fancy name had been derived. I went online to research the dish. Gudgeons are a traditional British dish, based on

Mrs. Beeton's recipe of 1861. They resemble the American dish called chicken strips in the fast food world. Gudgeons are made with strips of chicken breast cleaned and dipped in flour. They are then dipped in egg, followed by breading before frying. They are cooked thoroughly until golden brown.

I called Cathal's sister to let her know I would be in town. My email to Cathal went unanswered for days after which he said he doubted I would be hired for the job. Leaving my little girl with a big hug at Joanie's house, I promised to bring her the biggest chocolate bar. 'Mommy is going for a big job interview,' I told her. 'You have to do well mommy,' she said, not quite understanding the distance I would be flying for this interview. The travel plans worked well and I was able to rest on that Sunday in May which was Mother's Day. Monday morning I dressed in my best navy blue suit with white chiffon blouse. My hair was neatly primped into place, a douse of blush, eye makeup and powder dusted on, and the navy pumps were polished. However, my eyes burned. It was too early for me, but I had to stay alert.

The company's technical manager collected me early at the hotel and we drove through rural roads to get to the security gates. Then, it was through a small road on their compound, parking in front of a small, grey building. We climbed the narrow staircase of what looked like a prefabricated metal building to the main office. There, we were joined by the General Manager, a pale, tall woman whose father had started the company and built it from scratch. I went through my presentation which had been practised to perfection and the managers asked dozens of questions. They appeared impressed by my answers. At the end of almost two hours, we were done, and they went away for a brief discussion. When they returned, the owner said, 'We want to hire you for the job!'

The General Manager was excited. She held my hands and said, 'We think you would fit in really well and hope you will accept our offer.' The words reverberated in my ears like magic: 'Hope you will accept our offer!' She did not know how many months I had been searching and waiting to hear those words. I was in a daze for two or three seconds before I could compose myself and not drool over an offer that had not yet been made. I asked if they would pay for moving expenses, since I was coming from the other side of the Atlantic. The response was 'Yes of course'; and we left it at that. The company was to send a written offer to me in a few days. I only had to relax, hold my breath for a few days, and try not to bounce off the walls with joy.

I was finally getting the opportunity I was looking for: a chance to live and work in Europe. 'Joy of Joys!' I screamed to myself, 'Good job. Good job! You did it!'

Back in California that evening, I went to collect Tiffany. Joanie asked how the interview went. I erred on the side of caution saying I felt it went well but would have to wait for written confirmation. It was best to do this. Celebrating with the world without a written contract was foolhardy. With a confirmation in hand, then I could start making announcements.

As I fell asleep in my own bed that night my mind screamed, 'We're moving to Europe!'

13

ESCAPE TO EIRE

Planning the Move

My job letter came on May 12th, and I had to plan a move across the Atlantic in six weeks. This company would not hold a job for a foreign worker forever; I knew that. I had to push myself to organize the move, and push myself hard. 'Can you arrange to be here by July 1st?' the HR manager had asked. 'Of course,' I said. 'That's no problem at all.' How was I going to do it? I had never planned a cross Atlantic move in my life. Which moving company was I going to use? Was I seriously going to go through with it? Many moments of self doubt slapped me in the face. I had no idea who to turn to for support. Most people would have been terrified at the idea and would attempt to transfer their fear to me. My one supporter was my friend Joyanne who lived all the way in the United Kingdom. She knew everything about my job search. She had accommodated me in her home in Reading, listened to my stories, and helped me with my interview rehearsals. She would understand. I called her with the good news and as usual she said, 'Congratulations. Now get on with it!' That's what I needed to hear.

The company had provided me with a generous 12,000 euro moving allowance to spend as I wished. In my mind, all I had to do was sell my house, sell my car, get a moving company, find someone to look after Tiffany while I moved, and find somewhere to live in Dublin, Ireland. Who was I kidding? It was an enormous feat and the ultimate test in being organized and resourceful. I went online and found an article about moving house. The article described how one should write a structured plan for each week leading up to the move. The plan, however, was written for a three month move. I had to compress details into half this time. Week 6, Week 5, and Week 4 before the move were focused on removing unwanted items, cleaning and selling the home. This was the biggest task. In Week 5, I had to find a good moving company. They would certainly need several weeks' notice to plan and book space on a ship for the move. Week 3, I was to start packing everything. Week 2, I had to sell the car and sell any big appliances or goods I was not taking with me. Week One before the move, I had to mail any essential items needed on arrival. This was also the week to close bank accounts, if possible, and transfer utility accounts into the name of the new home buyer. When would I have to give up the keys to the home? Where would we stay? How could I manage travelling with my child and settling in a new country? I had so many questions with no short answers.

When was I to give notice at my job? The standard procedure was to give two weeks' notice. I did not think this would be enough to hire a replacement. However, I did not want colleagues at work to torture me with their own misgivings about a massive move. They would be afraid I could not sell the house or the car, or anything else on time. I decided to keep quiet until everything was finalized and I had my plane tickets in hand.

The property market had been booming for at least three years. However, there were signs of a slow down when I decided to sell. I asked my good friend, Derek, to help me with the sale. He had helped with an equity loan in the past and I wanted him to work some magic and get me out of California right away. We listed the house immediately. I was poised to make a generous profit but we had to look for buyers who were not in a chain. Yes, this meant buyers coming with cash or pre-approved for a bank loan; the golden buyers.

I cleaned every corner of the house, hosted two successful garage sales, and started selling off unwanted items on E-bay. I also had to decide which items, to take with me. The electricity in Europe was 220 Voltage. If I wanted to keep my stereo and other small electronic gadgets, I would need step up and step down transformers. It was back to E-bay again for these gadgets. I ordered three heavy transformer boxes that arrived in the mail. They were heavier than I thought they would be. However, I planned to take as many small electronic gadgets as possible. I was hiring a 40 foot container so it would have to be filled to the rim to be worth my while.

The first garage sale was advertised online and in the local paper for a bright Saturday morning. The night before, I priced and sorted all items, taking them down to the garage at the back of the house. Old toys, clothing, shoes, furniture, curtains and old linen were carted downstairs. Books, bathroom gadgets, and old kitchenware I did not like, went on sale. They were possible treasures for someone else. At 6:00 am I woke up, got dressed quickly, rolled up the garage door and moved my car to the visitors' parking down the street. I spread all household items around the garage neatly for potential buyers. Before I could even finish putting out items and pricing them, vans were circling the area. They loomed like vultures waiting for the kill. Potential buyers or observers in some cases, had the hobby of going around to all advertised garage sales to determine what they could resell at a later date.

'The sale starts at 8:00 am. I'm not ready yet!' I had to caution a few who came running up at 7:00 am. 'Just taking a peep', one vulture stated. She looked like she had a sharp eye and knew exactly what she wanted. These people were buying to resell at their own businesses. They would probably want everything cheap. Vicky, my 82 year old neighbour, who was always ready for business, rolled up her garage door too and put out her treasures. She came over a few times to see what I was hawking. The woman always wore her pager. 'In case my agent needs to contact me,' she would say. She was skinny and looked as if the wind would blow her over. However, her mind was active and she did not stay still for a moment.

Vicky was a seasoned tap dancer and took any gig that needed an "old woman who could move", as she put it. She had old music scores, tap shoes, and an old ballet mirror to shift. She was all about business despite the fragile appearance. Sales always brought the other neighbours out too. They would come to snoop around and say a quick hello. I was lucky to get rid of many unwanted items. One had to be ruthless in a big move. Transporting fond memories for the sake of it was not a smart option. There was no time to look into boxes of old books from University, so I decided to take them with me.

The frenzied home sale had begun. I was advised to remove all photographs and signs of ethnic bias and bake some bread and let the smell permeate the house. I had heard these gems of wisdom before. 'Put out fresh flowers around the house,' said Derek. There must have been a book somewhere called "Making a box look livable". My real estate agent's demands were extensive and it was a time when homeowners did their own decorations before selling their homes.

Once the 'For Sale' sign went up, we had to remember to be tidy at all the times. We had to wash all the dishes and put away dirty clothes every day. The daily discomfort was wearing me thin. Poor Tiffany could not leave her toys out. She could take them out in the evening after school, but they had to return into hiding before leaving home in the morning. Many of the really big toys were sold off in the garage sale. The remaining plastic cars and bikes were donated to the church in Camarillo. I was sure the Sunday school could use them for the toddlers. Tiffany was getting too old for them anyway.

Her favourite play computer, "Press a Button", was lost to an eager buyer of children's electronic gadgets. Derek suggested we stage an Open House one Sunday afternoon to invite potential buyers who drove around on weekends looking for a home. It was a favourite pastime for many locals. We had to tidy the house, bake some bread, put out fresh flowers, and then disappear for three hours. According to Derek, the first wave of visitors at any Open House were all the curious neighbours who wanted see what inside my house looked like. All the uninvited guests would come to find out what linen I used, what living room furniture I had in place, and how clean I kept my toilets. The Open House would make the neighbours confident of the value of their own homes. After the wave of neighbours, then the "Looky-loos" would come around. These people spent their Sunday afternoons roaming neighbourhoods for "Open House" events to get home decorating ideas and entertainment. A small percent of the visitors, would be potential home buyers. We had to focus on that small per cent and do a thorough sales pitch to them.

During my break from the house, I decided to also look around my neighbourhood for Open house events to see what the competition looked like. It was indeed an eye opener to find the most beautifully decorated homes for sale. Some other shabby representations were also available. Our units all looked the same outside. The main difference was how each homeowner decorated the small outer patio and of course the interior of the home. I was able to get ideas from the superbly decorated homes to improve my staging.

I purchased new drapes, linen, and bathroom decorations. The good news was I would be able to take away all of these items with me and we were due for an upgrade anyway. I received a generous tax return that year and I was able to buy a number of beautiful home fixtures without thinking twice. I had always wanted a four poster bed and decided to treat myself to a beautiful bed from a furniture store on Westlake Promenade. I would put the purchase on my credit card knowing I would be able to pay it off immediately. The store clerks in this establishment were aloof and snobbish as usual, I walked into the store. Pausing for a long time at a large mahogany four-poster bed with pineapples carved into the middle section of the posts, I asked, 'Is anyone working around here?' I said this loud enough so the sales clerks who were ignoring me, conveniently, could decide who was going to assist me. One woman walked the long distance of 10 seconds, across the floor. She was middle-aged, wore prim spectacles, and looked over the top to address me.

'May I help with something?' she asked. 'Yes. How much is this bed?' I asked. 'What other similar beds do you have on the floor? I would like to see your catalogue please.' She muttered that the bed was at least $4000 and it was expensive. I ignored the comment and pushed for the catalogue. I looked at other models and decided the one I had spotted first was the one I really liked best. 'OK, I will take this one. How soon can you have it delivered?' I demanded. 'Excuse me?' She looked a bit confused and was probably ready to go back to discussing the soap opera from the night before. 'Who writes up the invoices?' I continued. 'What's the estimated delivery date?' I made her hop into sales mode. She realized I was serious. Within fifteen minutes I had paid for the bed and delivery and left the store to rush back to work. The sales clerks were left gaping in amazement. It was their easiest sale that day with no real work involved.

I had to time the delivery and set up with the real estate agent so it did not clash with the visit by a potential buyer. I lived merely five minutes from my job. When the delivery truck called to say they were almost there, I ran out of the office swiftly letting them know I had to run an errand. The installation of the massive poster bed in my small bedroom really lifted the room to another level and I was sure it would instil confidence in a buyer. It was amazing what this small change as well as a new comforter with silky matching pillow shams could do to raise the value of a house. The buyer was not going to get the furniture but he could certainly imagine he had it.

Staging Once, Staging Twice, Sold!

House showing continued for two weeks then my agent suggested lowering the price just a little if I wanted to sell quickly. I was upset with him. I had taken out an equity loan the year before and I wanted to pay this off and still have a profit to take to Ireland. He pleaded and I resisted. Another house had come on the market in my row of townhouses. The seller had the same square footage but he installed a hot tub in the small foyer off the kitchen. That was not fair. It was my original idea and I never went through with it. Derek managed to get a chance to see the property and it looked great. We would have to come in below their price to attract buyers. He warned I could not be too greedy or I would never sell the house quickly. Reluctantly I agreed to lower the asking price. I was still poised to make a big profit. What was I worried about? That box was going to give me a good return on my investment. If I waited too long, the market correction everyone warned about, would come back to haunt me.

We lowered the price by $15,000. Viewing activity picked up again the following weekend with several appointments being made. I baked more bread, bought fresh flowers, and then disappeared for a few hours with Tiffany. The good news came at the end of the third week when we got an offer from two men who were moving from the East Coast and liked the little townhouse. They planned to redecorate the kitchen and work wonders with the place. They could do any renovations they wanted. I just had to get that quick sale. Many papers were signed, as if in a blur, with Derek and the Escrow Company. I asked for a three week escrow so I could have time to pack and get my belongings off the property. We also had to time the move two or three days before I went to Ireland. Timing was everything. The new buyers agreed to this and I heaved a huge sigh of relief. I could finally get on with the rest of my relocation list.

The Moving Company

During the home selling frenzy, I had contacted several moving companies for quotations. I combed the Yellow Pages for companies that would collect locally and manage a cross Atlantic move. Not every company was able to do this. My cousin gave me an extensive, one hour story of her moving company that packed toothbrushes and all toiletries in the same box as a toilet brush because they were all in the same room. No thank you; I wanted to pack small items for myself.

Two companies came to visit and do an assessment of all my goods before they would give a quotation. I asked for quotations of self packing, as well as paying for packing and unpacking service. Eventually I decided to go for a company that had partners in Ireland and showed a gold star in their Yellow Pages advertisement. The moving company's representative warned me that a dock workers strike was looming in the port of Los Angeles but it was probably nothing. Whether the dock workers were on strike or not, I had to remove my belongings and get to the other side of the globe. The house had been sold and there was no turning back. He indicated in case of a strike the goods would be safe in the 40 foot container until things settled down.

Having the experience of a cross country move from Florida to California helped a great deal. I knew all items had to be numbered and listed. The movers brought rolls of numbers for me to start working on this. He convinced me that they were excellent at packing and their service also included unpacking in Dublin. They did not want to be responsible for breakage of items if I had packed badly. It looked like a fair deal so the decision was made to pay for packing service for small items too. I was going to pack anything needed for immediate use and leave the rest to the experts. I made a deposit and the moving company was booked. They needed two to three days to pack and remove everything. The first day and a half was going to be spent wrapping, numbering, and taking inventory of all goods. I had to be there to sign off on the inventory. The last day, everything would be loaded into trucks and taken away. Only at the port would everything be organized in a forty foot container. This was different to the move from Florida to California when everything was removed from the house into the container and my car was driven into the container. The final packing was to be timed to the minute during my last few days in town. We would then have to go to a hotel in the area. I set the dates and promptly made hotel reservations for the last two nights. I could leave nothing to chance.

Announcements Two Weeks Before Moving

Letting everyone know I was leaving California and the country seemed more difficult than selling my belongings. Announcements had to be timed and phrased correctly. I also had to adjust the pitch of my voice. The tone had to be just right so as not to alert the listener that I felt tired of the California life-style and needed a new life. I had to be ready for the barrage of questions and the list of fears. There would be statements of envy about how I was going to Ireland, a mythical and magical place. My listeners would probably act out any other biases and experiences they had, based on my announcement of the move.

The immediate reaction of close friends and family was disbelief. 'You have a great job that takes you travelling to different countries!' 'You live in a beautiful neighbourhood and have a nice house!' 'What more could you possibly want? You have a sports car!' 'Your child would have to go to a new school.' 'Are you crazy? Have you finally lost your damn mind?' 'How could we come to visit you when you are thousands of miles away?' 'Who do you know over there? You would be alone in Ireland!' My wish was that people would be genuinely happy for me and for this unique opportunity that presented itself. A few were happy, but most were terrified. I chose to ignore most of the remarks and steadfastly planned and scheduling micro-activities.

A cross country move or a cross Atlantic move in some people's minds, was as permanent as death. They saw it as a course of no return. Some people reflected on their own situation with the knowledge that they would never make a change or never do anything to correct a life they disliked, no matter how bad things were. If they could not do it, why should I want to make a change? As I tried to battle with other people's emotions, I had to do my own planning and packing and battle with self doubt. Support was a scarce commodity. The most careful and well-timed announcement had to be that at the job. My resignation letter was typed at least a month in advance, but I decided to hand it in, only when the sale of the home was arranged. Why "jinx it" and risk making big announcements without a home sale? I imagined the interrogation from colleagues was going to be intense.

Two weeks before leaving, I presented my resignation letter to my boss, Tom. He was surprised and even more shocked when I revealed I was moving to Ireland! 'I'm looking for European work experience,' I said. 'Oh. You mentioned that some months ago,' he admitted. Well, in case he did not take me seriously in the past, he knew I was serious then. I wanted to get European work experience and if it was not with the Company, it would be with another firm. Mark, the Englishman made a few off-hand jokes about the Irish. British tended to do this. 'You would certainly have to learn to drink Guinness. They drink a lot over there,' he said.

C.J., my Chinese colleague was the most surprised of the group. 'How could you do that? How did you get a new job?' he asked dumb-founded. 'Well, I went online and applied for jobs,' I said. 'You are moving in just two weeks? Then you would have to sell your house,' he suggested. 'That's done. I listed it for sale some time ago. The escrow will close this week,' I said. 'You will have to get a moving company for such a big move,' C.J. continued. 'They're already booked. They came to assess my belongings last week, gave a quotation and will come to pack everything three days prior to departure,' I boasted at my efficiency. 'You will have to pack all your things. Oh, that will be a lot of work,' he said with a worried tone. 'I've almost finished packing. I've sold off unwanted belongings. The large suitcases have been packed and the moving company prefers to pack and label everything else to their specifications,' I summarised this major step in the move. 'You will have to sell your car! You will never be able to do that!' He seemed to triumph in the fact I had not done one task. 'Don't worry about that. I have been looking for a buyer'. The man was visibly shaken with the thought of moving and the amount of work involved. Thank goodness I told him my news after everything was completed. The effect of my story on his nerves was baffling. He sat back in his chair, exhaled, and reflected. I left his office wondering what madness I had just witnessed and moved on to the remaining staff with the announcement of departure.

Selling My Red Car

My beautiful, red Mitsubishi Eclipse with the sun roof was last on the list of items to sell. I had grown quite fond of this car and posed with her frequently while driving around from place to place. Back in Trinidad, many people gave their car a girl's name. An old car was frequently called Betsy. My red car had been purchased brand new and I used to refer to her as Mitsu, on occasion. For seven years I had driven the little beauty with the sun roof and shiny hood. Religiously scheduling oil and filter changes every 3000 miles, she was in mint condition. It was hard parting with the red baby; difficult indeed. I would usually hand wash and vacuum the car myself. Any stains in the upholstery were scrubbed and removed immediately. For the sale of the vehicle, I approached a "detailer to the stars". According to Joanie, many movie stars used this particular car detailing business; I had to go there. They did an engine wash, an under-body wash, upholstery cleaning and thorough detailing. They were able to buff away every scruff mark on the body. The shine of the red was irresistible. Inside smelled and looked like a new car. I was ready for the big sale. However, I did not know the first thing about selling a car. Should I list it in the newspaper? Should I list it on the internet? Or should I just go to car dealerships?

One friend said I should look at the blue book to see the car's value. It was seven years old being purchased brand new in Florida in 1997. I felt it looked like new and also I never had an accident. Surely that should count for something. I was running out of time. With two weeks to go, how could I advertise in the newspapers and wait for discerning buyers to examine and refuse my car. I took the easy option. I decided to drive into car dealerships and ask what they would give me for my shiny, red, new looking Mitsubishi Eclipse.

My search took me to a few car dealers on Thousand Oaks Boulevard. They all sold big named cars like Lexus, BMW, and Hummers. They had no interest in my economy vehicle. I decided to go closer to the heartland. I would go to Oxnard. Placing telephone calls to a few car dealers in Oxnard I asked what they would offer. I gave the year and make and said the car was in mint condition. Though the blue book said $6000, everyone offered $4000. I protested, but they said they would have to see the car. Most people would do a trade in. They seldom bought used cars outright in case they got a lemon.

One Week Before the Move

I left work during the lunch hour a week before my departure with the firm intention of selling the little car no matter what the offer. I made a one week reservation with a car rental office in Oxnard, so they could pick me up after the car was sold. I planned to drive the rental car directly to LAX as I left the State and hoped and prayed that everything would go as planned. The first car dealer was on North Oxnard Boulevard. The agent had no time for me. He looked out the glass walls at the car, asked the year and if I was ever in any accidents, and said $4000. I said thank you and moved on to the next dealer that was listed on Saviers Road near Five Points. I remembered this location in Oxnard, since I used to get lost frequently at this junction that led off in five different streets: Saviers, Wooley, North Oxnard, South Oxnard, West Wooley, and East Wooley Roads. Driving gingerly across the massive intersection, I was able to enter the car dealer's yard before a pickup truck swept past me. I entered and parked directly in front of the office.

Out came a tall dark man with cowboy boots, longish hair and a cowboy hat. He looked happy to see me and gave a vociferous greeting. The dealer must have seen a lamb for slaughter entering the yard that day. He rubbed his hands together. 'Are yuh tradin' in your purdy vehicle today Ma'am? Ah would luv tah drahve thayt little red car. It's sooo purdy.' Was I to tell him my plight or play the game of having ages to sell? He seemed to laugh with glee when I said I was not trading in anything. I had to leave town in a hurry and needed to sell the car. Oh, he was delighted. He rubbed his palms together even harder. His eyes gleamed. I got an uneasy feeling as the tone of his laugh changed. The evil used car salesman; he wants my car for nothing, I thought. 'Oh, ah kin help yuh with thayt!' he said with a drawl. 'Well I'm sure you can. What would you give me for this lovely car?' I asked.

I showed off about my knowledge of the blue book figures. He complained about the fact that he would be 'stuck' with my 7 year old car. He was not sure he could sell it. He would have to get it thoroughly checked and that was an expense to him. None of this was a concern and I knew it. Unfortunately, I could not think of anyone to give the responsibility of selling my car if I left it behind. I was forced to do the quick sale. I took his check for $4000, handed over the car ownership documents, and protested all the way. He called the rental car company to collect me at his office as he gleamed happily at his little red prize. "Ah cyant wait to drahve that there baybeee!" he drooled.

I got my rental car and rushed back to the office as if nothing happened. Inside I was crying for my little red Mitsubishi Eclipse that served me for the full duration of my time in Southern California. I hoped she would get an owner who took great pride in keeping her in tip top shape. It was a sad farewell for Ms. Red Car Long Legs.

I had to go through an exit interview with HR. The HR manager said she was sure I was planning the move when I was stuck in Dublin at Christmas time. I said it was pure coincidence, but she was not convinced. I had to give my reasons for leaving the company and positive and negative aspects of working there. I tried to be as amicable as I could. After all, I had the best professional opportunities of my life while working with this company. I did not know when again in my life I would get to travel the world first class, staying at the best hotels, or flying around in private jets. I had experienced the finest dining experience, with no expenses spared. All I had to do was work, and I really enjoyed my job. I had a great deal of autonomy to plan and implement programmes with minimal supervision.

The one negative happened a few months before when I found out that the men in the department earned at least $25,000 more than I did. That was just a minor detail that was overlooked ... just a small detail. I had gone to HR to complain and the answer was that I got the salary I had negotiated. It was no wonder the HR Director smiled when I told her the salary I wanted. She knew they were getting me cheaper than other professionals. To keep me quiet they had renegotiated an immediate $10,000 increase and a $25,000 bonus distributed in two lump sum payments. If I left early, I would be missing out on the second lump. My boss reminded me that I would not get the last $10k. 'That's OK,' I said. 'I'm not motivated by money.' He was shocked at my response. 'I just wanted to fly to Europe!'

Farewell Celebrations

My boss decided the department would take me out to lunch to say farewell. It was a wonderful gesture which meant a lot to me. Like a spoiled child I was annoyed with him for not finding me a job in the European arm of the business. However, it may have been outside his realm to do so. And in fact there was no benefit for the corporate office if they had to hire someone to replace me. I decided to mellow out and enjoy the farewell celebration. A lovely lunch and a lovely farewell coffee mug signed by all staff members in our group was a thoughtful goodbye gift. The mug made a great addition to my coffee mug collection. I never drank coffee but had a mug from every country and city visited. A few people from other departments came to my office to say farewell. Everyone had a story about an old uncle or grand parent who was Irish. It was interesting to see how the announcement of a move would bring some people out of their shells.

Jerry, the Senior VP of a large department, had never really spoken to me in the three years I spent in the building even though, I worked with colleagues in his department. We had exchanged the odd good morning and no more. Then suddenly when I saw him in the elevator, he remarked, 'I head you're moving to Ireland.' 'Yes', I said. 'Got a job with a company in Dublin.' He announced with pride, 'My father was Irish.' I replied, 'I can tell from your last name you're Irish. Well that's great. Will tell the relatives hello for you!' We laughed and went our separate ways.

Movers in Motion

The movers came to pack and double pack all my belongings. They wanted to pack all glasses using their 'special' method. I was asked to stop using all kitchen utensils, and only the basics could be used in other parts of the house. They planned to take two days to wrap everything and on the last evening the truck would come to start loading up. This was a frightening prospect. I did not know when I would ever see my belongings again. It was not easy deciding what documents I would have to take for immediate use when I arrived. Certainly all banking information and anything required to rent or buy a house could not rest in a box or container for months. All valuables like jewellery, deeds, and certificates had to remain within easy reach at all times. I had to decide on three categories of belongings: What to pack in suitcases for the trip, what to send in the mail, and what could rest in the 40 ft container. I wrapped my desktop computer in large comforters and blankets in a big box with pillows. Taking this box to the post office, I arranged to send it off in the mail to Dublin. I had to also mail important documents that could not fit in our suitcases. These I would need immediately upon arrival. The only address I had was the company's address. I confirmed with the company to use their address for delivery of my belongings and they agreed.

Where would I live when I first got there? It was going to be early July and summer in most temperate climates. I decided to put all winter clothes in the container. By the time I got my belongings in two months, it should be fine, I thought. I packed only summer clothes in my suitcases and bought two raincoats for the rainy days in Ireland that everyone spoke about so fondly. I bought a lovely red coat and the lime green rain coat, neither of which had insulation, but were certainly water proof.

I was determined to stretch the moving allowance to cover the moving company, the postage, the rental of the first month before I got my first salary, and the plane tickets for Tiffany and me. I could not take Tiffany with me the first few weeks of getting settled. So, I asked my sister to keep her in Atlanta until I was able to find childcare. I had to fly with Tiffany from LAX to Atlanta. Then, after a few days, fly from Atlanta to Dublin on a one way ticket. The planning and re-planning was wearing me out. How would I know what clothes to pack for her. She would certainly arrive a month later and it could still be summer. I packed her a large suitcase of summer clothes and then sent fall clothes which she would need when she arrived. Irish students were required to wear uniforms to school, so that simplified life considerably. As soon as she was registered in a school, I would buy the uniforms and her daily clothing would be settled.

I studied the street maps of Dublin closely on the internet. Cathal's sister suggested a good elementary school for Tiffany in a neighbourhood called Glasnevin. I went back online to locate the company, the school, and neighbourhoods where we could live nearby. I called the school principal to secure a place for Tiffany, and sent a written request. Places had opened up in Class 3, the level for 8 year olds. This meant that a place was available for Tiffany. I was a bit annoyed that she would not go on to Class 4 since she was already in Grade 3 in California. However, I stopped protesting when we learned she had to study Irish Language, Religious Instruction, Irish Dance and other subjects she knew nothing about. It was better for her to learn with the others at a relaxed pace. There would be no harm in repeating any work in a new and unfamiliar environment.

I asked my Aunt Audrey if she would fly with Tiffany from Atlanta to Dublin when I found a place to live. I was also in conversation with an in-law from Poland who would come to Dublin as an au pair during the early months when Tiffany started school. However, she could not come right away. My retired aunt agreed to stay with us a month while we got settled, and before Tiffany's school started in September. This meant booking more tickets to Dublin for Audrey, Tiffany, and the au pair. The travel allowance was being used up swiftly and the internet had become my best friend. I seemed to be booking tickets every day.

Again, I went online to determine where I would stay on arriving in Dublin. I searched for reasonably priced hotels in Dublin city centre. I wanted to be close to everything. It was the middle of summer with tourist from around the globe crowding to the city. Eventually I found a special deal at the Harcourt Hotel that first week in July. I did not want to stay more than a week at the hotel. My life in a new town always started at a hotel. The plan was to find a house to rent as soon as possible after arrival. I would stay in this house until I could buy my own house.

After booking the hotel, I then studied Dublin road maps online to find a house to rent at a midpoint between the school and my office. I spied a red brick Victorian house on Ballymun Road advertised as fully furnished with a bathtub that had jets. The rent was 1400 euros. By California standards, it was a steal for a large house. I contacted the agent by email and alerted him that I would be coming to Dublin the next week and wanted to set up an appointment. Everything was slowly falling into place. Needless to say, the last few days on the job, I did nothing much but tidy my desk and records so anyone following me could find things relatively easily.

I sent a mass farewell email to everyone I had visited in the Latin American operations. Goodbye messages came flooding in. Everyone expressed sadness in seeing me leave and wished me the best of luck in my future endeavours. It was such a heartwarming experience. So many said they would miss me. I tried not to be consumed by too much emotion. The decision to leave was made, but it was sad and I had to keep my focus. I was giving up a comfortable and secure lifestyle for the unknown in a foreign country. A two-night reservation at a hotel in Agoura Hills was ready for Tiffany and me to transfer all our suitcases when the moving company took our things. I continued to burn through that moving allowance but was trying to save some for when I arrived in Dublin. I hugged everyone in the department and left the office for the last time. The next day was going to be moving madness!

The escrow was set to close at 5:00 pm and I had to give up the keys to the house. Timing was critical. As soon as the movers took everything away, Tiffany and I would check into the hotel while a cleaning. This had to happen in time for me to deliver the house keys to the real estate agent. I was on my last shred of energy. I wanted to scream from the stress of planning and double planning. That escrow had to close properly because the profit of the sale was going to pay off two equity loans taken out the year before. I checked list after list and then created a new list with any outstanding things to do.

Everything worked like magic on our last day at Via Colinas in Westlake, California. The movers arrived early in the morning to whisk away our belongings. They were able to remove all the pre-wrapped furniture and boxes within three hours. I then called the cleaners to come in to tidy up. I felt like crying as Tiffany and I walked around the empty rooms for the last time. 'What's wrong mommy?' Tiffany asked. 'Tell your little room goodbye Tiffany. And your bathtub,' I said. 'I can't talk to a room mommy,' she replied. 'I know, but I'll tell my room goodbye,' I said. Farewell to the cathedral ceilings in the living room and the pretty dining room and wrap around patio. Farewell to the kitchen with its maple wood cupboard doors and the tiny courtyard leading off from the side. I would miss my little house.

We removed our suitcases and checked into the hotel in Agoura Hills. We were officially homeless. When again in life, I wondered, would I be a woman with a property and a car? That afternoon I handed Derek the keys and the escrow account closed successfully. The sale went through!

The Last Dance

On the Saturday I reshuffled our belongings in the suitcases while at the hotel. I then took care of last minute announcements and small details like another trip to the post office to mail items that could not fit in the suitcase. When I had told some PWP friends and work colleagues about our departure, a few of us decided to go out for dinner and dancing on that last Saturday night. Derek, my trusted financial advisor, real estate agent and friend decided he would take our group out to Universal City Walk for an evening out. We ate appetizers and had drinks. Then we decided to check out the dance spots for a laugh. All the packing and rearranging had taken its toll on my body. By midnight the fatigue set in. I could go no more. I begged off celebrating to go back to the hotel to sleep. My friend's daughter had been babysitting Tiffany at their house. The others protested, 'What are you going home to? Everything is packed and you are leaving for good!'

'You're probably right, but I can't keep up. Too tired …' I said. 'Are you getting old already? Stay out and party!' they yelled. The mind was willing but the flesh was weak. We said our farewells and I hugged my friends for what could have been the last time. We promised to keep in touch and some promised to visit us in Ireland. In the midst of the madness, Tiffany's dance school had their end of year concert and we were determined she danced as a farewell and tell the kids in her class goodbye. It was not as if I needed another responsibility. This show was on Sunday afternoon and we were booked to fly to Atlanta just after the concert.

Sunday we checked out of the hotel and went to the Thousand Oaks Performing Arts Centre for Tiffany's last dance with the California Dance Theatre. My plan was to whisk her away just after her group finished on stage. We could not hang around for the whole show. We had to return the rental car at LAX and catch our flight. I told one or two of the moms farewell and that we were moving to Ireland. They looked at me in disbelief. One mother who had helped me to watch Tiffany a few times after classes looked in a daze. 'What?' That was all she could muster. 'Yes. After the dance, we're heading straight to the airport. We'll have to rush, so just saying farewell in advance.' Tiffany pranced on stage with other ballet classmates as I waited backstage with a few mothers. As soon as she was done she changed into her own clothes, gave back the rented costume, and we ran to the car.

'Bye Bye California Dance Theatre. Thanks for many years of dancing. Goodbye Westlake California.'

I couldn't help but cry. I was happy for my new life but sad at the same time. We were driving off to LAX for the last time. I tried not to look back as we drove south on Highway 101. I would miss all my friends in California and the dry weather. We were moving to the green land of eternal rain. I was not going to miss the materialistic society. How much bigger did your house really need to be? Am I living in the best zip code or not? Would I have real friends or the zip code was the key?

I was leaving in search of real people who did not want to be movie stars. I wanted to meet people with a solid culture and heritage. California was full of transients like me, drifting in and out seeking fame and fortune. I was not sure what Dublin had to offer. However, the excitement of the new country beckoned. Everyone wanted to go to Ireland.

They must have known something I didn't.

ABOUT THE AUTHOR

Jennylynd (Lindy) James is an artist and writer with a long work history in the food industry. She received a Canadian Commonwealth Scholarship and studied Food Science at McGill University, Canada where she earned a Ph.D. Jennylynd worked for multinational companies like Dole Food Company and Boskovich Farms in California, and Keelings Multiples in Ireland. Originally from Trinidad and Tobago, she has lived in Florida, California, Quebec, Ontario, and Ireland. While in Ireland Jennylynd started a business promoting Caribbean food and developed a range of Caribbean style sauces and seasonings. She ran this business for five years with artistic flair. In Ireland she also discovered her hidden talent for painting and fine art.

When the Irish economy crashed on the heels of a worldwide recession, Jennylynd decided to fold up the business and move to Toronto, Canada. While living in Toronto she begun documenting her life's travels in a series of memoirs.

Jennylynd enjoys sharing her relocation stories in the hope of evoking an understanding of all the emotions involved in uprooting and living in a foreign country. She wants her stories of resilience and thriving to empower and motivate readers. Jennylynd lives in Bloor West Village, Toronto where she has embraced self expression in art, music and writing.